# Praise for *Going*

'Anyone with first-hand knowledge [...] find this story true to life . . . There's plenty to shock, but also black humour, camaraderie, sex, drugs and moments of poignancy wrested from a dehumanising culture.'

*Sydney Morning Herald/The Age*

'A light book with heavy themes . . . the issues tackled in this novel are important and urgent.'

*Books+Publishing*

'An alarming—albeit funny—glimpse into life beyond those white coats . . . a light, pacy read.'

*Who Magazine*

'When focused on hospital life, Henry's experience and expertise shine through, illuminating the difficulties her characters—and her real-life colleagues—face.'

*West Australian*

'A really good read . . . Steps are being taken to remedy the culture in teaching hospitals but, judging from this story, there is still a long way to go.'

Blue Wolf Reviews

'A book that has a vital role to play, *Going Under* is a conversation-starter, an astute and penetrating tale that strikes at the very heart of our country's health care system.'

Mrs B's Book Reviews

'An important, timely book. The story gets smarter and darker as it moves on, but that only adds to the enjoyment. Here is someone who gets [being a junior doctor], and has written about the experience clearly.'

Sam Still Reading

781 439175109

# about the author

S onia Henry is a doctor and a writer. She has been published in *The Australian*, *The Sydney Morning Herald*, *RM Williams Magazine*, *Kevin MD*, *Australian Medical Students Association Magazine*, *ANZ Journal of Surgery* and a variety of other platforms. Her debut novel *Going Under*, a fictionalised account of her internship, was an Australian bestseller. She is passionate about First Nations health and improving health equity for people who live in regional and remote parts of the country. She spends part of the year living and working as a GP in remote Australia, and is a council member of the Medical Benevolent Association of NSW. When not being a doctor or writing, Sonia enjoys travelling, swimming, good jokes and Portuguese wine (its inexpensive price does not reflect the excellent taste!).

# sonia henry
# put your feet in the dirt, girl

**a city doctor goes bush**

## ALLEN&UNWIN
SYDNEY · MELBOURNE · AUCKLAND · LONDON

Allen & Unwin
Cammeraygal Country
83 Alexander Street
Crows Nest NSW 2065
Australia
Phone:   (61 2) 8425 0100
Email:   info@allenandunwin.com
Web:   www.allenandunwin.com

*Allen & Unwin acknowledges the Traditional Owners of the Country on which we live and work. We pay our respects to all Aboriginal and Torres Strait Islander Elders, past and present.*

 A catalogue record for this book is available from the National Library of Australia

ISBN 9781761068072

Set in 13/17.6 pt Bembo by MIdland Typesetters, Australia
Printed and bound in Australia by the Opus Group

10 9 8 7 6 5 4 3 2 1

 The paper in this book is FSC® certified. FSC® promotes environmentally responsible, socially beneficial and economically viable management of the world's forests.

*This book is for three things. A person, an animal
and a place.*

*My friend, JG.*

*My dog, Buddy.*

*And the wild frontier of Western Australia,
and its red, red earth.*

Life isn't good here
Life isn't bad
Life hardly exists here at all
Those who belong nowhere belong only here
Beyond the 26th parallel*

Dave Warner, 'Waiting for the Cyclone'

*The 26th parallel is a line that divides Australia from east to west. It begins at Shark Bay in Western Australia, north of Geraldton, serves as the boundary between South Australia and the Northern Territory, and runs into the Pacific Ocean north of the Sunshine Coast in Queensland. Only around two million people live north of the 26th parallel, less than ten per cent of Australia's population.

# prologue

# sydney

Someone once said to me that entering the world at birth is like walking into a giant casino—from the moment you arrive, you're playing to lose. The more I thought on it, the more sense it made. Some people have a lucky streak that inevitably ends, some are stuck with bad cards from the get-go, and most move from game to game, winning some, losing some.

You could say I'd been having a prolonged good run. I was a doctor living in Sydney, I'd published my first book, and I was about to, pass pending, finally complete my training to become a GP, which meant job security and no more exams. Of course, no one's life is ever as as great as it looks from the outside, but, like poker, life is a game of bluff, and things appeared to be going my way.

The first bad card came in the form of an innocuous enough direct message from the Instagram handle @heartdoc_82. It belonged to a man who, being a heart surgeon, lived to cut open people's chests. That makes him sound like a psychopath—and maybe he is. Then again, I'm a person who responds to DMs from psychopaths who slice open other people's chests, which makes me sound a bit unhinged myself—and maybe I am.

I first met heartdoc_82 years ago at a hospital ball. My housemate Max was doing a cardiothoracic surgery term when we were both resident junior doctors, and heartdoc_82 was Max's registrar. On this particular night, Max and I were drunk, as was our entire table of friends. (You know those people who always get put on the back corner table at events due to their propensity to be troublemakers? That was us.) Medical functions made me nervous, and cheap wine was usually the best, albeit messiest, coping strategy.

Max, with a good dose of Dutch courage, walked over to heartdoc_82 to give him a piece of his mind about something work-related, and I followed him, determined to throw in my two cents worth.

Up close, heartdoc_82 seemed surprisingly benign, quite different to the monster of the operating theatre I'd heard about. My drunken intention of giving him feedback turned into a drunken bid to be friendly.

I can't remember what really transpired in our conversation that night. But if my vague feelings of concern the next morning were anything to go by, it was wholly inappropriate and extremely embarrassing. Thankfully, I was saved by the interjection of Max, who dragged me away with the zinger, 'God, stop this conversation now. We aren't having HIM OVER FOR A DRINK. And anyway, HE'S UGLY.'

'I'm right here,' heartdoc_82 said, sounding faintly amused, as I was pulled into an Uber and taken back to the safety of our rundown old sharehouse's toilet bowl.

I didn't run into heartdoc_82 again. So when, some years later, he slid into my DMs with a *long time no talk, your Insta is a little bare, I remember the hospital ball, lol,* I didn't think too much of it. I'd only downloaded Instagram to try to promote my book. This didn't work, as I never accumulated many followers, but it did provide heartdoc_82 with an avenue to get in touch. My friend Loretta, more experienced in matters of the 'gram than me, assured me that random reach-outs from people you haven't seen for years are perfectly accept-able and 'that's just the way Instagram works'. Clearly, I was behind the times!

Instagram messages with heartdoc_82 led to real messages (his suggestion), which led to phone calls (his idea), then FaceTime (his insistence), then emails, then a fully fledged virtual friendship.

It was a little weird that this bloke I'd met only once, when I was so drunk I could barely remember my own name, seemed to want to speak to me this much. But, I reasoned, I was a doctor who had written about the hardships of medicine, so maybe he figured he could be more honest with me than with most of his colleagues. I received quite a lot of correspondence from disenchanted medics, so heartdoc_82's reach-out wasn't too surprising.

The world of heart surgery sounded brutal, and he genu-inely seemed to need a kind ear. I'd always been a sucker for friendships with other lost souls in medicine, and I guess if you begin as friends you feel as if you genuinely know somebody, which makes the next step into an IRL relationship feel more natural. And that's how it went.

He was interstate for a while so he was also hard to keep track of: it was the nature of the job. It did mean, though, that our paths wouldn't unintentionally cross, but that didn't really matter, because communication was so easy, and regular.

'You're the only person I can talk to about everything. I've never met anyone like you,' he told me, after admitting he'd felt ashamed about not attending a patient's funeral. He'd wanted to go, he said, but decided against it for fear his colleagues may think less of him for showing emotion—something that was unusual, I was learning, for a cardiac surgeon. His life was also complicated in a way mine wasn't, but I was happy to listen and offer my own insights. Actually, I felt quite sorry for him. He had a child, I knew, and there'd been a nasty separation. This wasn't surprising—doctors have notoriously high rates of divorce, and their break-ups can be especially messy. A hazard of the job, apparently. Once, Loretta, suspicious of his fondness for texting and peculiar habit of only FaceTiming me from the hospital, made me ask him point-blank if he was still married and living with his wife. He flatly denied it, confirming the separation and bemoaning the struggles of co-parenting.

From the vague due diligence I'd performed with people who knew him from the hospital, it all seemed pretty legitimate. There was no reason not to believe him. His hours were weird and god, *so long*. There was nothing suspicious on his Instagram page—actually, there was barely anything on his Instagram page, which should have been a warning. But I just thought he was busy, and not very sociable. And he was so young, for the terrible responsibility he had: a fully fledged heart surgeon shy of his 40th birthday. It amazed me, his proximity to life and death at such a tender age.

He also had a strange melancholia about him, a sadness in his soul. And what's more irresistible than someone who needs saving? The heart surgeon who needed his heart saved. As someone prone to the fantastical (which means I can also be a bloody fool), I didn't stand a chance.

I felt as if I had known him for years. I was so surprised by our common beliefs, despite occupying opposite ends of the same profession. I was a GP and at heart a bit of a creative, the court jester of the medical world, and he, as a cardiac surgeon, was the undisputed king.

I cared so much about my patients, about making them feel acknowledged, about not missing a result, but in comparison with this cardiac surgeon, this part of my personality felt like a sign of weakness. Less hardcore people like me, I figured, became GPs, whereas doctors who had the capacity to crack open other humans' chests, like him, became surgeons.

In his presence I played down the difficulty and nuance of my job, and made him laugh (he had a fantastic laugh) with stories about my patients' odd requests, which broke up the endless stream of coughs and colds.

His stories, on the other hand, fascinated and terrified me. They also made me wonder about what kind of a person you have to be to exist in that world, to have so much faith in yourself that you could pick up a knife and stick it inside a human heart.

Meeting me was, he said, *meant to be.* Fate. *You enamour me,* he texted me, which was a bit flowery, but I found his effort to impress me with words dorkily charming. Without me, he said, he felt like nothing. He told me that for the first time in his life he could laugh about things. He could talk about work. He could cry. He could be vulnerable, and that was something he wasn't used to, this man who wielded a scalpel on the organ that keeps us all alive.

The fact that he seemed to have fallen for me very quickly and wanted to move things along very fast disconcerted me. He bought me books. He started making suggestions like, 'It would be nice to meet your parents.' He said finding someone creative in the more sterile world of medicine had shifted something within him. While I wrote poetry, he started to follow poets on Instagram, and tagged me in a post that said *She had given him colours while the world had left him grey*. I thought it was a bit chintzy but it was sweet, and touching. Why would he make all this effort if he didn't need to? Only people you trust and deeply care for are good for those sorts of intimacies, right?

Any lingering doubts about some of his more questionable behaviour—and there were doubts—were always assuaged when I confronted him. Sometimes, it seemed like he was two people. He could go from tearing up over what he told me was a life spent ticking boxes he no longer wanted to tick, to laughing with me over some of my better jokes, to lapsing into cold silences for no apparent reason.

I was also uncertain about why his marriage had ended. When he admitted to me it had been a combination of a series of mistakes and it all happening too soon, this worried me even more. If he hadn't been certain about getting married and starting a family to begin with, as he told me, then why go through with it?

And the heart surgeon thing made me worry too—my hobbies were writing and travelling and getting drunk at the pub. The hospital was a place I had left as soon as possible to disappear into general practice. On the other hand, heartdoc_82 didn't seem to derive much pleasure from anything aside from operating (and that I had my doubts about), and talking to me. I remember once saying to him during one of his strange personality changes, 'If I pushed my finger through your skin, I feel like inside there'd just be nothing there'. He seemed to reflect me back at me, like a strange two-way mirror, rather than be a person of his own. It was like that poem 'Antagonish', by William Hughes Mearns:

Yesterday upon the stair,
I met a man who wasn't there!
He wasn't there again today,
Oh how I wish that man would go away!

I remember reading that and feeling unsettled, because somehow I understood it. I sensed it, this oddity within his personality. But every time my rational self took over and recognised these incompatibilities and creepy feelings of unease, he'd morph into this person I genuinely liked, at the flip of a switch. (*Lesson one: trust your instincts.*)

He always apologised when he upset or unsettled me, which reassured me—surely bad people didn't apologise? He wasn't used to discussing his emotions, he was used to control, I was different from him. He started seeing a psychologist, at my behest, to work through his issues.

He'd also got me at a bad time, *but don't they always?*

Prior to the fateful day heartdoc_82 slid into my DMs, a few things had been going on. Someone close to me had been very sick, and I'd been acting as their medical liaison for the better part of two years. Even though the worst was over, it had taken its emotional toll.

At the same time, my long-distance relationship had finally worn me down and we had separated. Although I didn't miss the distance, I missed everything else and I was probably a bit lonely. My fellowship exams were coming up in a few months, and until I passed them my life was effectively on hold. I had by this point sat so many exams in my life that I couldn't even count them, and in the meantime somehow published a book I was still doing publicity for.

I'm not complaining—these were great opportunities—but we only have so much fuel in our tanks at any one time, and I wasn't very good at recognising when the empty light was flashing. I suffered from the absolute inability to ever say no, so I never did. Yes, yes, yes. Then more yes.

I was terrified that if I didn't take every opportunity offered to me, people would think I was ungrateful. I was terrified that if I wasn't thorough enough with a patient, they'd either die of something I missed, or I'd be sued and end up in the paper with a headline about my negligence.

Living in Sydney, the harbour city, looked good on paper, but it meant money was constantly tight. People think doctors and writers are rich, which is a laugh: if it were true then I, as both these things, should have been lying on a beach in the Bahamas. Instead, I was working extra shifts at night at the private hospital to save money, all of which was going on exam prep courses. The exams cost around twelve thousand dollars, and the chance of passing all three of them was around 40 per cent. I had never failed an exam, but in the lead up the possibility was all I thought about. Even as I slept, I had constant night-mares about having to re-sit.

The poker face I wore, as if I held all the aces, was starting to crack.

When I did pass my exams, there was no happiness, just the toxicity of pure, unadulterated relief. I didn't just hate the way medicine controlled my life (had I not passed those exams, I don't know what I would have done), I secretly resented my gender and wasn't immune to the pressure to somehow 'have it all'.

I was a female doctor. If I gave up medicine, all I'd be was a shrew who didn't have a family. And if that life was my choice, if I just didn't *want* kids, I would still be a shrew, but one who was also selfish as well as somehow defective. I didn't know if I wanted children, but I refused to not have the option. So in the middle of training, exams and writing books, I put my fledgling body and bank balance through three IVF cycles to freeze my eggs. I treated it like another exam I had to pass, walking out of the IVF clinic and heading back to work. I made jokes with my fertility specialist that he and my accountant were the only men I did honest business with. I was a woman heading towards my mid-thirties and doing my best to stop time in its tracks, just the way men could.

With a packed schedule of patients, I also didn't have enough minutes in the day to properly consider how all these things might be wearing me down, and decided, as usual, that the only way out was through. That's why when heartdoc_82 appeared—this person who was so unbelievably interested in my life—well, it threw me off course. I spent my days talking and listening to other people and all of a sudden here was this person who couldn't get enough of listening and talking to me.

Fate, he reminded me, this was fate. Him and me: meant to be!

But there's a reason fate has a reputation for cruelty. As it turned out (there's a plot twist coming, if you haven't already guessed), it was all one big fat lie.

Social media brings nothing good—ain't that the truth. Mel, who I had trained with, messaged me one night when I was doing a late shift at the private hospital for extra cash, wanting to have a whine about work. Feeling gossipy, and remembering she'd been heartdoc_82's resident at one point, I confided in her.

*You'll never guess who's charged into my life,* I wrote to her.

She remembered heartdoc_82 all right, describing him as a 'power-hungry shithead' (that made me laugh), but it wasn't just that she remembered. And the next part didn't make me laugh.

*Babe, I don't think he's separated anymore,* she texted me. *It looks like they've been back together for ages and his wife just had a baby. I'm sure she's in my medical mums-and-bubs FB group.*

It's hard to describe what it feels like to be sent screenshot after screenshot of somebody else's life, a life that prior to this moment you had been told didn't exist. The 'separation' was a bold-faced lie: the day he was ardently professing his love to me for the first time, I discovered, rather unfortunately, was the day his wife had given birth to their second child. Their shared family existence played out in front of me in the daily uploads she had made of their lives. She was a prolific poster, and while she was happily showing her private Facebook group her new baby, her husband was pretending neither of them existed.

That night I lay in the on-call room at the hospital. Between buzzes of my pager, I reviewed—in a strangely clinical way, where I was in my body, but at the same time watching all of this from above—his family's weekly grocery shop (he and his wife shared a fondness for shiraz and nice cheese); the way his child had come into the world; a lengthy post about cloth vs. disposable nappies; and photographs of him with their children and dog on wholesome-looking farmstays. This was the man who had told me how lonely he was, how difficult separation and co-parenting was, but how it had all been 'worth it as they had both realised the marriage had been a disaster', and how since meeting me, finally, his life had made sense.

I think something in me changed when I saw all of that. It wasn't just the lying to me; it was that a person could have the ability to lie so completely to themselves. It was impossible for me to comprehend how someone could choose to live that way. Everyone lies, I know that. People lie and cheat all the time. Less-than-ideal, random hook-ups happen in high-stress workplaces frequently, and in those sorts of situations, assuming it's consensual, everyone usually knows where they stand.

This wasn't like that. It was like he had sucked my blood dry, and all under completely false pretences. 'Emotional rape' is a harsh term, but that's the best way I can describe it. Above anything, I had been such a good friend to him. I knew better than anyone what it was like to feel alone as a doctor—how friends became your rock and shelter. I had felt so sorry that he didn't seem to have that support like I did; he had seemed so genuinely, desperately alone. When it turned out he wasn't alone, quite the opposite, it was horrifying.

Nothing, for me, was more important than friendship, and he had taken that friendship from me, and tossed it away as if it meant nothing. The carelessness and ease with which he told all of those lies absolutely astounded me. It felt like he had, rather bullishly, infiltrated my life for the sole purpose of dismantling it.

'I was happy to be mates with the guy! We could still be mates today!' I said to my friend Blake, who ironically, I suddenly remembered, was the person who had told me the line about life and casinos. 'But he just wouldn't let up!? Why? He knew it was all bullshit, but he just wouldn't leave me alone! Why?'

'He must have liked it,' Blake said, shrugging. 'He can't be normal. All that lying would exhaust a normal person.' Then he paused, looking frightfully moral. 'I mean, I'm a Catholic. Whatever people think about Catholics, we do have a strong sense of guilt. He obviously doesn't, having chosen to do all of this.'

True enough. You aren't a bystander in your life—you make choices. And this was what heartdoc_82 chose. The deception, the duplicity, the grand declarations, all while he was at home with a newborn and running a cardiac operating theatre— maybe he just liked it.

'Couldn't he have just, you know, gotten a hobby?' Loretta said, with disgust, as we sat on her couch reviewing the mums-and-bubs Facebook photos of him with his newborn.

But heartdoc_82 did have a hobby, we discovered, it just wasn't badminton. So many affairs he couldn't keep track of them. Flying to different countries to tell other women he loved them. Sleeping with junior residents and senior colleagues and nurses and, it seemed, well, everyone! All while being able to function as a cardiac surgeon with a young family and a friendly smile. The happy young family whose whole existence, I reminded myself, was built on a lie.

It was a very bad time. To say I was disillusioned is to put it mildly. Even worse than the facts of it were the throwaway lines that came from people I knew when they heard the bare bones of what had happened: 'He's a heart surgeon? What did you expect—he'd have a woman in every port.' Or, 'But surely you must have known.' And then there were the vague remarks like, 'Well, they just want their cake and to eat it too.'

No one, aside from close friends, told me to tell his wife. Ranks close in these situations. 'Why hurt her with the truth? Think of the kids.' (Why hadn't *he* been thinking of the kids?) 'Maybe she knows, maybe they've got an *arrangement*.'

Is this marriage, I wondered, this tacit acceptance? It didn't seem like much of a way to live, and it confused the hell out of me. I felt like a child, as though one day, perhaps when I was an adult and doing adult things like getting married and having children, I would understand. My parents weren't like that, but maybe they didn't understand either.

Heartdoc_82 said, when I confronted him with the evidence of his lies, that he made himself sick, and that he hated himself. He carried on with reams of false promises and lies and tears, his modus operandi that by now was becoming a broken record. Then he returned to the operating theatre to repair the next heart on the table. The guy's motto must have been 'compartmentalise and carry on'.

With the passage of time, the anger abated and common sense took hold, and I wondered if heartdoc_82 was, deep down, very unhappy. Happy people surely don't choose to live that way. I thought maybe he was in a position I feared more than anything: he was trapped. Trapped by the prestige and difficulty of his job, trapped by a life he found himself in (chose to be in, I reminded myself), and lacking the personal strength or will to front up to it all. Perhaps the best way he could find to deal with his (self-inflicted) chains was by using other people to distract himself and drowning in a sensible one to three glasses of Barossa shiraz.

Or maybe, he just liked it.

No matter what logic I used to try to explain this situation to myself, it didn't change the fact I was desperately confused. I felt like I was shrinking. I had lived for nearly twenty years in the heart of Sydney, the big city I had craved to be in so much, and now my life was becoming increasingly small, then smaller again. It doesn't take much for your world to go from being charmingly cosy—knowing the guy who owns the corner bottle-o almost too well because of how much you see him (his name is Brett, by the way)—to being so miniscule you feel like you can't breathe.

He was everywhere (heartdoc_82, not Brett from the bottle-o, who, in the interest of honesty, was also probably (definitely) too present in my life). It didn't matter that he wasn't physically in Sydney: the memories were attached to my brain like molasses to horse chaff. The hospital we'd both trained in. The people we both knew. The extent of the deception made me question everything. I'd meet new people and look at them and think, Are you leading a double life? My friends told me they were vicariously traumatised—one was dating a new man and, when he was a bit vague about making plans on a weekend, she said to me, 'I mean, I now assume "busy" means that he's probably spending Saturday with his non-existent wife and kids.' And the worst thing: walking past the hospital on my way to Coles, or the pub, or a coffee shop, and seeing other girls who, by then, I knew he'd done the same thing to. Oh, there were lots of us, I discovered. An entire rolodex. But no one said a word; we just walked past each other in the street.

During this period I developed a love for the work of the Portuguese writer Fernando Pessoa. I drowned myself in his writing; the melancholia and fatalism appealed to me—he seemed as stuck in his own head as I was. Fernando seemed to understand. He was, after all, the man who had written 'if the heart could think it would stop beating', which seemed sort of appropriate.

With grim determination, I made plans to leave Australia. Finally, I had my fellowship letters and the ability to work across the globe. I lined myself up a job in Dublin, with the idea to live part time in Spain and Portugal, and write my European blockbuster.

I told my friend and housemate, Roy, that I was done with this life, and started to pack up my room in our old Darlinghurst apartment. Escape was imminent. It would be my birthday in three days, and I would be landing in London, then crossing through Italy into Spain. Finally, I thought, I would be free. I am a writer after all, I told myself to justify this mad plan. This is the kind of thing writers do, right? (Who did I think I was? Elizabeth Gilbert?)

A series of very expensive gifts showed up in the post, all of which were promptly returned to their sender. The apologies continued, heartdoc_82 said he never stopped missing me, and I couldn't understand it. I threatened to tell his wife everything, which didn't seem to scare him as much as it should: *I deserve this*, he wrote to me. *My life is a fucking mess.* A comfortable mess, evidently.

'If I don't blow this apart, it'll never stop,' I said to my friends.

'He never wants this to stop,' Loretta replied, grimly. '"I've been crying all day, Sunny," "I'm reading books about narcissism to educate myself, Sunny,"' she went on, her cheeks going red, in a high-pitched imitation of heartdoc_82. 'COME ON! It's all bullshit! Nothing scares this guy away. He's UNBELIEV-ABLE.' And then, her coup de grace: 'I mean, heart surgeon? So what if he's saving the babies or whatever shit he spews out to manipulate you? We know now, in his case anyway, heart surgeon is just code for FUCKING PSYCHO.'

I squeezed out a laugh, but deep down, I knew she was right.

So I stopped it. I ended things so absolutely there could be no going back. It's the only way to do it with those types of people. It wasn't graceful or dignified or cool-girl or any of the ways that powerful, independent women are meant to end things, but I ended it. I had no choice, not only because of the obvious—he wasn't my friend and never had been, so continuing a friendship wasn't an option—but also because he was atrociously manipulative. He'd already tried to call for the ostensible reason of talking about work, because he was having a hard time at his current hospital. I guess he knew that my role as a 24/7 doctor counselling hotline offered him an angle to stay in my life. Or he simply enjoyed having me there to listen to his problems, and thought he deserved my care and concern. Whichever it was, neither was good. So with one fell swoop, I dropped the axe.

Goodbye.

I hoped that going to Europe, being on another continent,

would cure everything. When in doubt, get out, as my dad likes to say.

But in the poker game I was already losing, I was to be dealt a final bad card. Well, the entire casino was. Two days before my flight out, Covid-19—a novel strain of coronavirus, a virus I had stared at underneath a microscope in medical school, and coincidentally the only virus I remembered in microscopic detail, probably because of its shape and the word 'corona' being Spanish for crown (it was as romantic as a virus could get)—was declared a pandemic and the borders were closed. No one was getting in or out, least of all me.

Suddenly, I was stuck. At least my boss kindly said, in all the confusion, that I could keep my job. So every morning, instead of wandering around cobblestoned European streets, I got the train to work, somehow survived the day, got the train home, then prayed for sleep. Then repeated it all the next day. By now we were in the middle of a global pandemic, and I was right there on the front line.

I'll never forget the patients who weren't able to get their mammograms as breast screenings closed to protect people from the spread of Covid-19, and the patients who missed their probably lifesaving chemo treatments, and the woman who was trapped with her physically abusive husband in lockdown, and who rang me, crying, from her car. The ten-year-old girl who had developed such bad anxiety that she now described leaving the house and seeing the outside world as 'like being inside a video game'. I also remember a small moment of amusement when the new receptionist asked if I could do an overdue pap smear over telehealth. I explained that unless the phone receiver had a special speculum on the end, I was out of ideas for that one.

Everyone was terrified. My colleagues who worked in hospitals were waiting for the waves of unwell people, but as a steward of the community I was still dealing with people being ... well, people. At least, I told myself, I still had a job. I wasn't like my patient's son who had tried to take his own life in Melbourne after he had lost his business for the second time, or his father, my patient, who under the cover of darkness had driven to the Victorian border to take his destroyed son home so he could watch over him 24/7. My patient looked sick with fear when he disclosed this to me, as if I was going to ring the police and report him for a breach of lockdown.

'He tried to kill himself,' he said. 'My son. My only son. He was alone down there, with no money and no help. The mental health wards were jam-packed. What would you have done?'

I didn't answer him, because I knew what I would have done, the way anyone reading this knows. We can't change our human-ness, regardless of our job titles or of pandemics.

My patient told me that he often just sat there watching his son sleep. When he left, I put my head down on my desk and I cried. The tears felt good, in a way. At least I was feeling something.

I was in the position of knowing how important it was that the pandemic didn't spread, as well as seeing the tremendous human cost of our response. This probably wasn't so good for my mental state either, but I coped the way I usually coped. I kept going to work, simultaneously drowning and saving myself in other people's problems. Perhaps heartdoc_82 and I had that in common.

When all this was over, Max told me that it was like I'd disappeared for a year. I was so lost in the river of stress, exams,

Covid and all of those horrendous lies that I started to question what was real—whether I was real.

I was always horrified by the suicide rates among doctors, but that had been something I only *wrote* about. Now, uncomfortably, I knew how they got to that point—standing in front of a train or calculating how many micrograms of fentanyl they'd need to make it all go away. The holes in the swiss cheese were all lining up, and suddenly I felt dangerously alone. Not in an obvious way, but deep inside, in that part of myself that no one could really see: it was the monster we all have there, waiting to be unchained.

I felt like I was about to meet my maker. My mum had always liked to say that I was a lucky person. But maybe I had played all my cards, and my famed luck had finally run out.

And so, despite all I'd objectively achieved and all I'd been blessed with, that's how I, at that exact point in my life, quite ashamedly felt, and that's where I found myself.

Flat out of fucking luck.

Game: over.

I didn't leave Sydney because, as a medical professional, I had a keen interest in serving remote Australia, or due to a particular passion for the health of First Nations Australians. Back then, at that very low point, it was for entirely selfish reasons that I ran away. Remote areas can attract saviour types, friends of mine who live out there have told me, but I can assure everyone that the only person I had any intention of saving, in the beginning, was myself.

The next day I joined a locum agency that specialised in finding work for GPs in remote areas around Australia. A clinic, the lady from the agency emailed me, urgently needed a doctor in a town in the middle of the desert. Everyone else was working from home, working *remotely*, so I, staying on theme, took a job in the literal remotest part of the country. It was as far west as I could go. The Portugal equivalent of my own country.

'I'll take it,' I said, in total desperation.

So, this is the story of how I ended up flying thousands of kilometres across the country, alone, to take a job as the solo doctor in a mining town of 300 people in the Pilbara region of Western Australia. It suited me. Western Australia is 2.646 million kilometres square. In the Kimberley, the north-ernmost region of the state, there are more crocodiles than people. In other words, it's a big enough place for someone trying to stay lost.

So I left, with the plan to do 40 days in the desert for my sins, surrounded by the red earth.

It turned out I would stay much longer than 40 days.

# part 1

# western australia

Ever been in a desert before? Then you wouldn't understand. But Christ did. He understood the peace, the solitude, the immense impersonal hostility that cleanses the soul. Was it the starkness of the red centre of this country that brought a man face to face with reality?

Hammond Innes, *Golden Soak*

I wake up feeling extraordinarily depressed and realise I haven't packed. *Another day in this life.* I am flying across the country and I have no idea what the weather is even going to be like.

I throw half my wardrobe into a suitcase, and order an Uber. The driver looks at me with something between suspicion and awe when I explain I am going to the airport.

'I haven't taken anyone to the airport in three months,' he says.

It's deserted when I arrive. I wander around, fighting a sudden urge to find myself some roller skates and career down to the Qantas terminal, wahoo-ing, and yelling 'I'M FREE!' Everyone—me and the three other people in there—avoids each other. Stickers for social distancing are everywhere, and all the shops are closed. I try to remember my last flight to Europe, and all the life and happiness I saw around me. Now, I am in the Qantas mausoleum.

There are only two flights on the board, one to Perth and one to Melbourne. I sit at Gate 16 with the other people who have somehow arranged exemptions to be allowed into the Kingdom of Western Australia. There's a big sign up that screams *THANK YOU DOCTORS*. It shows an attractive young woman in blue scrubs. It then flips to *THANK YOU GPs*, and features a portly middle-aged man with white hair.

When we land in Perth, we are greeted by people wearing full personal protective equipment. The passengers go through one by one as we are temperature-checked. About fifteen policemen wearing rubber gas masks are sitting at little desks interrogating my fellow passengers as to the legitimacy of their paperwork and why they want to enter the great state of Western Australia.

The Kingdom of WA idea seems less like a joke now. I feel like I'm stepping into Bhutan, rather than just another state of Australia. I remember, a few years ago, the Western Australians wanting to secede and become their own country, and my dad remarking, 'They're different over there.' We both mumbled something about 'mining interests' with knowing glances at each other, the way most people who aren't from WA do.

I approach the desk. The policeman, through his gas mask, gestures for me to stay behind the line. I obey. He reads my paperwork three times. He calls over another policeman, also in a gas mask, to ask his opinion.

'I'm a doctor,' I say, hoping this will grant me some kind of magical instant entry, even though he must already know that from my forms. 'I'm going to work in the Pilbara.'

They decide, finally, that I have provided enough information, and the first policeman stamps some papers with enthusiasm.

'I'm just checking I'm exempt from the fourteen-day quarantine?' I ask the policeman. 'Apparently, my agency said, doctors who are working where I am are?'

This is true: the two doctors who came before me had been able to start work immediately. The pandemic has gone into a bit of a lull in WA, cases are down and everything is opening up. It's also such a remote place that I will be the only doctor for miles, so, as the agency pointed out, it makes sense to start work straightaway.

He looks at me. 'I think they're changing that,' he says. 'You need an email from the chief health bloke.'

I find the million emails on my phone and show him all of them. He shrugs. 'Like I said, they're reviewing it—but looks okay to me'. I try to ignore the faint sense of unease descending upon me. Either way, he lets me through.

After collecting my bags I stumble outside, searching for the airport motel I am staying in tonight before I fly 1500 kilometres north to Karratha the next morning. I finally discover I can call the motel and they will fetch me. Someone else is going to the same motel, it turns out: a man in an Akubra hat, who appears beside me. We don't speak to one another, but he silently lugs my bag onto the bus when it arrives. I thank him, which he ignores.

'Where are you from, love?' the driver asks me.

'Sydney,' I say.

'What are you doing in Perth?'

'I'm a doctor,' I explain. 'I'm working up in the Pilbara for a few months.'

He turns around to look at me, even though he's still driving.

'A doctor?'

'Yeah,' I confirm.

'What kind of doctor?'

I'm glad for both of us that I can say 'GP', and everyone can relax a bit. For some people, the idea of a female doctor is stressful enough. Based on their strange responses, I gather that a female surgeon is altogether too much.

He sounds relieved. 'You been out there before?'

'Never,' I say. 'This is my first time in WA.'

Akubra Hat stares at me without saying anything.

'Bit different up there from Sydney,' the driver says, ominously. 'What are you running away from?'

I take a leaf from Akubra's book and don't respond.

I am dropped off at the airport motel, which is reminiscent of the facilities at a school camp I went on when I was fourteen. I drag my suitcase through a little garden of fake rocks and let myself inside Cabin 215. I set my alarm for the morning.

What, I ask myself, in god's name am I doing?

The next morning my phone is packed with messages from my dad, who is concerned about me driving alone from Karratha to the Pilbara.

*The flight doesn't land till 1 pm. Maybe stay in Karratha overnight. Remember, don't stop the car for anything except a marked police car. Is there a satellite phone? Is it a 4WD? Why can't you get the bus?*

My phone then starts beeping with messages from my mother. She has somehow googled the address and phone number of the local policeman in the town I am going to: *His name is Sergeant Osborne. Call him if you get stuck. There's also an open-air cinema there! Did you take your tennis racquet? There's a court!*

I have horrifying images of my phone going dead, my parents being unable to contact me, and me rolling up to the town I am meant to be the solo doctor in to discover Sergeant Osborne has already had the pleasure of liaising with Mum and Dad over the phone, even though I am nearly 35 years old.

I stumble onto the bus to the airport. The man at reception gives me a free coffee. He tells me the earth is so red out where I'm going that people often find it seeps into their skin, and takes weeks to really wash off. The police show up. The man at reception whispers that they come by three times a day to check people are obeying quarantine. If they're not, he says, they're arrested.

I thank him for the coffee, uneasily, and the bus takes me back to the airport. Akubra Hat appears out of nowhere and sits next to me again. We don't speak, as is our arrangement. He lifts my bag off the bus, silently.

The airport is a hive of flights. Compared to Sydney, which was deserted, Perth is buzzing. I look on the departures board to see destinations I've never heard of, aside from in Australian folk songs: Karratha, Fortescue, Paraburdoo, Albany, Esperance. So much for the flight ban, I think. One thing is immune to Covid-19 and that's mining money.

I get another text from Dad asking me why I'm driving instead of catching the bus; it's the fifth time he's asked me this. I walk on to the plane, pleased I can put my phone on flight mode. With the world in chaos, it is a relief to fly over the wide red earth. I look out, admiring the rivers and rocky hills from above. By the time we descend into Karratha I am feeling, for the first time in months, quite excited.

These positive feelings last until I am shouted at by a woman in an orange vest after I illegally snap a photo at Karratha airport. I don't know why it's not allowed but assume it's got something to do with protecting mining interests. I am by now convinced Western Australia is completely beholden to its mining industry, which means the whole country is. How had I never realised this when I was living on the east coast? No wonder they wanted to be their own nation! I am standing inside the economic engine room of Australia.

My feelings of awe at the sheer power of the land I saw from the air are quickly replaced by overwhelming fear as I realise I have to drive alone through the desert. I haven't driven a car for twelve months. (Mini the Pooh, my bright red Mini Cooper Cabrio convertible, was written off after a lady in a Prado rammed into me from behind.)

A taxi driver drives me away from the airport and drops me outside the deserted Karratha medical clinic, where my chariot, a Subaru Outback with a concerningly large bull bar, is waiting for me, along with a safe deposit box containing the key.

'Have you bought supplies?' he asks me before he leaves, when I explain I am going well in the heart of the Pilbara.

I look at him.

'There's one tiny shop out there, and the prices are really jacked up,' he informs me. 'So I'd get everything you need here.'

But it's getting late. It's going to take me three or four hours to get out to my destination, and it's already 2 pm. I have appalling luck when it comes to getting lost and car troubles so three to four hours could easily turn into five or six. I decide I value my life and sanity more than my bank balance and a diverse cuisine, forgo the supermarket and climb into the car.

Two things strike me. First, there's no phone charger, and my phone is on 40 per cent. I curse myself for forgetting to charge my phone overnight, an unbelievable oversight: I must be stressed. There's also no GPS in the car, nor a satellite phone, despite what I'd assured my parents. Not that I'd have any idea how to use a satellite phone even if I had one, I remind myself.

I sit behind the car wheel and consider the situation. I am 5000 kilometres from home, and 1500 kilometres north of Perth. I am about to drive hundreds of kilometres, alone, with a phone that might die, through the most ancient part of the world, which may or may not have phone reception anyway. I haven't driven a car for twelve months, and I don't know how to change a tyre. I have nothing on me aside from an old stethoscope and a suitcase full of ill-considered clothing. I open the glove box, to check if perhaps there might be a Gregory's like the one my dad uses. There isn't.

With some mental gymnastics, I decide that the Subaru Outback is an enormously reliable vehicle, and that if I leave now, I should get to the town while it's still light. I come to some kind of acceptance that if the car breaks down or I run into an animal or I get lost, there's a chance I'll be assisted by some well-meaning truck driver, and there's also a chance I'll be raped and murdered, becoming another statistic on a deserted highway in Australia. I regret with every fibre of my soul that I ever watched *Wake in Fright*.

I wonder why I didn't ask more, or any, questions when I accepted this job. Questions like 'Is there a phone charger in the car?' and 'Is there phone reception in the Pilbara?' or even 'If the car breaks down who do I call?' Is there a WA equivalent of the NRMA, I wonder? How many people have died on this particular stretch of road? What was the exact manner of their passing?

I put the name of the town into my ancient iPhone and hope for the best. The map tells me I am 3.5 hours away. My hands are sweating and I wish desperately I had listened to dad and arranged to catch a bus. If there even are buses.

I turn on the car and drive to the highway. At first, trucks intermittently shoot past, but as I get further into the desert they thin out. I've been on the road for nearly an hour and still haven't seen a single other car driving in my direction, only going the opposite way, away from my destination. This is a relief of sorts, because I don't have to worry about potentially murderous drivers seeking out solo females in Subaru Outbacks creeping up behind me, but it also worries me. Why is everyone leaving?

I try the radio but all I get is static. I flirt with the idea of playing some music from my phone but remember my draining battery. I sing to myself, which is of vague comfort. I notice a dead cow on the side of the road and am amazed cows can even exist out here—the land is so dry. All I can see is red dirt, and the occasional mound of arid grass over red hills. The horizon is endless.

The highway goes on and on, deeper and deeper into what feels like the core of the earth's crust. A lone car appears behind me. All I can think about is *Wolf Creek* as the driver seems to get closer to my rear, but mercifully I realise they just want to overtake.

I eventually make it to the roadhouse my parents had told me about, where they'd instructed me to stop for a breather. Mum had described it, drawing from what she'd found on the internet, as a gorgeous little wooden café serving hungry travellers. In reality, the roadhouse looks like the setting of a snuff movie for unsuspecting, naive idiots from Sydney driving through the Pilbara alone.

Another two hours and another dead cow pass by. Miraculously, just as I see the sign for the town, my phone hovering at 4 per cent, a bus appears ahead of me out of literally nowhere. It is unbelievable—I have somehow located the bus I have spent the entire journey regretting I didn't catch.

I follow the bus down the turn-off, and the road turns to dirt. I relax, knowing that inside the bus are likely lots of people and a responsible driver who knows how to do useful things in the desert, like change a tyre. I allow myself to, finally, properly look at my surroundings. It's not particularly pretty, but it's like a person who, although they aren't classically beautiful, has something about their features that makes you unable to look away. They completely arrest you.

The land of the Pilbara took me hostage, I think, from the moment I first really laid eyes on it.

Everything feels old. Looking back, I can't think of anything else I was conscious of aside from the knowledge I was in a very, very old place. The last time I felt something close to that was when I was walking through an amphitheatre in the remnants of Pompeii a few years ago. I remember standing there, at the entrance to the main arena, with the distinct, unshakeable feeling that I was standing in a place where people had suffered, and suffered terribly.

Here doesn't feel like that. It just feels, well, so old. Older than anything I can comprehend, almost older than humanity itself. I realise that humans were in this place long before the Roman Empire, and the earth I am driving on existed even longer ago than that. As I stare at the red mounds and the earth, I have the sensation that I am seeing the beginnings of time itself. And the land, it seems to echo its heat towards me. I feel a marvellous sense of peace. The fear I felt on the open road melts away completely.

A large wedge-tailed eagle flies above the car, crowing into the air. I can't believe it, but here I am, in Australia, feeling magic I have never felt before. I am in the cathedral of the outback, the most sacred place I have ever been. This is why people talk about the power of the land. Because the land is alive, here, speaking to me.

I have the uncomfortable feeling that I am on sacred earth and soon I will be approaching a mine that tore it up for money. It isn't right. Not in an academic sense of being wrong, because it's wrong to destroy artefacts or country that gives us insight into the formation of civilisation, but because it just isn't right. The same way we know, logically, that it isn't right to take a knife and slash it across our wrist, but until we see the blood and feel the pain we don't really *know*.

You can't understand the land of the Pilbara from a newspaper article or a book, or even a story like I am writing now. You have to go there and feel it and hear it speak to you. And then you will come close to understanding, but only a little. To see the land bleed, for money and mining and modernity, I cannot begin to imagine what that does to the hearts and the spirits of the original people who were and are so connected to this red earth. But until I went there, I didn't know. Whatever 'woke' views I espoused at dinner parties in Sydney, I didn't truly know, and I am sorry for that.

I continue driving behind the bus in a bit of a daze. The earth stretches for miles in all directions, as red as drying blood. I am really here. In Sydney I had started to live in the dangerous place between the past—what could have been—and the future—what should be. It didn't leave much time for the present. But here I have no choice. The earth was here for millions of years before I was alive and will be here well after I am gone. I am nothing but a speck, a whisper of a life, crossing over a power and history I can't put into words. I have nothing but the present moment. That's what the earth does to me. Every plan, every worry, every feeling I have is insignificant compared to this.

The feeling starts to melt away as I follow the bus into the town. Desert Town, I now realise, isn't really a town. It's more like a collection of demountables and some house-lined streets, all of which look as if they could be lifted up by cranes and moved away over a few days. I remember reading an email about the job that explained this is mainly a mining town, with barely any other residents. There are three big mine sites nearby, the email said, so everyone in Desert Town works for one of the mining companies that own them. I didn't think too much about what this meant at the time, but now I suddenly understand. I have moved to a place set up for the sole purpose to blow things up under the ground. Everyone is here, I remember the line from the movie *Red Dog*, for one reason:

MONEY.

I drive to the end of the 300-resident town, which leads into a paddock of red dirt that goes for miles before disappearing into the horizon, and call my parents.

I open the window. It's bloody hot.

'Yes, I've made it,' I say to Dad. 'I ended up behind the bus.'

Dad is thrilled. 'I said you needed the bus!'

'Sure.' I hang up without bothering to explain that the bus didn't appear until the last 30-kilometre stretch. I try to find the email with instructions on where to go, and somehow struggle into some kind of administrative demountable. I wander past a couple of men in mining uniforms to find two women in mercifully efficient looking polo shirts. No one knows who I am or what I am doing here, so I show them the email. This works. I am given a key to my apartment with some vague instructions on how to get there.

'Don't worry, the place is so small you can't get lost,' one of the women says.

I try to explain that I'm not sure whether I'm meant to be self-isolating for 14 days. They look at me blankly.

'We don't know anything about that.'

I decide that if no one knows anything, including me, then I can't be arrested for a crime, and I walk back to the Subaru.

I find Block G, Unit 2. It's essentially in a shed—these types of accommodation are called 'dongas', I discover from a quick google of *mining town accommodation shed*—but at least there's air conditioning. There's no Wi-fi, no cutlery and no washing machine. I assume this is standard because I'm in a mining camp, basically. Not being particularly domesticated, I'm not overly fussed. At least it's clean. I sit on the bed. Forgetting my promise to Roy and Max back in Sydney that WA will be a good detox for me, I find myself desperate for a wine.

I find the supermarket, even though I'm not technically sure if I'm allowed outside. The taxi driver in Karratha was right—the prices are really jacked up here. I pay $30 for a bottle of Margaret River white wine, even though it's probably worth nine.

I walk back to G Block and try to ignore the three signs I pass that scream warnings about cyclones. I take the wine and a packet of chips back to my shed and sit down inside. I realise

14

that because there are no glasses I'll have to drink out of the bottle. When in Rome. Except I'm not in Rome. I'm in the middle of the desert, thousands of kilometres from anywhere.

I start to wonder if someone will call me to let me know that I'm meant to present to work at a certain time tomorrow, or at least to clarify the quarantine business. I look out the window to see the police station opposite and the medical clinic next to that. No one is in there because it's a public holiday.

I field texts from my friends in Sydney. Everyone wants to know what it's like out in the Pilbara.

*Is the accommodation nice? Send photos!*

I am too embarrassed to show them my shed and just say it's very dusty.

Finally, my phone rings. It's Fiona, my locum agent, who is safely in Sydney, making a decent commission from my trials.

'So, there's just been a bit of a problem with your paper-work,' she tells me cheerfully. 'Apparently they're changing the rules about who's exempt from quarantine, but it should all be sorted out by tomorrow morning when you're meant to start. The last two doctors were fine. How's the accommodation? Do you have food?'

I look down at my wine and chips.

'Yeah, it's all right,' I say. 'So am I allowed to go to work tomorrow? The paperwork the policeman gave me at the airport says I'm exempt but he reckons it definitely is changing, and no one here knows anything.'

Fiona sounds a bit uncertain but still admirably positive. She tells me I am quarantined until tomorrow morning so can't go outside. Apparently there is a phone number for food delivery in the mine site handbook on my bed.

'If you go outside you'll be arrested,' she tells me chirpily. I don't tell her I've already been outside to go to the super-market. I stare out the window at the deserted police station.

Fiona reassures me she will contact the miners' mess and dinner will be delivered to me in half an hour, and tells me not to worry about anything.

Two and a half hours pass. I call a variety of numbers in the handbook but no one picks up, likely because it is WA day. I'm starving.

I look at the police station again, considering my options. It's still lifeless. I decide to risk it and walk up to the admin block. The ladies in polo shirts jump back, as if I have the plague, when I explain I am meant to be quarantined but also don't want to starve to death. One kindly arranges to get me a chicken curry from the kitchen. They assure me another meal will be delivered in the morning. I take my curry down to my shed and curse myself for not asking for a glass to drink my wine from. I take a swig from the bottle, and go to sleep dreaming of red dust and cyclones and birds, flying high above me. Part way through my dream I find myself trying to catch a bus, out of the Pilbara. The bus never arrives.

I say to a bird, 'Let's go.'

The bird replies, 'We can't.'

'Why not?' I ask, as the dust swirls around me.

'We're waiting for the bus.'

The bird is Vladimir, and I am Estragon. Waiting in eternity, for Godot's coaches to take us home.

I wake up wanting a coffee. I don't want to risk leaving again because Fiona hasn't called to tell me I'm safe to integrate into the community. But I'm also thirsty. I waste time googling *is it safe to drink water in the Pilbara* to find no definitive answer. I am dry as a chip, though, so decide to risk it. The water tastes like warm milk.

I find the handbook and call the info line, and miraculously someone answers. I explain I am the town doctor and don't know whether I can leave quarantine yet and would someone mind awfully bringing me a cup of coffee?

There's a silence on the end of the phone.

'Love, I would help you in a heartbeat,' the bemused voice tells me, 'but we're based in Perth. So it'll take a long time to get a coffee to you up there.'

I get another phone call from Fiona as I sit in my shed, staring out at the medical clinic through the window. No word yet about the quarantine. She is still positive it will be sorted out this morning so I can attend work, which is sitting there, about 8 metres away.

I'm wondering whether I can take off my uncomfortable work clothes when I'm interrupted by the phone ringing.

'Doctor Henry? It's Nurse N, from the medical clinic.'

I am relieved.

'Can I come in yet?' I ask.

Nurse N sounds irritated. 'No, not yet. But I need your help with a patient.'

She starts rattling off concerning phrases like 'loss of vision' and 'severe headache'.

I explain it's very difficult to assess over the phone, and ask to speak to the patient. Before then I try to ascertain whether he needs urgent transfer.

'Is he stable? Are his obs stable? Is he febrile?'

There's a silence, and I wait to hear the answer, reassuring myself that at least if obs (meaning his vital signs, blood pressure, respiratory rate, temperature, oxygen saturations) are all right, things probably aren't too out of hand.

'Are you there?' I ask again, confused by the lack of response.

Nurse N admits she has forgotten to take his blood pressure and temperature. I start to develop a headache. The patient comes on the phone.

'Hi, doc,' he says.

I ask how long he has been having visual changes.

'About six months,' he says cheerfully.

'You've been having trouble seeing for six months? What about the headaches?'

'Oh, I've had them for years, doc. I get migraines. I just want a medical certificate.'

'Are you nauseous? Vomiting? Is this headache different to usual?'

He starts to answer me when there's a knock at the door of the shed. I stare at the door as the patient takes me on a journey down memory lane, recounting every headache he's had since he was thirteen.

I answer the door while asking him if he's had any head trauma recently. There's a policeman standing there. I'm relieved. This must be Sergeant Osborne.

'I'm Acting Inspector Johnson,' Not-Sergeant-Osborne informs me. 'I'm back to Sergeant tomorrow. The rules have just changed and we aren't sure if your exemption is valid anymore. I'm just here to check you're obeying quarantine.'

I can hear the patient talking into the phone.

'I've just got the policeman here,' I explain as I move the phone away from my ear.

'When can I go outside?'

'Not till Sergeant Osborne comes back and sorts it out,' Acting Inspector Johnson informs me. 'Tomorrow. So if you go outside before then I'm going to have to arrest you.'

We stare at each other through the screen door.

'You haven't been outside, have you?'

'Of course I have,' I say, by now thoroughly tired of this ongoing confusion about my quarantine status, when all I want is someone to tell me what the story is so I don't inadvertently break Western Australian law. 'And you would have seen me. You're directly across the road!'

'You went outside?'

'I have no food or any supplies,' I point out. 'I can't starve to death, can I?'

Laughter floats out of the phone, and I remember I'm still in the middle of a call.

'Do you think I can arrest you for getting food?'

'You tell me. You're the policeman!'

'I'll turn a blind eye just this once,' he says generously. 'But don't do it again.'

We eye each other off as he walks the 8 metres back to the front door of the police station.

'Don't blame you, doc,' the patient says as I return to the call, 'I wouldn't want to starve to death in a place like this either.'

I spend the day fielding phone calls about patients who are being seen in the clinic across the road. Nurse N informs me

that even if there is an emergency I'm not allowed to physically see the patients; if I do, I will be arrested and fined. I ask if
perhaps she can escort the patients to my shed so I can see them
through the screen door.

'Rules are rules,' is her opening line when she shows up at
my shed to introduce herself. She lets herself in, despite the fact
I am apparently riddled with coronavirus, and looks around
with surprise. 'This isn't where the doctor normally stays,' she
says. 'Normally you're in the VIP apartment, in Q Block.'

I'm relieved. An upgrade would be nice.

'Can I move there, then?'

She looks at me. 'Doubt it now,' she says airily. 'They never
move people once they're settled. That's a pity for you, isn't it?'

Nurse N has green streaks in her hair and wears matching
light-green scrubs, like an exploding lime. Nurse Lime, I will
call her.

I resign myself to the shed. Nurse Lime tells me she will
check with Acting Inspector Johnson if she is allowed to take
me on a tour of the town, and breezes out.

As the day goes on I take more calls from the clinic, including one from a depressed miner who tells me that he's lived in
Desert Town for nine years and he's totally over it. I've been
here for less than 40 hours and I understand how he feels.

Nurse Lime reappears at my shed and informs me through
the screen door that Acting Inspector Johnson has allowed me to
go on a tour of town but only if I go in my own car and don't get
out anywhere. Nurse Lime leads the way through the red dirt in
her truck, stopping occasionally to show me the sights.

'And here's the morgue,' she says, pulling up next to me and
rolling down her window.

'Do we, ah, often use the morgue?' I ask.

'I've ordered a whole heap of new toe tags,' she says casually, as if she's announced there's a fresh plate of scones available at the tea party.

We progress to the 'airport', which is a field of red dirt with a falling-down fence. 'This is where the flying doctors land to do a retrieval,' she tells me.

This is a relief. Anything that signifies help and assistance calms me.

'If they're caught up and we have to tube a patient or anything like that, we do that in the clinic while they're on their way,' she tells me, again in a maddeningly casual tone, as if she's said something of no consequence.

I start to feel a little unwell. Intubation means throwing a tube down a patient's windpipe to keep them breathing. It's something anaesthetists and emergency specialists do—not, in my opinion, locum GPs with no help, in clinics with no hospital, in the middle of nowhere.

Besides, I haven't tubed someone since supervision during my emergency term, which was years ago. The criteria for this job clearly said 'general practice with basic emergency experi-ence', not 'anaesthetic-level trained'.

'What?' I say. 'We tube people here?'

'I think we could give it a go if we had to,' she says, looking at me almost challengingly.

I imagine being alone in a field of dirt as Nurse Lime screams at me to intubate a dying miner, me intubating their oesophagus and them dying anyway. This is too serious a misunderstanding; I can't just ignore her words and hope for the best.

'I won't be tubing anyone,' I say firmly, meeting Nurse Lime's eyes. 'If that's what is expected, I've been misled. I won't be able to stay.'

I decide that depending on how she responds, my next phone call will likely be to my locum agent and my next move will be straight back to Karratha airport. I am a well-trained doctor, but I know my limitations.

Nurse Lime quickly backs down, though, and mumbles something about the flying doctors being pretty good at getting there on time. I return to the shed and start calling Max and Roy.

'Don't be ridiculous.' Max, 5000 kilometres away in the safety of Sydney, sounds horrified. 'Of course you can't fucking tube anyone! Just bag valve mask them if it comes to that. And, for fuck's sake, call the flying doctors or whoever it is you call out there. Jesus. That sounds terrifying!'

Roy echoes his sentiments. 'She's just testing you,' he says, wisely. 'Stick to your guns. Don't be a hero. You're a GP. Just be a GP. This isn't *M\*A\*S\*H*.'

Then 5 pm hits and the phone can't ring anymore. I wash out a cardboard coffee cup I found earlier, relieved I now have a vessel to drink the wine from. I pour it to the rim and sit on the bed.

There's a knock at the door. It's Nurse Lime, still resplendent though now in head-to-toe mauve.

'You're being moved,' she says. 'Chop chop!'

Q Block is a palace compared to the shed down in G Block. The best bit is an outdoor area that looks directly across onto the heart of the Pilbara. The word 'heart' captures it, I think as I stare out the screen door. Red, red, red. Blood-red dirt that stretches as far as my eye can see. In the distance, the dirt folds itself into little table-top mountains, which the sun creeps behind. I see a sole tree, home to what seems like hundreds of corellas, who look warily over at me. I'm so taken with the landscape I forget Nurse Lime is standing there watching me. I thank her profusely. This definitely beats the shed.

Later that night, Holly, the head receptionist at the clinic, and Sam, a remote nurse who has done fifteen years of hard yakka out in these parts, appear at my door. I try to explain no one is really sure about my quarantine status, but they tell me I have no choice but to let them in, because they need to explain how the telehealth program works. The medical clinic was also under the impression I could start work straightaway, so has been scrambling to somehow arrange telehealth even though they've never used the system before.

'The other doctors before you didn't have to do quarantine,' Holly says, 'so we don't really know what to do, but it's okay, we can sort it.' Sam is calm and seems equally unfazed by having another new doctor land in her workplace: she looks me directly in the eye. I feel a wave of relief that Sam is working with me, and instinctively sense that she will be someone I can rely on if (when?) it all turns to shit. Holly is reassuringly efficient, and looks infuriated when I tell her Nurse Lime kindly arranged my transfer to Q Block.

'What? No she didn't. She would have kept you down in G Block if it was up to her. As soon as I heard you were in that shithole I rang the head of admin services and had you moved up here. Unbelievable!'

Holly starts explaining the politics of the medical clinic, and then they ask if I drink. My expression must give me away because they start laughing.

'Don't trust doctors who don't drink,' Holly says, looking at me with approval.

They tell me that my paperwork still hasn't been sorted out, and the rules seem to be changing every other hour and probably won't be made any clearer even with the arrival of Sergeant Osborne, so it'll be telehealth until then. Holly says she'll drop round in the morning and sort me out with the video link-up so I can meet the patients over camera.

'It's a really good new program,' she assures me. 'It'll be like you're in the room with them.'

'What? I can't hear you!'

'Which ear is hurting?'

The patient looks confused—at least, the bits of his face that aren't blurred do. He starts yelling into the camera about his ear, which sounds painful. I am unable to help as the screen has suddenly gone fuzzy. When it rights itself I find myself staring at Nurse Lime's bosom, swathed aggressively in green.

Her face comes into view and she assertively informs me the patient is not happy with the standard of care he is receiving over telehealth. I point out that if I leave Q Block I will be arrested, and also that I am not responsible for the quality of the connection.

I field emails from Holly, Sam and Nurse Lime all day. The patients, to their credit, adapt to telehealth relatively well.

They ask me if I am in Perth. I explain I am about 100 metres away but due to the Covid protocols I am unable to see them in person.

I deal with a depressed mother, a suicidal miner, a child with a horrible MRSA (staph) infection, and a woman whose pap smear has shown a high-grade cervical lesion. The woman accuses me of not knowing her medical history and gets teary until I explain I have no access to her file and am flying by the seat of my pants, so to speak, over the video call. I call the specialist in Perth to ask if there's anything else I should do except repeat the pap smear in one year. He can't remember the patient and seems confused that someone is calling him from the Pilbara, of all places.

'I feel sorry for you,' he says kindly, when I explain the nearest (small) hospital is 400 kilometres away. 'I couldn't do it.'

The next patient wanders into the call drunk, and asks if I can check his testosterone levels. He is slurring and red-eyed. I tentatively ask if he's meant to be working on the mine site but he reassures me it's his week off.

'I've only had one beer,' he explains.

I don't feel it's my job to ask if he's drunk, particularly over video, so I ask why he wants his testosterone checked.

'My friend had his checked and his was low.'

'Do you feel your . . .' I pause, trying to think of any objective medical signs of low testosterone, '. . . testicles are, ah, on the small side?'

'No!' He looks offended. 'They're huge! I've got great balls!'

'Good. Good,' I say. 'What about any chest, ah, fat? Do you feel you might have breasts?'

'What?! I don't have tits! Why are you asking me this?'

'I'm just trying to ascertain if there are any objective signs that your testosterone is low,' I explain.

We stare at each other over the video screen.

'I get tired and I feel depressed,' he says proudly, slurring into the camera. 'I know it's my testosterone.'

Throughout the day Nurse Lime appears at my door without knocking, barging in despite the fact I am meant to be quarantined and no one is meant to come anywhere near me. She barks instructions at the same time Holly emails me to tell me the next patients have arrived.

I begin to realise that half the patients have complex issues that have been only perfunctorily followed up because the longest any doctor stays here appears to be a grand total of four weeks.

Something mildly positive occurs when my last patient of the day appears in the video. He looks like something out of an old Hollywood Western, in both his outfit and his extremely attractive appearance. Conveniently, he has a back problem and insists on lifting up his shirt. He's wearing an Akubra and a big belt, like a proper cowboy—no, ringer, I mentally correct myself. One of the first things Holly told me was that I'd be dealing with a few of these types, and that my Sydney-sider use of the word 'cowboy' was offensive; 'ringer' is a more advanced type of cowboy, she said, and it's the proper and only term to use out here. The ringer is covered in red dust, with blonde hair that flops over his eyes. He asks where I'm from. When I tell him Sydney, he says with surprise, 'Over east?'

I am so charmed by his broad Australian accent and his

referring to the city of Sydney as 'over east' that I am momentarily lost for words. He says he is also from Sydney, but 'got into a bit of trouble over there', which he doesn't elaborate on. He tells me he spent some time in 'the Territory', which I for some reason find unbelievably interesting. I learn that he flies mustering helicopters on the cattle station half an hour away. I don't know what mustering is but I nod knowledgeably. He asks what a doctor from Sydney is doing out in the Pilbara.

'I guess we're all escaping from something,' I say, lightly.

He reads the room, or the video. We stare at one another. 'Everyone who comes out here is running away,' he says, sounding very old all of a sudden.

I don't feel like elaborating, but neither does he. I tell him he needs a CT scan and he can't ride horses. He says he will anyway. I tell him he can't drive or fly helicopters. He says he is driving a few hundred kilometres to Carnarvon tomorrow, to pick up a chopper he'll be flying back to the Pilbara.

I tell him we have reached an impasse, but I'm perfectly happy to see him when his back gets worse. He smiles and puts his hat back on. Miraculously, I feel slightly alive.

The day ends with Nurse Lime once again barging through my door, for—it seems—the sole purpose of telling me that the flying doctors will do a way better job than me, and that she has regularly had to tell doctors what to do when they have failed over the years. All I can think is how relieved I am that I'm quarantined and, therefore, don't have to accept awkward invitations to see the town again—the morgue was quite enough for one tour.

That evening, with little else to do except finish my one precious bottle of Margaret River white, I'm onto my second glass when Holly and Sam roll up, in high spirits. I'm worried about getting caught socialising by Sergeant Osborne and, despite a negative Covid test that morning, I still don't feel as if anyone really knows what's going on with the quarantine, so I stand near the window, motioning them to step back. They make the reasonable point that Nurse Lime has been barging in on me all day, and that it really makes no difference because they have all been working at the same clinic since 8 am, and have to see me to give me all the scripts to sign and show me how to operate the computer system, which has been crashing intermittently all day. I don't fight them; I'm so discombobulated by this whole situation I'm relieved for the company.

The wine has buoyed my spirits and I make the cheery point that at least I'll only be on call every second weekend when I am out of quarantine, so I can maybe, you know, see a bit of the Pilbara. Sam and Holly look at me sadly as they explain the doctor in Desert Town is actually on call 24/7 and that I am actually only *off* call every second weekend. I start to feel the sinking dread again.

'How many times would you have, you know, a really bad emergency?' I ask Sam.

'Not often,' she says reassuringly. 'Once or twice.'

I am relieved. 'Twice a year is fine.'

'Oh, I meant month,' she tells me. 'Once or twice a month.'

I finish the bottle with gusto. Then my phone starts to ring. I am shocked to see it is Nurse Lime. I look, hazily, at Sam and Holly, who assure me I am not on call right now.

'Don't answer it,' Sam says, after checking her email from management, which confirms the doctor is not on call after 5 pm when in quarantine. 'They can call the flying doctors.'

Despite my being lapsed, my Catholic guilt and general doctorly need to ask 'how high?' whenever anyone says 'jump' kicks in. I answer the phone sounding, based on Holly's thumbs up, marvellously sober.

Nurse Lime is panicking. There is a patient in the clinic with abdominal pain, who is doubled over screaming in agony. She has tried three times to put in the cannula, despite her informing me earlier in the day that she is an expert in the procedure. She sounds too flustered to give me a set of obs but, finally, my brain starts to work and I ask for the patient's name and age. She can't remember that either, but someone else yells his name from wherever she is inside the clinic.

Holly snaps to attention. '30-year-old ringer who's a hard drinker. Last year he was flown to Perth with pancreatitis,' she whispers loudly.

'Remember ringer is an advanced cowboy,' she clarifies, rather snobbishly, seeing my brief look of confusion. 'They get offended if you call them cowboys.'

'Yes, *I know*,' I reply, 'I'm familiar with the lingo now!'

With some prompting, I elicit the information Holly has just told me (ringer, hard drinker, history of pancreatitis) from Nurse Lime. I explain I can't come into the clinic because I will be arrested. She tells me to ring the nearest hospital, which is 400 kilometres away.

'Can't you do that?' I ask. 'I don't even have the patient's details.'

Nurse Lime yells some obs down the phone. They aren't good—he needs a transfer. I call the 'local' hospital to see if I can somehow get him shipped to them, but no one answers. Meanwhile, the cleaner takes over the phone at the clinic's end, acting as a go-between and sounding more and more panicked.

'They usually don't answer,' Sam says, swigging a pre-mixed gin that has miraculously appeared from her bag as she watches me trying again to reach the hospital with an empathetic expression. 'Plus it's too dark to drive, and the ambos don't drive after dark because of the cows on the road.'

'Ambos?' I ask hopefully.

'It's just volunteers who drive the ambulance,' Holly says, shutting down any last hope I have of any other professional aid. 'They're not, like, paramedics.'

'So where the hell do I send him then?' I ask them, holding the phone away from my ear as the tinny voice of Nurse Lime begs for assistance.

'Royal Flying Doctor Service,' Sam says. 'It's your only option I reckon.'

'Are you sure I can't go in there?' I ask, desperately.

Holly shakes her head. 'If you take one step inside the medical clinic you'll be arrested, management already told us.'

The absurdity of the situation finally hits me, and, in lieu of being able to do anything else, I leap into doctor mode.

'Get bloods, blood sugar, ECG, fluids,' I rattle off to Nurse Lime on the other end of the phone, 'and with his history and lack of facilities, we've got no choice. Call the flying doctors and explain.'

She tries to make me do it myself, but I point out I don't know the patient's weight, have no notes in front of me, and am incapable of examining him from the prison of Q Block.

The mood rather ruined, Sam and Holly sneak out the back to avoid any of the townsfolk spotting them fraternising with the quarantined doctor. Nurse Lime continues to call me all night. Finally, at 4 am, I hear the plane. The pancreatitic ringer is spirited away, still, by the sounds of it, alive, and probably more sober than me.

I vow I will contact my locum agent as soon as I sober up, to ask exactly what the on-call situation is in quarantine.

I put my phone on silent, leaving the medical team of Nurse Lime and the cleaner to go the rest of the morning alone, and pass out. I dream of red nothingness stretching into nothingness, yachts floating along a river in Europe, and all the things I am trying to forget.

The days in quarantine start to merge. Between meeting the people of Desert Town over the camera, all I do is watch episodes of Agatha Christie TV adaptations, and drink wine with Holly and Sam when they pop over after work to give me new pathology and prescription forms. I make them sit behind the back fence while I sit on a chair outside my screen door, so we sometimes have to shout to hear each other, which they think is hilarious. I don't mind—I like my new friends. I also like the view from my backyard, which is an endless desert of ancient dust.

One day, careful not to be seen, I walk out of my back gate towards the red earth stretching for miles in front of me. I remember Holly's advice to stomp on the ground a few times to frighten the snakes away, and nearly have a stroke when I think I see a snake as I dance along the desert, but it's an old tyre. I walk for maybe twenty minutes into the nothingness, then realise that I am stinking hot and if I go any further I will probably die. I stare into the sky and feel the intensity of the Western Australian heat.

How First Nations people survived for thousands of years in this place becomes a source of absolute wonderment to me.

I remember photographs in textbooks at school of First Nations Australians being transported with chains around their necks. Standing there, in the sun, looking into the endless red heat, suddenly I feel impossibly cold. The same feeling I had driving into the Pilbara returns sharply. People shouldn't be made prisoners in a place they live and breathe, a place that represents only eternity. I understand for the first time something of the sins of my forefathers. I am alone, in a desert, with no newspapers or politics nor anyone I can convince of my righteousness. But the truth is in the land, and again I feel it surround me. Who am I to ask this place for forgiveness, I wonder, when it is so powerful and I am so small. I walk back to Q Block, feeling uneasy.

'It's the juju,' Holly says wisely, when I explain my uncomfortable epiphanies over a few pre-mixed gins on opposite sides of the fence that evening.

Roy calls me from Sydney later and I start explaining the juju. As soon as I do, though, my phone cuts out. Every time we reconnect and I mention it the same thing happens.

'This is fucking freaky,' says Roy, who's sitting in our apartment in Darlinghurst. 'Whatever you do, don't bring any of that home. And don't take any rocks or anything. I've read about this. It brings so much bad luck!'

Roy rings off, saying he feels the spirits through the phone line—even though he is 5000 kilometres away—and is going to burn some sage to 'cleanse our apartment'. He recommends I do the same, but I have no sage, only my thoughts, which aren't sage enough. And the dying light, whispering to me in the dusk.

I survive my two weeks of quarantine with no major catastrophes. Some entertainment is provided by Holly, who after two years of working with Nurse Lime is at the end of her tether, and brings me her formal complaint letter about the clinic, which I peruse with interest. Holly is a writer of simple clarity that I find oddly insightful: *Nurse Lime doesn't listen to understand, she listens to reply*, heads up the third paragraph. 'Good line,' I say, with admiration.

Part of me dreads being allowed out of my apartment because I will be the only doctor on call literally for hundreds of kilometres. From now on, I don't have the threat of arrest as an excuse to avoid any hair-raising emergencies in an under-resourced, questionably staffed medical clinic in the middle of the Pilbara. I ask myself why I felt the need to throw myself into this potential catastrophe: couldn't I have just gone on a yoga retreat to find myself instead? Then I remind myself that Covid means no group yoga for anyone, and also that I am hopeless at yoga.

I leave Q Block at 7.45 am. I am amazed at the world of Desert Town, which I haven't seen for two weeks. It's a tiny community set among a giant, expansive mound of red, red dirt. I stop at the turn-off where the sign says *Medical Clinic* and stare ahead of me. All I can see is dust, sky and flying white birds, and all I can hear is the sound of nothingness. It's the start of winter back in Sydney but in the Pilbara it is summer. Not summer, I correct myself: the dry. Here there are only two seasons, the wet and the dry. The place is so enormous even the seasons have to be simplified.

I walk inside to be greeted by Sam, who wants me to look at her dog bite.

'You know it was Danielle's dog,' Holly tells me, rolling her eyes. Danielle is the cleaner, who seems to occasionally—with the pancreatitic ringer, for instance—double as a nurse. 'It's been like this for weeks. You need to go and see someone,' she tells Sam.

Sam asks me if there's anything I can do. I look down at her leg, where a big hole lies underneath her dressing.

'Bit awkward, isn't it?' I ask. 'Working here with the owner of a dog who attacked you?'

Sam shrugs. I focus on the dog bite. It looks awful.

'How long ago were you bitten?'

'Three months.'

'You've had this hole in your leg for three months? And you've just, what, kept dressing it?'

I force Sam into letting me swab her dog bite and tell her that as soon as the result is back I will call a plastic surgeon in Perth. Sam regales me with stories of her other literal and proverbial scars, including a scorpion bite on her other leg. She's been a remote nurse for over a decade and has the marks to prove it. I have been in the Pilbara for two weeks and technically haven't been outside until now, so I try not to overthink anything right at this moment.

I write Sam a script for some antibiotics and hope for the best.

One by one, the patients start to trickle in, some of whom I have already met over telehealth. They gape at me. Holly explains they've never had a doctor there under 60 and usually they're men, so that may explain it. I also wonder if it might be my fashion sense—despite having a clothing addiction and a wardrobe the size of Antarctica, like all hoarders I don't make use of what I accumulate: instead, I wear a variation of the same crumpled denim shirt and cotton skirt every day. My one concession to being in the desert is my pair of suede country boots, which I wear like a badge of honour, despite having bought them in Sydney. This honour is taken from me when the patients astutely inform me this style of footwear has become a city thing and most people living out bush can't afford to buy them anyway, so I just look like a fuckwit.

Sam tells me by late afternoon that the patients think I am a decent sort of doc but am too young. When she tells them I am nearly 35 they are blown away. I make a point to tell Roy back in Sydney that his Botox technique deserves a medal.

My last patient is a man who comes in with a bit of a headache. He is about to start his next swing, which I learn is a term for seven-day mining shifts. I'm interested to learn more about this, so after questioning him about his headache and doing a rudimentary neuro exam I ask him about his job, and life. I don't know much about mining at all, I realise. This feels ironic, because even after two weeks I am starting to understand that all the money in Australia sits under the ground. The ground is a suitcase, and the iron ore bundles of cash inside it.

'So it's an open-cut mine, right?'

He nods. 'I drive one of the operators.'

'Not such a bad life,' I say. 'I guess the money is really good, right?'

'It is,' he says, and then tears start rolling down his face.

The ten-minute consult about a slight headache turns into 40 minutes. By the end of the hour, I'm also blinking back tears. He's depressed and alone, dealing with his kids being in Perth while he works for a company that, as he says, cares only about 'bums on seats' and moving iron ore out of Australia so they can sell it to China to be galvanised and then buy it back. I get him an appointment with a psychologist in Karratha, three hours away. The waiting list is two months long. I tell him to see me every week until then.

Suddenly, I feel it: the isolation. But it's different to the loneliness that had started to engulf me in the city. I just had no idea. Like any other Australian who lives in a coastal city, I really have been totally blind to what is happening in the land I have called home my whole life.

He tells me I am the nicest GP he has ever met, which genuinely touches me, but I brush it off.

'No, you really listen,' he says, before he walks out the door. 'Thank you for listening.'

I feel the same sense of inadequacy I've been feeling since medical school. It's easy to listen. It's everything else I feel like an imposter at. Good doctors are physiological genii, deft with the scalpel, and capable of interpreting complex CT scans with one eye closed. Any idiot can listen.

'But if you don't listen, you'll never know what's wrong,' Holly points out, when I sidle up to the front desk to share my thoughts. 'All that other shit you can learn in a textbook. Or call someone if you need help. It's the listening that makes the difference.'

It sounds simple when someone else says it. And it makes sense in this silent, constant, endless expanse of red earth and fading sun. It is, in an insane way, like being back inside the womb. Which is an odd thing for me to say, considering I hate the loaded term of 'womb', the ideal of the mother and all the associated stereotypes that come with that.

But that's how it feels. This silent, open space, completely devoid of judgement, that sits there, seeing everything and everyone, from the beginning of time until the end.

The land of the Pilbara does nothing except listen. The sense of peace that comes from that is wild in its power. I walk out of the clinic and stare at it, at those flat tabletops of land and the never-ending, burnt horizon.

The land hears everything. It offers no solution, no direction, and no blueprint for how to live. It is just there. Listening.

Sometimes, as a doctor, that is all I can do too. And there must be something good in that.

That is one of the first lessons the country there taught me. I would do well, later, to remember it.

Stop, listen, heal.

My room starts to become a revolving door of crying patients and front desk starts to get suspicious. Holly and Sam ask me what the hell I'm doing to them in there.

'Never seen so many men crying since you got to town, doc,' Holly says.

'Maybe it's something about your face,' Sam adds.

I realise that I am counselling everyone else about their problems when I have dumped myself here to try to escape my own, but at least it gives me other things to think about.

I have an unexpected bonding moment with Nurse Lime, who I see standing in the medication room, shaking her head at her phone. I ask her what's wrong.

'My sister wants to get married and have another baby even though her relationship is on the rocks,' she says, looking disgusted. 'She shouldn't have even had the first with him, it's been that bad. A month ago she was leaving him! I don't know what's changed!'

'Maybe they've patched it up,' I say, having little else to offer.

She ignores that. 'You know what I'm going to tell her?' She turns to me, looking determined.

'What?'

'That marriages don't save relationships and babies don't save marriages,' she says. 'That's what our parents tried, and it was a nightmare for everyone involved.'

I'm blown away. She looks at me, for the first time since we've been working together, directly in the eye.

'You know, Doctor Sonia,' she says, 'what my sister needs to understand is something that took me years to learn.'

I wait.

'Pain isn't love,' she says, holding my gaze. 'It's just pain.'

I let that sink in.

'That,' I tell her, 'has to be one of the best lines I've ever heard.'

She nods, briskly, and turns back to the medication shelf. After that, Nurse Lime and I actually get on okay. Like me, she clearly has her own reasons for being in the desert.

They ask me to stay for an extra month, then a day later they ask me to stay another month after that. The self-isolation period has meant remote locums are difficult to fly interstate.

I feel a sense of foreboding as I hear myself agreeing to the extra time. The medical clinic, despite the improvement in my relations with Nurse Lime, and our being staffed by approximately seven people and situated 400 kilometres from anywhere, is starting to resemble a major teaching hospital in terms of its politics.

I feel bad for Holly, who essentially runs the entire medical centre but is only given the title of receptionist. She is constantly battling Nurse Lime and the other nurses, fly-in fly-out (FIFO) employees who seem to stay for a few days then vanish. As a doctor, I have to pick my battles. Everything, I realise one day as I run from my regular patients to a girl who is having an asthma attack in the emergency end of the clinic, is down to me. I understand where Holly is coming from, but I also can't get the nurses offside: all it takes is them not having my back in one horrible emergency and we're all screwed.

Holly and I have led completely different lives, and yet we discover we genuinely like one another. She is very honest, which I appreciate.

That's the problem with doctors, I think. Even if a lot of us aren't very happy, there's something in us that makes us pretend. Maybe it's the years of hell, through medical school and training, then, when you finally finish, all the power and money. You start to live as a construct of a person, rather than just being who you want to be.

You finish training, marry another doctor, open your rooms, start making money and hang out with your doctor mates, half of whom are as messed up as you. Then you find the best private schools and send your kids there. You're never home, because you're at work, playing the good doctor and paying for your doctor life—the mortgage and the holidays—so then you have one affair, and maybe more. And it all looks so perfect. It all looks so fucking perfect. Until one day you wake up, and you realise you've lived somebody else's life, for reasons you don't entirely understand.

I don't want to do that. The thought is overwhelming, intense.

*I don't want to live that life. I am not going to live that life. That is not my life.*

'I don't know what I want,' I admit to Holly one evening as we sit sipping pink gins in her backyard. 'I'm 34 years old, and I don't know what I want. But I don't want that.'

'I'm 34 too,' she says, 'and you've done way more than me. God, look at all the things you've done. You've been a physio, a doctor, you've written a fucking book for fuck's sake, and seen the world! You've seen the whole world!'

But it isn't true. Holly has done a lot too. She brought two kids up largely on her own, because her husband was a FIFO worker for the mines. She put herself through a nursing degree at 30. She runs a medical clinic in the middle of the desert, and has two very well-adjusted children. She's also strong, and resilient. She says it how it is, which takes guts.

It's amazing that so many people just refuse to speak plainly, or to be honest with each other, or themselves. Maybe you have to go for the desert to learn how.

'I think you're so brave,' Holly continues, 'coming out here alone, just doing it.'

'The truth is,' I tell her, 'I'm not brave. I'm just exhausted. It's stupid and self-indulgent and I don't want to be. But that's the truth of it. And I don't know how to feel better, so I guess I'm here, just, I don't know, being here.'

'Well, you're the coolest doctor we've ever had,' Holly says encouragingly. 'And I'm glad you almost had a breakdown.' She grins at me. 'Because it brought you here to meet me. I for one am really glad you're here. And one day, maybe soon, maybe not, you'll feel better. Until then, we just have to keep going to work.'

We start laughing. I see myself from above, in a giant map of Australia, and get my phone out to google where I am. I zoom out and show Holly.

'Can you believe this is where we are?' I say, awed. 'This tiny place, in the middle of just miles and miles of—'

'—fucking dust,' says Holly, a native of the Pilbara with the vocab to go with it. 'I can't wait to move back to Perth.'

Everyone always wants to be somewhere else. I was always like that, too: there was always somewhere else to be, someone else to meet, another horizon to conquer.

It's not as if I've found the place I want to stay forever now. I have literally pulled up stumps in the Pilbara because I just had to go somewhere. But there's something about the remoteness, the colours, the sheer size of the place. It's impossible to explain.

I don't feel great, or even myself, whoever that is these days. But as I walk home from Holly's backyard, feeling a slight buzz of pink gin and praying the phone doesn't ring—I'm likely close to the limit the only on-call doctor should stay under—I think that at least, for once in my life, there is nowhere else I want to be. I am so far away that I feel safe and, in a strange way, protected.

I must have really needed this, I think, as I lie down and close my eyes. It almost scares me, how far I needed to go to feel only a little bit better. Either way, it's a relief. As I go to sleep, the desert surrounds me. I am being cradled by the earth. It's not like I go down on my knees and ask God or whatever it is out there for help. But in a way I suppose I do. And the earth listens. It listens.

And it doesn't lie. The land does not lie.

I stare at the results in front of me. I try to tell myself it's nothing—the abnormality is so mild I can probably just disregard it. But then I remember the other results, exactly the same results, on . . . how many patients now? Ten? Probably closer to twenty, I think. Or 30?

I jump out of my chair and walk to the back of the clinic to find Sam.

'Have any of the other doctors working here noticed these weird persisting low white cells and neutrophils? Like in a lot of the patients?'

She considers the question. 'I think one of the other GPs a while back thought it was a bit strange,' she finally offers. 'But they were only here for two weeks, so . . .'

'. . . never followed up,' I finish. *Typical*.

For someone who was never the world's bravest doctor, I am starting to become a real advocate for remote medicine, and becoming increasingly vocal about the terrible discrepancies between here and the city. I go on a loud rant about how the mining companies have enough money to tear apart the earth but can only provide sub-par medical facilities.

'And where's our blood gas machine?' I demand of Sam. 'You said it was arriving the first day I got here!'

'It's stuck somewhere outside of Perth,' she says, shrugging.

'How can they expect us to manage emergencies when we don't even have anything to show us the patients' electrolytes or haemo-globin levels?' I ask her, feeling as if I want to tear my hair out.

Sam looks sympathetic. 'It's just the way it is out these parts, doc.'

'This is Australia! Not out the back of war-torn Syria!'

'It's better here that Kalumburu,' she points out.

'That's not a defence!' I feel my face going red.

How, I ask Holly as I stand in front of her reception desk, can Australia justify the amount of money the mining companies and government are making out of iron ore but at the same time not even give us a fucking blood gas machine? And where the hell are the specialists?

Perth, she tells me.

'Not helpful!' I point out. 'Perth is nearly 2000 kilometres away!'

Sam, who has appeared behind Holly, looks a little pained, and sips her coffee.

'What's with the way they pay all these miners all this money to live out here, knowing FULL WELL they're lonely, depressed boozers? There's absolutely no help or proper counselling, aside from their company counsellor, who they have to sign a waiver for, that says the counsellor can tell the company anything! Like, that's fucked! No wonder I'm seeing the worst liver function I've ever seen. It's the golden handcuffs, I tell you bloody what.'

Holly walks over and tells me to shut the fuck up because one of the managers is sitting in the waiting room.

'They're probably a depressed alcoholic too!' I whisper, glaring at everyone.

I don't care, I think to myself as I call the next patient in. I am a doctor. I work for the patients, and am guided by my own sense of ethics. I might be stuck in a mining town, and not pissing off the mining companies is probably looked on favourably by the owners of the clinic, but that does not mean I am beholden to these underlying politics. I am a doctor, which means I serve only one group of people: my patients.

Wow, I think. Pride, as opposed to fear, in my role as a doctor.

'We're starting an audit of sorts,' I announce to the meagre staff. 'Every blood result in the next week that comes back with low white cells or neutrophils, we are recording. I'm going to stay back tonight, and every night this week, and go through all the results from the last three months.'

'And then what?' Holly asks, looking excited, as if perhaps we may be onto a major medical discovery.

'I don't know yet,' I say. 'But maybe it's something.'

Maybe there's some kind of weird cluster. Maybe it's the iron ore. Maybe we are all going to get cancer and die.

'Just try not to breathe too deeply outside,' I say ominously, 'and stick to the bottled water.'

Holly almost chokes. 'Don't tell me you drink the water here?'

'No one told me not to!' I say defensively. Fuck. I've been drinking this disgusting water for weeks now.

'It's just calcium,' Holly assures me. 'It won't kill you.'

She says that now, I think darkly. I go into my room and start googling *iron ore and leukaemia*. God. The results are terrifying. I came here to be reborn, not to die! I take deep breaths. I'll just go straight to the shop after work and get some bottled water, I think. That's a good, practical way to approach this.

Eight hours later I appear at the local (only) shop to purchase some water bottles. I consider my options. I notice a big 15-litre plastic bottle, like the ones they use at football matches, or take in the back of 4WDs going into the desert. Surely that's more practical than buying a bunch of water bottles. Not to mention more environmentally friendly. It seems a little late to be considering the environment, as I am literally living in a bowl of machinery and iron ore, but I'm happy to do my bit where I can.

I lug my giant bottle out of the shop and run into Arthur, a patient of mine with a bung elbow.

'Refilling the clinic water cooler? It's 7 pm. Can't that wait till tomorrow, doc?'

'It's for me,' I explain. 'I'm a bit . . . suss on the water here.' I don't inform Arthur of my suspicion that a leukaemic cluster secondary to all the iron ore we are ingesting is probably floating over the town, like a big nuclear cloud.

'Oh, do you have a water cooler at your place?' Arthur looks impressed.

'No.' I look at him. 'It's just for me to, you know, drink out of.'

He looks at the giant water plastic water bottle, which I am struggling to hold.

'Might have to get a big straw, doc,' he says, chuckling. 'Bit hard to pour out of something that big.'

Arthur doesn't know what he's talking about, I think, as I nearly break my arm trying to haul the water into the back of the Subaru. How hard can it be?

An hour later I am cursing myself that I didn't buy 1000 small plastic water bottles, and realising that my city-person

environmental concerns are no match for life in the Pilbara.
I try to winch the huge bottle up so I can pour some water
into a small cup, which results in me knocking the cup over
and sending the enormous plastic vessel packed with 15 litres of
water rolling along the kitchen floor, water spewing out its top.
I settle for propping it up and bear-hugging it, gingerly tipping
some water directly into my mouth as I half-crouch, half-stand
under the sink.

I am, I realise, very, very alone. I also realise, as I stand there
with my brow furrowing, that Arthur was spot on. What I need,
I think ingeniously, is a very long metal straw, or maybe even a
piece of hose . . . if I leave that in the giant water cooler, I can
literally just roll out of bed, put my mouth on the hose piece,
and drink up the glorious, non-calcified, clean water.

Brilliant! I just need to get some hose.

I am so proud of this idea I almost look around, wanting
someone to tell. Heartdoc_82 enters my head. He is probably
still in theatre, sewing together a damaged valve, or elbow-deep
in a chest cavity. And here I am, excited about the prospect of
fashioning a giant straw out of a rubber hose just to have some
clean water.

At least I'm damn well surviving in this place, I think to myself
as I clean up the broken mug and wander into the bedroom
to watch some *Miss Marple* on my laptop. 'The only way to
survive, is to adapt, survive, overcome,' my Year 9 geography
teacher used to tell us. Mr O'Dwyer could be a bit annoying
but his catch cry has never felt more relevant.

Adapt, survive, overcome. With a giant drinking hose, like a
modified bong, inside a big plastic container meant for water
coolers. In the middle of the desert. It's all becoming very biblical.

Mr O'Dwyer did some time in the seminary, from memory, so he'd undoubtedly be proud.

I can't remember when the dreams started. Quite soon, I think, after I got to the Pilbara. I've gone through phases in my life. Sometimes I have vivid, vivid, dreams, sometimes there's nothing, and other times, I have powerful hallucinations. It wasn't until I confided in my friend Nina, a GP in Dubbo, who had recently read a book by the neurologist Oliver Sacks, that I found out what they were.

'You have hypnopompic hallucinations,' she told me, looking excited. 'Sacks writes about them!'

Hypnopompic hallucinations are extremely vivid, usually visual dreamlike events, although they can also be tactile or auditory. They can seem real and are often frightening. They plagued me through my years as a junior doctor, even inspiring a chapter in my first book, where the main character has a recurrent dream (nightmare?) that she is sharing a bed with a corpse. It wasn't always corpses for me. Sometimes it was spiders, or men standing in the corner. The proverbial monsters under the bed are the things we fear the most, I suppose.

I haven't had these sorts of experiences for a long time, but in the Pilbara, the vivid dreams start again. This time they're different from my other dreams. The things I see are distinct, stranger, less concrete. That's probably why I can't recall exactly when they started, just that they have, and that I often wake up unsettled. Sometimes I find myself standing next to the light switch in the early hours of the morning, the fluorescent glare flooding my little apartment. I see snakes on the floor, sometimes the shadow of a man. More than once, I see a baby, crawling along the carpet near my bed. For many days I think I forget the dreams, or only half-remember them, until they start to happen more frequently.

I'm more tired than scared—between my nightly visitors and my phone ringing at all hours I'm not getting much rest, and I need it. I think about taking sleeping tablets, but then I fear missing a phone call. At least twice a week, sometimes more, I'm woken up by the dreaded sound of my phone ringing.

So, I put up with the dreams. I assume it's the crack in my subconscious, trying to tell me something. But I don't understand the nuance, so I just have thoroughly disturbed sleep instead.

Holly comes into my room. The pathologist from PathWest is on the phone and apparently it's urgent. No doubt it's about some horrendous blood result. Pathologists only ever ring GPs if they've seen something horrific and need to alert them immediately. I forecast what I will do. Call Karratha, I think. But it's late afternoon. Fuck. Too late for the road ambulance. No one can travel out of the Pilbara even two hours before dusk because the risk of hitting a cow or other animal is too high. I'll have to call the patient in, but god knows where they are. On the mine site, or drunk and dying somewhere. That means calling the flying doctors. Who probably don't have any planes free. Which means . . . me. Me and a very sick patient, alone in an under-resourced medical clinic in the middle of the desert.

'Hello?'

'Hi, Dr X,' I say, cringing internally. 'It's Dr Sonia Henry. I'm just returning your call.'

'Thanks for calling back.' He sounds relieved. 'This is going to sound a little strange.'

I nearly laugh thinking of how much higher my threshold for what's strange has become since I arrived in Desert Town.

'Go on,' I say.

'Ah, it's about the unusual blood results.' He sounds uncertain, which is relatively unusual for a pathologist.

'For which patient?' I prompt.

There's a pause.

'Um, well, for nearly all of them,' he says, now sounding excited. 'So we started calling it the "Pilbara neutropoenia".'

I can't believe it. Someone else has noticed the low blood counts. I am not going mad. I have clearly made a MAJOR medical discovery. Me, Dr Sonia Henry, humble GP and discoverer, with the pathologist from PathWest, of the Pilbara neutropoenia. Hundreds of lives saved. An inquest into iron ore. A new water supply. A masters, maybe a PhD. Or maybe we are all about to die.

'I know! I was wondering if I should be calling public health! Will they be coming out here? I've started a bit of a casual audit, but I can write something up! Should I call the Department of Health, maybe?'

'Well, we were going down that road,' he says, sounding hesitant, 'but then we started looking more closely ... and I think ...'

'You think ...?'

'I think ... well, we all think, at the lab, that the blood is ...'

'The blood is ...'

'It's heating up,' he says, awkwardly.

My Nobel Prize and my new, exciting career at the forefront of medical research explode. Ka-boom.

'Heating up?'

'Yes. We think there's an issue, either with the storage at the clinic or with the plane.'

For a second I don't understand what he's talking about. The bloods are driven from the clinic to the processing centre, aren't they? And then I realise the processing centre is in Perth. The bloods are driven, but only to Karratha. Then they're put on a plane to Perth, where they spend another two to three hours before being driven to a lab.

*How did I not realise this?*

Such simple things like blood processing, as a doctor in a city, or even in a regional area, you just take for granted. But out here, small tubes of blood needed to go on planes.

*Even the blood is fly-in fly-out.*

It turns out the Pilbara cluster is likely down to nothing more than bad storage—the bloods heating up causes these anomalies to occur. That said, as we both agreed, we couldn't necessarily put every result down to that.

'What if there's a true leukopenia,' I ask, 'that isn't because of the blood heating up? Or would have been there anyway?'

'I guess you'll just have to re-test all of them,' he says uncertainly. 'Would that be hard?'

I picture the endless list of patients. 'I'll figure something out,' I say half-heartedly.

I go out to announce the news to my colleagues. As disappointed as I am not to be onto a groundbreaking discovery, this does mean I can give up on late nights spent trawling through blood results, and also that it's unlikely we will all die from drinking the water.

'But you got yourself your big 15 litres!' Holly says, stifling a laugh. 'All for nothing!'

'The water does taste like shit here, though,' Sam says bluntly. 'Once you get your giant straw you'll be right.'

I make a mental note: buy a hose—or at least chop off someone else's.

I drive back home to Q Block. It's going to be another long night of *Miss Marple*. Thankfully, there are close to fourteen seasons of it. My phone rings. It is my mate Kristina, calling from Melbourne, which is currently in lockdown. She has miraculously gotten a job in Denmark and is fleeing Melbourne's curfew.

'They're actually letting you out?' I ask her.

Kristina replies in the affirmative. She reports all she had to do was a tick a box that asked when she wanted to return to Australia.

'What did you tick?'

'2030,' she says cheerfully.

Kristina has been through a break-up and, like I was, she's ready to escape. I envisage the place she is going, the canals and colours of Copenhagen.

'How's the desert?' she asks.

'Oh, you know,' I say, looking up and at my 15-litre water container, sitting rather menacingly on the kitchen bench, 'dry.'

After I say goodbye, I think about settling into *Miss Marple* but the talk of Europe has unsettled me. Or awakened me. So instead, I get up, grab my swimmers, pull them on and head to the local pool.

It's empty. Just me, and the black line, and the blue phosphorescent water, and the dying sunlight. I swim, stroke by stroke, lap by lap. At the end of every 25-metre stretch I turn around, see the fading red light of the sky above the red desert, and keep swimming. I think about everything and I think about nothing. I fight with the water yet, impossibly, I float.

And then, by chance, something miraculous happens. In the pool, this oasis in the middle of the dust and the dirt, a new love affair begins.

Occasionally, I have tried mindfulness. I used to tell my patients to do it and I liked to practise what I preached. I knew meditation was good for me, but it was a struggle. It was often easier to sink into a bottle of Brett's wine than a deep breath when I wanted to empty my head of pesky, repetitive ruminations on things I couldn't change. I knew I would feel better after it, but for some reason it was so hard to do. I think my best effort at practising mindfulness was four minutes.

I never really understood how to live in the moment because I loved sticking myself in the past or the future. But in the pool, I am so effortlessly present. I feel my arms and my legs, I feel and listen to my breath. In, out, stroke, turn, in, out, hit the wall, turn, keep going.

I swim 1 kilometre. When I hit the wall at the end of my 40th lap, I pull off my cap and goggles, and sink to the bottom of the pool. I sit there in the coolness of that amazing water. I let my hair float, and I feel this overwhelming sense of calmness, and deep joy. It reminds me of being a child, and the sleep that would come over me when I laid on my bed after a day at the beach. My mother always took us swimming. It didn't matter where or what time. There's something about being surrounded by water that's almost like a kind of subconscious throwback to being inside the uterus. Who knows what it is, but whatever it is, I have found it again, and the pool is my salvation.

I float home, feeling better than I have in months.

My feelings of zen last only until 8 am, when I present to the medical clinic for the day's work. Holly is fighting with one of the agency nurses, or Nurse Lime, or both—it's hard to tell—and there's a lot of door-slamming and not-so-quiet mumbling of 'she's a fucking bitch'. Danielle is worried that Sam is going to sue her for the dog bite and has made me write her a medical certificate so she can go home 'sick with stress'.

Meanwhile, I am trying desperately to find Sam a plastic surgeon in Perth who will take her case. Her leg is looking worse and worse and I'm starting to wonder if the bite is causing her to become septic. I call the lab, who tell me there's a pending result. I check the file.

'*Staph. pseudintermedius*,' I read. 'That's new.'

Sam asks me what the hell Staph. pseudintermedius is. But I have no fucking idea, so I google it, to discover it's a bacterium specific to . . .

'The mouths of dogs,' Sam reads over my shoulder.

I read more. Apparently on lab culture it closely mimics normal staph aureus, your run-of-the-mill skin bacteria, and thus it's never properly treated.

'Mate, you need to go to Perth. This is fucked.'

The hole in Sam's leg is big and red and oozing. She's tried a million different antibiotics. She asks me if I can debride it, meaning cut away all the dead tissue in the hope it will heal.

'You must be joking,' I say in disbelief.

I ring a plastic surgeon in Perth, who takes one look at the photos and hears my tale of dog bacteria and words like 'Staph. pseudintermedius' and 'we live in the middle of the Pilbara', and tells me to call an infectious diseases specialist.

A few phone calls later I get Sam an urgent appointment in Perth on Friday. We assume she will be gone for a few days, maybe a week.

She informs management, who work hundreds of kilometres away in Karratha, and I read more about Staph. pseudinter-medius, which is actually pretty interesting. It is, I learn, quite rare for it to cause a non-healing wound in a human. I wonder if it's worth collecting all the notes, in case I could ever write it up as a case report.

I read some other studies on the transmission of dog bacteria to humans. Looks like in all these cases the dog has also been swabbed to prove it's the source. I wonder if Danielle would mind if I swabbed her dog's mouth. I waste half an hour asking Holly if she thinks I could text Danielle and ask her to bring her dog in, and then I realise that our human swabs may not work. I wonder what the pathologist would think of a path form labelled *Fido (dog)—mouth swab.*

'There's a vet in Karratha,' Holly says, looking thoughtful. 'They might know what to do.'

I ring the vet, who tells me my best option is to get swabs from the dog's mouth (!) and have them processed through

54

her lab. She tells me it will cost around $120, which Sam instructs me to bill to the medical clinic because it was the cleaner's dog who caused it, but I offer to cover costs—this may be my ticket to scientific fame and glory. The leukopenia was just the bloods heating up, I think, but this is different.

I decide I will call Danielle and ask her to bring in her dog next week for testing. Just as I am about to lift the receiver, the door opens and a semi-familiar looking young blond man walks in, dressed in an Akubra, station shirt and jeans and covered from head to toe in red dust. It's the super-hot ringer! Back from Carnarvon! In person, not over telehealth!

'G'day,' he says. 'I've got an appointment.'

Holly, not subtly, nudges me in the ribs, making me cough.

I hustle him into my office.

'Nice to meet you in person,' I say to the ringer, whose name is Linus, a bit awkwardly. 'How's the back?'

'Fucked,' he tells me.

'Did you end up stopping horse riding?'

'Nah.'

'And you went all the way to Carnarvon to pick up a helicopter, and then flew it somewhere?'

'Yeah.' Linus looks a little sheepish. 'Kinda had to, ya know.'

'Well, it's hard when you have to work,' I agree.

I examine his back. Backs are mercifully easy for me. For a few years before I was a doctor, I was a physio, doing mainly sports injuries and backs. Backs are familiar, a reminder of a time of my life that felt easier, simpler. I look at his flexion, extension and rotation and his straight leg raise.

'I think you've irritated your disc,' I tell him. 'And with the fall from a running horse and the referred pain you're getting, we should send you for a CT.'

'But that's in Karratha,' Linus says, looking a bit downcast. 'By the time I've sat in the car for hours driving there my back will be even worse.'

He makes a good point. The tyranny of distance isn't just about how far away Australia is from the rest of the world. Here it's also an internal issue, I think.

'The tyranny of distance, hey,' he says.

I look at him. 'That's just what I was about to say.'

There's a silence.

'So, what's a writer from over east doing out here anyway?' he asks me.

I look at him sharply. 'How do you know I'm a writer?'

He admits to googling me after our last appointment. He tells me he's read some of my articles, and he thinks I'm not bad. He has downloaded my book but will reserve judgement until he reads it in its entirety. I feel something between amusement, irritation and interest.

'It's fair enough to look surprised,' Linus tells me, reading my mind. 'A lot of ringers don't read anything.'

'I'm not casting aspersions!' I say.

'I read a lot,' he informs me. 'Not much else to do out on a cattle station.'

'What do you read?'

He looks thoughtful. 'I'm going through a Russian phase at the minute. There's something about the melancholia that appeals to me.'

I feel my head tilt slightly, only half-believing what I'm hearing. 'Really? And which in particular of the greats appeals?'

'Chekhov I'm pretty into,' he informs me, 'and I've read all of Dostoevsky but that was a while back so I need to revisit

him. I haven't got to Tolstoy but that's only because he hasn't
got to me.'

Is he joking?

'*War and Peace*, the c★★★, got stuck in the post,' he explains
colourfully. 'It takes ages to get here. It's got to come from a
bookstore in Perth.'

Not joking.

'Have you read any Tolstoy?'

'*Anna Karenina.*'

'"If you look for perfection . . ."' I begin.

'". . . you'll never be fucken content," Linus finishes, with a
flourish.

I blink a few times. I'm not saying that any particular person
of any particular kind should read any particular type of book.
That's what is so wonderful about books and humans, after
all—there is such a broad variety of each. But I have to say, I did
not expect to be quoting Tolstoy and hearing about another
person's love for Russian literature, here, in a tiny room in the
middle of the Western Australian desert, or for the purveyor
of all things Russian to be a 26-year-old cowboy ('ringer',
I mentally correct myself) covered in red dust, whose every
second words are 'c u next Tuesday' and 'fucken', and who lives
in a tiny donga out on a cattle station, with nothing around him
except earth and cows.

'With a name like Sonia you would know this stuff,' he says,
appraising me. 'Eastern European?'

'Half-Ukrainian,' I say, by now believing him to be almost
psychic.

He looks me in the eye. 'Worked with a few Ukrainians on
export boats,' he explains.

'Right,' I say, shifting. 'Let's get you this CT scan.'

His back must be hurting because he agrees. I print off the form and give him some advice. He looks like he is about to stand up to leave, but then hesitates.

'Anything else I can help you with, comrade?' I am trying very hard not to smile too broadly.

'Um, it's my nose.'

I look at his nose. Looks all right to me.

'Yep? What about your nose?'

He tells me, rather hesitantly, that it has been bleeding for the last month, on and off.

'Why do you think that is? Has anything happened to it?'

'Well . . .'

I wait.

'I was punched,' he finally says.

'I thought you came here to get out of trouble,' I point out. 'I seem to recall you saying that's why you left Sydney.'

'It was . . .' he pauses, 'um, a consensual punch.'

'How,' I ask him, genuinely interested, 'does one go about being consensually punched?'

'I've got a mistress back in Sydney,' he explains, as if this is something I must hear all the time and should, therefore, understand the medical implications of.

'So . . .'

'Well, you know, we were . . .'

'In flagrante,' I say. I don't doubt he understands. As well as knowing Latin legal terms, the guy probably speaks fluent French.

'That's right.'

'The blood must have been a bit of a mood-killer,' I say wryly. 'But each to their own, I guess.'

He asks, rather flirtatiously, if I have any vices. I consider the question.

'I'm far away from all my vices out here,' I finally decide upon. 'Much like you, if your mistress is all the way back in Sydney . . .'

'Touché,' he says.

'Oh, you do speak French, then, do you?' I can't help myself.

'German, actually.'

'Why did I ask?'

We both grin.

I take a good look at his nose. We meet halfway: he agrees to avoid any nose-jarring activities and, if the bleeding hasn't eased in a week, to cop another CT.

'Only other time I got a punch that good was when I was arrested back east,' are his parting words, 'but I've avoided coppers since then.'

'Not bad behaviour, though.'

He winks at me.

I usher Linus out of the doctor's office, shaking my head. The people you bloody meet. German-speaking, Russian literature–reading ringers with mistresses and rap sheets. As you do.

Holly and Sam rush in, looking enthralled.

'He has swagger, that boy,' Holly says, impressed. 'Total. Swagger.'

'What happened?' Sam asks enviously.

I say nothing, only wink at her lasciviously.

Her eyes widen. 'Whaaa . . . ?!'

'I saw him about his back, you idiots! Now leave me to finish my notes!'

Our laughter echoes around the entire clinic, until Nurse Lime comes down to ask why we're having so much fun.

'Just practising high-quality patient care,' I say. 'Not much else to do out here, is there?'

Holly, Sam and I have lunch at the local tavern. My weekend off call is coming up and I can't wait. I hover at the bar as I order my lunch, and ask Andy, the tavern bloke, if they do Aperol spritzes.

'Not for now,' I reassure him, seeing his look of confusion. 'For the weekend.'

'What's an Aperol spritz?' Sam asks, ordering a burger.

'God, mate. Come on.' I look at Andy. 'Can you explain?'

'I don't know what an Aperol spritz is either, doc,' he says.

I sigh.

'If you tell me what's in it maybe I can make one?'

'Prosecco and Aperol and, you know, spritz,' I say, feeling a glimmer of hope.

'We've got sparkling and vodka?'

'You may as well just get a vodka soda,' Holly points out, not unreasonably.

I ignore her. 'I suppose I could have it sans the Aperol,' I agree.

They both stare at me.

'What?' Holly says, flatly.

'Sans the Aperol. Without the Aperol.'

'Why not just say "without"? You people from over east, honestly . . .' Holly shakes her head. '*Sans*. Seriously.'

'Don't you ever say "sans"?' I demand of Andy.

'Nah, doc,' he says, apologetically. 'Maybe we can make you a cocktail and call it an Aperol Sans? You know, in your honour.'

'That's actually very kind of you, Andy,' I say. 'An Aperol Sans, sans the Aperol.'

It feels like a metaphor for my life.

Sam asks me if I want to go to Craft Club that night, but since I've already agreed, uncharacteristically, to attend a Tupperware party with Holly's friend May (who also happens to be the Desert Town librarian) on the weekend, I tell her that this might be enough for me in terms of overly domestic activities.

*A Tupperware party. Who am I?* I try not to think about it all too much. Lord.

'They drink at Craft Club,' she says, trying to tempt me.

'I'm on call,' I point out. 'I'd have one but I can't really drink in front of the ladies. They're all patients, remember?'

I ask Holly if she's going.

'Holly doesn't go to Craft Club,' Sam says, sounding a bit uncertain.

'I used to,' Holly says, looking annoyed, 'and then Lauren's sister told me I got a bit aggressive on the red wines, so fuck them, I never went again.'

'Well, Lauren's sister can't talk, she loves a drink,' Sam says.

'Who's Lauren?' I ask.

I gather from what follows that if we were in an American movie and Desert Town was an American high school, Lauren would be the prom queen and her husband, Dave, prom king. Dave is the president of the sports club, which is 'a big honour', according to Sam.

I've got life all wrong, I can't help thinking as Holly and Sam discuss the politics of Craft Club and its latest disastrous-sounding meeting. I could be married to a hot guy with a couple of kids, running Craft Club and helping the other half with his sports club. I could be perfectly satisfied with that, and live a fulfilling and involved life. Instead . . .

'Come over for dinner if you don't go to Craft Club,' Holly offers, misreading my thoughtful expression as loneliness. 'Colm is finished his swing and he's smoking fish. It'll be good.'

Colm Calhoon is a bit of an enigma in this place. I've only met him briefly in Holly's backyard, when he's either been on his way to work or heading to bed after a shift. He doesn't say much and Holly tells me he never socialises with anyone. He works as a drill blaster, exploding huge swathes of ground to bring up iron ore. But that's not what interests me the most.

What interests me is that Colm, I know from the snippets Holly has told me, is from Tipperary, Ireland—probably not so much of a surprise with a name like Colm (pronounced 'Collom', Holly explains) Calhoon. It could be that I'm missing overseas travel, but I don't think it's just that. I've always liked the Irish. I like the way they resisted the English, and I like their spirit. I think what I like the most is their love of home. There's something comforting and consistent about the Irish. Even in their wildest and bloodiest days, they remained steadfast in their identity.

I sit in Holly's backyard, drinking gin and patting her dog Bongo. Holly is mouthing off about work. Her kids are coming in and out and she tells them to go and play inside, because we are talking about adult things, which just means we are swearing a lot. Her daughter has made me a necklace of purple and pink beads.

'I'll wear this to work,' I tell her. She beams.

I admire her easy innocence, and aura of happiness.

'Maybe I should have popped out some babies in my 20s like you,' I confide to Holly, 'and then figured myself out after that. The longer I wait, the less I know what I want, and the more impossible it all seems.'

'My cousin, who's totally loaded, had kids at 42,' Holly, ever the pragmatist, says. 'Don't worry about it.'

At this point Colm emerges with the fish. It is excellent. When I tell him I'm from Kings Cross his eyes light up.

'Lot of Irish lads round there,' he says, laughing. 'And Bondi.'

'Certainly are,' I agree.

We talk about Sydney, and we talk about Ireland. Holly tells me in her characteristically blunt and honest way that Colm came from a poor family, poor as dirt.

He laughs. 'Now I'm making this stupid amount of money blowing up the ground in this place,' he says. 'Blowing up history. You Australians don't seem to care so much for history.'

'You actually need to go and see the doc,' Holly scolds him. She turns to me. 'Colm's got Wolff Parkinson White Syndrome,' she continues, looking a bit furtive, as if the mine medic manager has tapped the backyard. 'He has these weird episodes sometimes.'

'You need to get that checked out!' I say, feeling panicked. 'Are you seeing a cardiologist?'

'Yeah,' he grumbles.

'Well . . .' Holly looks at me. 'They picked it up in the emergency department in Perth, that's where they realised he had it, and he saw the cardiologist briefly.'

'Briefly?'

'Well, it was just accidental. He was in there because he fell off his motorbike, and they saw this weird thing on the ECG. First they thought he just had supraventricular tachycardia, but then the heart specialist bloke came and spoke to him, and said he had Wolff Parkinson White, and then booked him an appointment to see him in his rooms.'

'When's the appointment?'

'Next week,' Colm says to my relief, looking annoyed. 'I have to take three days off work'.

Colm's accent is so thick I can barely make out his words, yet I understand everything. I like his lack of pretence. He offers to take me shooting.

'Just cans,' he assures me. 'I shot a roo once, and it turned out to have a little baby in the pouch. I felt shite, I tell you what. Never doing that again.'

'Roos are pests round here,' Holly says. 'But, after that, Colm couldn't do it.'

'You ever shot a gun before?' he asks me.

'Once,' I say, 'on a holiday in Vietnam. It was part of a tourist tour.'

'Any good?'

'Hopeless,' I admit. He laughs again, that magical Irish laugh. I see the leprechauns jumping out near the washing line. Bongo growls.

'We'll take you shooting out in the Pilbara,' he assures me. 'Not something you can do so much in Kings Cross.'

I imagine telling Max and Roy I am going out shooting in the Pilbara, of all things.

As we sit there eating smoked fish, drinking gin and talking, I have a sense of impending longing and of sadness. It's as if I know that many months and years from now, I will miss this place, and these people. And I will miss the lilting Irish accent and the heat of the red earth, and the smoky trout and the warmth of new friends who will become old.

I am caught in the in-between. In Desert Town, I am in the never-never. The freedom in this place is completely indescribable—I still haven't found it anywhere else. I think that's because it doesn't exist anywhere else, except there.

I am simultaneously battling the mining company about Arthur's elbow, and an orthopaedic surgeon in Perth about the knee of another patient, Hank. I notice I am starting to become a little shorter over the phone. Usually, I'm so terrified of appearing rude I am overly nice, which I don't know does me any favours. Sometimes it feels like people expect doctors to be a little abrupt, and because I rarely am, it gives them just enough rope to hang me with. I've dealt with enough assertive receptionists and overworked nurses and registrars to last me a lifetime. But here, I am learning fast.

I sit there listening to Arthur, who, to put it medically, has the hard shits.

His elbow is stuffed, rendering his ability to drive a mining operator pretty useless. He tells me that after nearly three decades of loyal service, he's over it. This injury happened at work and he deserves a compo claim, not to be blamed for it all. We have a rather existential discussion about being loyal to people or things that actually don't give a rat's about you, and about what that does to a person.

'It makes 'em very fucking angry!' Arthur yells at me as I try to take his blood pressure. I tell him to try some deep breathing, which he ignores.

'My supervisor is a c***,' he says, not bothering to hold back. 'So it'll be a fight. It'll be a fight.'

We shake hands in solidarity at the end of the appointment, and I assure him I am here, with my printer and letterhead, for the fight.

He stops outside to talk to Hank, who is on crutches. They exchange heated words about the mining company and the injustice of it all.

'How's the knee, Hank?' I ask timidly as he hobbles in, eyeing off his crutches, his enormously swollen knee and his grimace.

His look tells me everything.

Hank's knee, to put it very medically, is stuffed.

'You need a total knee replacement, Hank,' I tell him. 'The arthroscope hasn't worked. It's not the surgeon's fault, it's just your knee. It's kind of fucked.'

'Can you call him?' Hank looks desperate. 'He's stopped taking my calls.'

I bite back a laugh. Hank, his orthopaedic surgeon, Dr T, and I are stuck in a triangle of avoidance. None of us wants to hear from the others, but we are all at the mercy of Hank's knee, which just isn't getting better. If anything it's getting worse, and now both Hank and I have the mining company on our backs, asking us when Hank can get back to 'being a bum on a seat', as Hank put it, and moving some goddamn iron ore to make them more goddamn money. (Okay, so that's not quite how the HR person phrased it when they rang me, but there was a lot of corporate bullshit like, 'We're just *concerned* about Hank.')

'Cath doesn't want me on these bloody pills anymore,' Hank grumbles, 'but without them I can't move. Now I'm becoming a pill-head. I need to see the surgeon. He did this! He needs to fix it!'

I take a big breath. I'm going to have to call Dr T in Perth. Again.

It's a mercifully brief conversation.

The silence, when I say it's me calling about Hank's knee, is so thick I can cut it with a knife.

'I know neither of us want to be having this conversation, Dr T. But Hank's knee is stuffed,' I say bluntly. 'I'm sending him to Perth for a total knee replacement. I can't keep him up here.'

Dr T blusters a bit about trying an ultrasound-guided corti-sone injection.

'Have you ever been to this part of the Pilbara?' I ask him, thinking how the clinic doesn't even have a blood gas machine, let alone an ultrasound, let alone a pharmacist who can supply cortisone.

'No,' he admits.

Thought so.

'Okay, so, it's really in the middle of nothing. Picture nothing, then multiply by it by even more nothing. That's what Hank and I are working with. Nothing by nothing by nothing. I'm sending him to Perth.'

There's another pause.

'I can see him next Monday,' he says, suddenly, to my surprise, sounding totally defeated. 'I'll get my receptionist to arrange it with him.'

I hang up. 'Hank, you're going to Perth.'

'You really gave it to him, doc,' Hank says, sounding impressed.

I think back to being a junior doctor, terrified even to make a phone call to a registrar because I knew they'd be mean to me. I remember my final exams, how I'd quaked in my boots. And here, I'm ordering orthopaedic surgeons around as if they're my interns. I honestly didn't think I had it in me.

Hank leaves, and I remember, slightly uncomfortably, a conversation with heartdoc_82.

'I thought of you the other day at work,' he had said to me. 'It was like you were sitting on my shoulder.'

'Oh yeah?'

'The scrub nurse handed me the wrong retractor,' he began.

'And . . .?' Being given equipment is a common event in any operation; now and again you're bound to get the wrong piece of metal.

'I had to catch myself,' he explained. 'Normally I stand there with my hand out, waiting. But suddenly, I had this image of you, staring at me.'

'Sorry,' I say, 'can I just clarify: if a scrub nurse inadvertently hands you a slightly-too-small retractor, or whatever, you don't just say, "Oh, sorry, Mary, I need the other one." Instead, you stand there in silence, with your hand open, and the whole operation stops, and you don't say a word, not a single word, you just wait for her to figure it out herself?'

'Yeah,' he said.

'So the operation could pause for, what, five minutes? Longer?'

He shrugged. 'Depends how long it takes for her to figure it out.'

There's a silence.

'Mate,' I said, 'that is fucking psychotic. That is insane. That's control-freak psycho 101.'

He looked almost defensive. 'I realise that now. Hence, when it happened the other day, I thought of you and how you'd respond to that, and I didn't do it. I just acted like a . . .'

'Normal person?'

'Yes,' he said. 'Like a normal person.'

I shake my head. 'Jesus.'

And who knows, I think now, remembering my frustration with the orthopaedic surgeon and the managers of the mine, maybe he felt like if he was too nice, people would start taking the piss. It depresses me to think that we all exist in a world where we feel we have to be overtly nasty to stay ahead of the pack. I thought the way he had behaved was totally abnormal, but maybe in the environment he was in, normal just wasn't really possible.

About 30 kilometres down a dirt track from Desert Town is a huge cattle station owned by Rick and Jacqui Prohart.

I know this because it was one of the first things Nurse Lime told me when I arrived. From what I could gather by her tone, the Proharts are VIP PATIENTS. Sam, too, was clearly impressed by their status as 'station people'. 'You know if Mrs Prohart is in the clinic that she's really sick,' she informed me. 'They're tough out there. They live on the land. They're station people, you know.

Station people.' I don't know anything about cattle stations or station people but I thought it sounded kind of dramatic.

Then, on a Saturday morning at 9 am, just as I'm about to get off the treadmill and go for a nice long swim, my phone rings. It's Sam, who is first on call.

'What's up?' I say, trying to keep running as I talk.

'I just got a call from Rick Prohart,' she tells me. 'Apparently Jacqui is sick as a dog. He's bringing her in from the station now, so they'll be at the clinic in about half an hour. I think you should come in too.'

Sam is an extremely capable nurse, one of the best I've ever met, and normally doesn't call me unless she's really stuck. But I get it. This isn't any old patient (even though we are meant to treat everyone the same). This is one of the PROHART FAMILY. STATION. PEOPLE.

I decide to forgo going home for a shower and head straight to the medical clinic. When I walk in the back door and look down at my outfit—gym shorts and an old T-shirt with a giant Mickey Mouse on it—I wonder if I should have reconsidered.

I walk into the little emergency department to see a woman lying on the bed and a man beside her wearing an Akubra and a linen shirt with a logo that says *Yardi Station*.

Sam has already put in a cannula and taken bloods, which unnerves me a bit. Cannulating patients gives you an important-looking task and is a good way to jump in before you have to really consider anything. But thanks to Sam's efficiency, this has already been done. Everyone looks at me as I enter the room and I realise my appearance means that no one recognises me as the doctor.

I clear my throat. 'Hi. My name's Sonia and I'm the, ah,

doctor covering. Sorry about the way I'm dressed. I was at the gym,' I explain, 'and Sam called me, so I came straight in. But it looks like she's, ah, got everything under control.'

I fear Mrs Prohart does not seem that impressed. Mr Prohart offers me his hand and I see him staring at my T-shirt. If this was an old movie or TV show featuring a country practitioner, I'd have a black bag and a nice shirt and tie. I'd also, I realise, probably be a man. It feels like we all come to the same conclusion at the same time: I don't look like anyone's idea of a doctor, but we are in the middle of nowhere, and I'm the best we've got.

Mrs Prohart isn't too sick, but she's got a very nasty gastro and she needs some IV fluids and some tests. The problem is that the test results won't be back for days, so I um and ah about whether or not to go against the guidelines and just treat her with antibiotics. There are some weird bugs running around this part of the desert, making my city-person medicine pretty useless at times, and the guidelines I'd normally follow totally irrelevant.

We decide to rehydrate Mrs Prohart and keep her in the clinic for a few hours, try some anti-nausea meds and see if she settles down.

I excuse myself to go and have a shower and say I'll return in a little while. She thanks me. Before I leave, I am so curious I can't help myself.

'So, you guys live out on the station, right?' I ask.

Mr Prohart nods.

'Gosh, I'd just love to see a cattle station,' I enthuse, feeling a little as if I've stepped into an outback Aussie movie. 'I mean, it's just so amazing, right? The land, the station . . . wow!'

'Doc's a writer,' Sam says, to put my enthusiasm in context for the bemused-looking Proharts.

'I could probably sell a romance about station life pretty easily,' I say, thinking out loud.

Mrs Prohart, already looking a bit less peaky with the fluid plumping her up, starts laughing.

'You're very welcome to come and have a look around one weekend when you're not on call,' she says.

'Really?' I say, 'Yes! I'd love that!'

They both try not to laugh too hard at my enthusiasm.

'I'm going to buy an Akubra,' I tell Rick, who, still laughing, is looking at me is if I've come from another planet.

'Where you from, doc?' he asks me.

'Sydney,' I say. 'Kings Cross.'

The Proharts' eyes bulge.

'You're a long way from home.' Mrs Prohart looks at me. 'What on earth brought you out here?'

'I wanted a change,' I say, telling my truth/lie again.

A change is an understatement—my life has been completely transplanted. But to think, I muse on the drive back to Q Block, of all the things I wouldn't have seen if I had stayed in Sydney.

The desert is teaching me things. It teaches me that the only constant in life is time. Not even in the sense of a clock or a watch, but in the fact the sun will go down and the moon will come up and then the sun will come up again. Short of an asteroid destroying the giant orbs that dictate the day and the night, they will move no matter what. It's what you do with that time, if you're lucky enough to have the freedom to play with it—that's what matters. The desert doesn't care—it will be there regardless, waiting for you, until you're ready to step into it.

I attend the Tupperware party, and last about 45 minutes.
I turn to May, my librarian friend, who is protectively cradling
a bottle of white wine. 'Do you think men go to Tupperware
parties?'

'No,' she says. 'They're either out shagging other women or
playing golf.'

Some joy is delivered in the form of a phone call from an
unknown number miraculously turning out to be Brett from the
bottle-o in Darlinghurst. I didn't even know he had my details,
and am touched beyond words that he's jumped on the blower
to check I'm still alive because I haven't been into the shop for
so long.

I explain I'm in the middle of the WA desert, at a Tupperware party.

'Fuck,' Brett says. 'I'd say don't drink too much, but ...'

I still to this day can't tell you what Tupperware even is, but
that night I make a promise to myself that as soon as I get back
east I will go into the bottle-o and thank Brett for his concern
about my wellbeing. People say a lot of things about Sydney,
but anyone who thinks it's a careless, unfeeling city has never
been to that little liquor store on Darlinghurst Road, where the
kindness flows right along with the wine.

The next weekend Mrs Prohart invites me out to see the cattle
station. I don't have a car with 4WD so enlist Holly to drive us
in her ute.

We drive out of Desert Town and take a turn down a road
that doesn't even look like a road. The dust is red and the sun

is high. The Pilbara, I think. Bloody WOW. I sit up as we drive past what I think is a . . .

It can't be.

I turn to Holly. 'Is this a train station?'

She starts laughing. 'Well, sort of.'

I can't believe it. In the middle of the desert, in the middle of Western Australia, suddenly there's a train station?

'Where's the platform?' I demand of Holly, whom I have titled 'Pilbara expert' and constantly annoy with annoying questions.

'It's not really a normal train station, it's to take out the iron ore.'

'There's a train station just for iron ore?!'

'Yep.'

'They can't afford to get a blood gas machine for the people who work for them but they can pay for a modern train station to transport chunks of metal? God, they're a pack of fucking c★★★s,' I say, referring to the mining companies without thinking, and without meaning to use such an offensive word. I look up, horrified.

'Sorry!'

Holly is laughing so hard she's crying. 'How do you think they get it out of here? And also, now you sound like you live in the Pilbara,' she says.

We arrive at the station.

I suddenly feel very alive. That's what the land does. It just surrounds you. It is so big, and I am so small. And here are these people who live on and with it.

'This is just all so bloody fantastic,' I say to Holly.

'Yeah, well, it's only because you're a doctor that we're here,' she says. 'Limey would be spewing that we've been invited out to THE STATION.'

'I know my title is officially doctor,' I say, looking over at her, 'but we both know it's actually battler.'

Holly, despite herself, grins.

As I step on to the Proharts' cattle station in the Pilbara, about to meet people who three months ago I had never even considered the existence of, I have a true sense of living my life, and expanding the small corners of my brain that have become too closed, and too dark.

How much, I think as I take in my surroundings, *things have changed*. For a moment I feel an immense sense of gratitude at how lucky I am to be able to change my home and life in the space of one flight and a number of weeks.

'Change is as good as a holiday' is a throwaway line but, for me, it is becoming lifesaving.

Cows, I muse, looking at the giant animals walking slowly in front of me, are not so lucky. They are at the mercy of us.

As Holly and I drive towards the homestead (homestead!!), a plane flies overhead.

'That'll be Rick,' she says.

'They've got a plane?'

'Most stations out here do,' she says. 'They're so big, you need air.'

I just nod.

Mrs Prohart comes and meets us, and ushers us inside. She has baked scones, at the sight of which I nearly fall over.

'Thought I'd better do the cattle station thing, you know,' she says, grinning.

I start laughing, relieved by how down to earth she is.

'Have to impress the doctor, you know,' she adds, and then I realise she may be having the same thought about me.

Lunch on the station is surprisingly normal. Mrs Prohart is thrilled I am a writer but I warn her my book is full of swearing and failed sexual encounters so she shouldn't expect a station romance. 'It's not quite *The Thorn Birds*,' I can't resist saying.

Mrs Prohart takes us on a tour of the cattle yards, and introduces me to her son, a rodeo rider who is standing by the fence with a cowboy hat and bandanna around his neck. We shake hands.

'You'll give your mother a heart attack with the rodeos,' I tell him.

I can't believe I'm shaking the hand of the son of a cattle station who rides rodeos while standing next to a large cattle yard that looks out over the mountains in the distance. People think they've seen land in Australia, but you haven't seen anything until you've seen the stations in WA. Mustering out there takes days, planes, horses and helicopters. The place is easily 1,000,000 acres squared, and all that earth is bordered by the giant mounds of the Hamersley Range. When you see such a huge place, you think less about ownership (even though out here everything is owned by either the mining companies, pastoral leases of stations, Gina or Twiggy, with some land given back to Indigenous land councils), and more about how ancient the earth is. Contracts and property and money—they seem ridiculous when faced with all that power and time. I'm in two minds about the mining companies: their relentless pursuit of iron ore makes me nauseous, but with mining comes money, and money for a lot of people. Without money it's hard to survive, but the land and the people who lived on it were here long before someone figured out how to dig up the elements inside it. On one hand, there's mining and money and the element of iron; on the other, the elements of fire, water, earth and air. Where are the riches greater? It's like asking if someone can buy the universe, although I'm sure there are some who would try.

Afterwards, Holly and I drive back to Desert Town, both agreeing that our day out at the Proharts' was a huge success.

'Mate, we've made it,' I say as we drive past the outdoor movie theatre (big screen in the desert). 'Invited out onto the cattle station. And they were so nice! I mean, you know, they probably know Twiggy Forrest and stuff.'

'They do,' Holly says.

'Bloody hell,' I say. 'Here we are, really in the Kingdom of Western Australia. The frontier. The wild west.'

Holly is laughing her pants off.

'The way you put it makes me almost excited to live in this bowl of red dust,' she says dryly. 'Let's go and have a gin.'

It's my weekend off and Lauren, prom queen of Desert Town, has, through Holly, invited me to the re-opening of the sports club, which has been closed since the onset of Covid-19.

'I just need to be supervised,' I say to Holly nervously. 'You know what I'm like after a few too many. I mean, you've met Dennis.'

Dennis is my alter ego after too many vinos, aptly named after Dennis the Menace.

Holly assures me with confidence that she will closely supervise both me and Dennis, and everything will be kept in hand.

I am not sure about the credentials of my supervisor, who likes a drink as much as, if not more than, both me and Dennis, but I feel scared enough of the mining company and the wives that I'll probably want to go home early anyway.

'I'll cap it at three wines,' I say confidently.

The sports club is actually a bit of fun. Queen Lauren and her friends (all of whom are my patients) are enthusiastically throwing back rosé as if it's water. They are all dolled up and look fantastic. I realise I am genuinely enjoying myself, and I'm on my way to get my fourth wine when Holly sees a group of people walking in. It's the Prohart kids and their cattle station mates. Holly, tipsy, calls them over. I almost don't recognise the son of the station without his hat and bandanna.

'Hey!' I say. 'I met you today. Your mum was really nice to have us out there.'

We get chatting. His life is so different to mine; I want to know everything.

He tells me about a recent trip across the Nullarbor and I am enthralled. 'Do you use a compass? A map? Follow the sun?' I demand.

'Nah, well, just Google Maps if it's working,' he says. I start laughing. Then he starts laughing.

We talk about the rodeos. He rides broncs, not bulls.

'Do you wear a helmet?' I ask, for want of anything else to say. Novice riders wear helmets, he tells me; apparently, once you proceed to expert you can go without. 'Sans helmet,' I say, smiling. 'Better hope for your mum's sake you remain a novice forever.'

He asks why I live over east. I still haven't quite gotten over the labelling of the entire other half of Australia as 'the east' but

I am starting to get it. When you're in 'the west' or the 'Kingdom of WA' as I like to call it, everything does feel very far away . . . On one side, there's the east; on the other side, the world. Oddly enough, I feel closer to the world being in the Pilbara than I do anywhere else in Australia, and I guess by sheer proximity I actually am—it's quicker to get to Singapore from here than it is to get to Sydney.

'I don't know, I just live there. My life is there.'

As I say the words, I realise I don't even know if they are true anymore.

'What do you think of the, ah . . . eastern states?' I ask.

'Cold and overpopulated,' he says bluntly.

'Do you travel much?' I ask him.

He tells me he has never left Australia, and generally doesn't leave Western Australia. 'Why leave the best place on earth?'

'You're like a walking Western Australian cliché!' I tell him.

We are interrupted by Queen Lauren appearing with a bottle of prosecco.

'Are you guys on a date?' she asks, tipsy and merry.

I start laughing. 'Sure, in the most romantic place in the world: the sports club.'

I sneak a look at him. He's nice-looking, this son of a cattle station owner: this station person. Rodeos, cattle, land . . . It's all very different from the things I'm fleeing from in my own head and, suddenly, the thought rather appeals.

Lauren enthusiastically forces a glass of prosecco into my hand and floats off towards the shrieks of the other ladies who are thrilled by the prospect of a real cocktail after months of only Andy's beer and house spirits at the tav.

'How old are you?' I can't help but ask.

'25,' he says. 'How old are you?'

I swear, living on the land makes them seem older.

'Um, 32,' I say.

I wonder why, if I was going to lie, I didn't lop a decent amount off my age. *Idiot.*

Holly, who has been in the thick of it with the shrieking ladies, comes over and asks if we can risk buying another bottle of wine. As my supervisor, she seems to think I am safe in the hands of the station's son, and so we agree that one more bottle between a few of us is more than sensible.

'I'll head home after that,' I say, classily. Holly agrees. One more bottle.

I must be on a boat. Somehow I've ended up on a boat. In the middle of the Pilbara. Maybe I'm on a little barge, going down the river? I must be, because that would explain the overwhelming . . .

I put my head up, and the world spins. I am not in a good way. I open my eyes. Mistake. Glaring light, but miraculously—a large bucket!!

I hug the bucket, and throw up what feels like my entire body, but is really just a combination of cheap rosé, prosecco . . . and tequila?

'Urghhhhh,' I say. I turn my head, trying not to think too much, and find myself face to face with . . .

'A horse?'

The horse looks at me through an open window. Its eyes are wise and all-knowing. And tinged with judgement, as it watches me drop my head into the bucket again.

I am between a horse and a bucket. I want to laugh, but my head hurts too much.

'What are you staring at anyway, horse?' I ask the horse, who does nothing except chomp on its lower lip. 'Haven't you ever had a big night out?'

Probably not, I think. Not many places for horses to party around here. Not many places for anyone to party, and yet, amazingly, I seem to have done so.

'Are you talking to Jeffrey?'

I am startled by a voice behind me.

Considering I don't know where I am, I am almost frightened to see the owner of the voice. It could be variety of disastrous choices. At least, I think, I don't appear to be anywhere that even slightly resembles a mining donga, or a mine.

'I got you some Berocca and Hydralyte,' the voice, which has a broad Australian accent, tells me.

Music to my ears! I have ended up in hangover paradise. Horses, buckets and Berocca!

I turn around, reasoning that anyone proffering Berocca has to be an ally, and see the 25-year-old son of the cattle station, with whose mother I was having tea and scones only yesterday, in my role as the visiting general practitioner.

'Your mum doesn't know I'm here, does she?' is all I can think of to say.

He starts laughing. 'Don't worry,' he says. 'I put you to bed on the couch, with the bucket.'

Then, even though my head is pounding and I feel like I want to die, I start laughing too.

We spend the day watching movies about rodeos and drinking Berocca, and later he takes me to the river, where we swim underneath the giant sky. I am among the elements here: water, earth, fire. For dinner we eat steak procured from the very cattle station I am standing on. He designs leather products: saddles, belts, bags. I admire the intricacy of his craftsmanship.

Out at the river we are caught out by Queen Lauren and King Dave, who look thrilled to be witnessing the fall from grace of the local GP with the son of one of the biggest cattle stations in WA.

I turn to him after they leave. 'So people can just roll up? Isn't this your land?'

He shrugs. 'It's big enough,' he points out. 'Blackfellas can hunt on it, people from town can come to the river.'

I realise it again, the sheer size of the place. I look up. There is the red of a large mountain above me, to my side the flowing water. There is everything, and nothing, for hundreds of miles, until you hit the Hamersley Range. And here I am, sitting next to a guy who rides broncs and is telling me about his collection of retired cowboy hats.

'This is the best day I've had in a very long time,' I say honestly.

Danielle looks at me suspiciously as I enter the medical clinic on Monday. I am buoyed by my new friendship with the station people and am feeling relaxed.

'You look happy today,' she says, scowling.

'Where's Holly?' I ask, smiling at her. She jerks her head, signalling that Holly is, worryingly, out the back of the clinic with Nurse Lime.

My relaxed, peaceful cheer is soon interrupted by a red-faced Holly flying towards the reception desk. Her hair floats after her, like Medusa's. She looks furious.

'Fuck this place!' she scream-whispers at me. 'I've had enough! I'm going home.' She storms out, but not before turning around to ask me if I can write her a medical certificate for acute stress leave.

I wonder whether to bother going down to ask Nurse Lime what's going on but I assume it's a permutation of the same thing that happens every day. I wish Sam was back, but last I heard they were thinking about doing a skin graft for the dog bite so I'm not likely to see her in Desert Town anytime soon.

I decide the best thing to do is see my first patient, and call her in.

It's The Sailor, thankfully. One of my semi-regulars and a nice kid. Her name is actually Harriette and I only say 'kid' because she's 28 and looks eighteen. I call her 'The Sailor' because of the small tattoo that peeks out from under her shirt—the outline of a yacht, which amuses me because we are so far from any water. She's quiet, but not in an aloof way, just in a quiet way. I like her a lot. In some strange way, she reminds me of me. She's young, and female, and she's alone out here in the desert too, working in a job dominated by blokes. I wonder, for a moment, why she's here. Then I toss the thought aside, because I know the answer. She's here for the same reason any of us are here: a change, or money. Or at least, to make enough money to make a change. She raises her eyebrows at me, and I realise she's witnessed the entire episode between Holly and Nurse Lime.

'Holly is the best manager they've had in ages,' she says.

'I've heard,' I say. 'But you know . . .'

'Workplace politics,' she says, grinning.

Somehow, fifteen minutes later, The Sailor and I have stopped talking about her blood results and slightly high cholesterol and oddly low sodium. These aren't tests I'd normally run in someone as young as her, but she's First Nations and therefore at risk of serious illness at a much earlier age. But after going through every result, painstakingly trying to explain each one—and giving her a good ear bashing about smoking—we've started talking about where we would be if we could be anywhere.

Sometimes in general practice, even if you're running late or very focused, with some patients you find yourself having a chat. It doesn't happen with everyone, and some days it barely happens at all. But I've found, in my life, that these chats always happen when I need them most. A moment of familiarity, a point of interest, a sudden connection and link of humanity.

With The Sailor, of all people, I talk about the place I love the most—Europe. It turns out The Sailor doesn't really want to stay in the desert. I'm in awe of the land but I get where she's coming from. I'm here now, but somewhere deep inside I still dream of that other world, of blue water and floating yachts and snow-covered peaks, of language after language and cobblestone roads and the lights of big, chaotic cities where nothing ever closes and people languidly drink wine, talking with their hands.

'I've got a twin brother, right?' she says. 'We used to build boats together, just, you know, pieces of wood. Out of our uncle's garage in Freo. Anyway, we got pretty good at it, and he kept saying, "Sis, we should take this yacht, get out of Freo, sail around the world."'

'I wondered about the origin of the tattoo!' I say, delighted.

She grins, and lifts the sleeve of her shirt, showing me the thin black lines of billowing sails.

For a second, it's like the ink jumps off her arm, the yacht taking flight. I look up. The window in the clinic isn't huge, but it's big enough to see what's outside: the red, the sky, the endless dust.

'Imagine sailing out of here,' I say, hearing the wistfulness in my voice.

'I think about it all the time,' she tells me, mirroring my own thoughts.

'Does your brother work in the mines too?' I ask, curious. 'It must be cool, having a twin brother.'

She smiles. 'It is cool and, yeah, he did work in the mines, but he left. He did what he said he would, and went across the world. He got a job building boats, for the richest people on the planet. Last I heard from him, he was in the Algarve, before that the Costa Smeralda. He built a yacht for Greg Norman! Can you believe that?'

'Wow.' The names of these exotic, far-flung places conjure up images so intense that it's like being offered water to drink after staring at a mirage for too long.

'A blackfella from Freo, who used to play at woodwork with me in a garage, now building boats for Greg fucken Norman.'

'It's absolutely superb,' I say, and I mean it.

'He keeps asking me to go over there,' The Sailor tells me, 'and I'm thinking about it. Once this Covid shit goes away, what's stopping me? Better than sitting on an operator for a mining company that cares about—'

'—nothing but money,' I finish.

'You should do it,' I tell her. 'We should both do it. I'll write books in Sardinia and you'll build boats. And we can have a beer on that amazing water, and remember the time we talked about this in the middle of the iron ore–filled Western Australian desert.'

'I'll see you there, writer,' she says, grinning at me impishly. 'I promise.'

'I'll hold you to that, sailor,' I say.

We both smile. Here I am a doctor, and she is a miner, but there I will be a writer, and her a sailor. The other life, devoid of all the other expectations placed on us both as women, waiting for us.

After The Sailor leaves, with her scripts and her path form and an appointment booked for next week, I ignore my waiting list of patients for a second, and sit there staring at the dust, thinking of someplace else. I close my eyes and imagine it— that future, that land, that feeling of being exactly where I want to be.

My first patient the next day is a man in his late forties who is rude and abrupt. I'm tired and don't feel like an argument so I agree to test his testosterone, even though there's probably no need, and dole out whatever he wants. Until he says he would like a prescription for Viagra with twenty repeats.

'I don't even think the pharmacy in Karratha stocks twenty boxes of Viagra.'

He argues with me until I tell him that even if I write a private script for twenty Viagra it's going to cost him a bomb, so maybe we're better off doing it my way—that is, prescribing the amount recommended by the pharmaceutical benefits scheme.

I inwardly sigh. Ten years of uni and training, working in the middle of nowhere to try to broaden my horizons, a pleasant smile and a 'how can I help you?', all to be abused for not giving some middle-aged white dude twenty repeats of Viagra.

I decide to move on. I try to tell him his triglycerides are concerningly high and ask if he wants to discuss that, but he tells me to get stuffed instead.

'The Viagra is all well and good, but if you have a heart attack, no one is going to be having any sex at all,' I point out. He ignores me, and then asks if he can be bulk billed because I 'haven't really helped'.

General practitioners, like Max says, really are at the coal face, in more ways than people realise.

I walk out to reception and watch Viagra Man go out the door. Holly turns to me. She has officially resigned but has agreed to an extra four weeks before leaving.

'I hate to tell you this . . .' she begins, looking apologetic.

'Oh god, is he putting in a complaint?'

'Even worse.'

I feel my heart sink.

'He's the pool maintenance guy,' she says.

'Oh, fucking great,' I groan. My one reprieve in this place, and the guy watching me through the black glass of the pool changeroom has just demanded 120 tablets of Viagra that I refused to give him.

'Maybe you could go back to the treadmill?' Holly offers, looking sorry for me.

I am at work and tired. It's the dreams. Every night now they plague me. Holly tells me it's the desert causing them, but I'm starting to feel as if I am being teased by—not a malevolent, but a cheeky spirit of sorts. Every patient who comes in asks, 'Had a big night, doc?' because I'm yawning so much.

'Poor sleep,' I say, imagining the snakes on the floor and the man standing in the corner that have been plaguing me at night.

That afternoon a patient comes in complaining of an ongoing cough. I go through his history and do an exam—nothing so remarkable but he's always working with dust so I decide to send him for a chest X-ray, which will take days to come back.

In the middle of my explaining this to the patient, I feel a yawn coming on. I try to suppress it, but it doesn't work.

'Tired?'

I sigh. 'I'm sleeping terribly,' I say. 'I have these wild dreams.'

'What kind of dreams?'

'Hard to explain,' I admit. 'They're not your typical nightmares, it's more like I see things ... It's like my brain is tormenting me.'

He looks at me closely. 'Have you tried the salt?' he asks me. I think I know what he means. Roy back in Sydney always used to say that if he felt any bad vibes he'd sprinkle rock salt on the windows and door frames, to repel spirits. Roy also taught me some helpful tips for the spiritual, rather than medical, use of sage, and filled me in on a variety of other superstitions. Who says that doctors don't have imaginations!

'Does that stuff work?'

He nods and explains he is First Nations. 'It's the spirits,' he tells me, confirming what I've suspected since I got to the Pilbara and the night visions began.

'But why would they come to me?' I ask. 'I'm here as a doctor. I'm also not a bad person—well, not too bad anyway— and I feel like I come in peace. Shouldn't they, you know, kind of know that?' For a brief moment I remember I am in the middle of a consult, but push the thought away. Suddenly, he has become doctor and I the patient.

He laughs. 'They're not trying to hurt you,' he says. 'They're just curious. It's your eyes.'

'My eyes?'

'They like things with different sorts of eyes on them. You've got these light green eyes. That would interest them.'

'Aha,' I say. 'So, what should I do? Get different coloured contacts?'

He smiles. 'I'm not being rude, doc, but the spirits also tend to like a good lookin' woman.'

I'm so taken aback I start laughing. This is madness. But I believe him: he seems to know exactly what I am talking about. He tells me to dust rock salt (it has to be rock salt) along any entrance to my doors and windows, which should deter them. I can almost see Roy's smile at this advice all the way from Darlinghurst.

I sigh. 'I hope this works.'

I don't know what it is about the way the two of us connect, but his dark eyes lock onto mine. I have heard before, from patients and others, about curing troubled souls and smoking ceremonies and First Nations healers. When I mentioned the dreams to May and Sam, they told me there was a woman in town who did something along these lines, but Holly told me on the sly that this woman was white—with white-man magic, she said, don't bother. Holly offered to link me up with a local

First Nations healer but I felt awkward, and also like it wasn't my place, as a white person, to ask for help from ancient magic.

It's like this patient senses I need help, but don't want to ask. He tells me he is a healer, and that if I like, he can perform a quick healing.

I say yes.

If anyone had walked into the consult room that afternoon, they would have seen the GP, stethoscope around her neck, sitting in a chair as a tall man stood over her, speaking an ancient language and moving his hands along her hair and face and head, along her body all the way to her feet, without actually physically touching her at all. For a moment I wish I'd locked the door, but I figure it's the Pilbara and so what? Anyway: I want the dreams to stop.

I feel odd when I stand up afterwards, dizzy or something.

'You'll feel a bit weird for about an hour,' he explains. He tells me there were a few spirits attached to me, which he told to leave.

'Right' I say. 'Wow.'

'There's one more thing,' he says. 'I'll probably have to come over, so if you see a big black man standing in your place, don't worry, that'll just be me. It'll be early, around 1 or 2 am.'

I consider what explanation I could offer to anyone who sees my patient rolling up in the wee hours of the morning. But then, if it's part of the healing . . .

'No, I'll come there in my mind,' he says, guessing my thoughts. 'So don't be worried, it's just to check they've all gone. You'll just go back to sleep.'

'Right,' I say again. 'Thanks, um, thanks for this.'

'You heal me, I heal you,' he says, and grins.

'Of course I'll bulk bill this appointment,' I say. 'I mean, considering the mutual healing that's gone on.'

He grins. 'Thanks, doc.'

'No worries. Where's your Country?' I ask, curious.

'Shark Bay,' he tells me. 'You should go there, it's a good place.'

It's just one of those things. I can't rationalise what happened in the clinic that day, or why I had my dreams; all I can do is know that they did happen, and that something else happened a few nights later at around 1.30 am.

I'm not dreaming—I don't think I am, anyway. But I can feel it happening again, something waking me up, me being there, in that weird half-world where you're not asleep but not quite awake either. I see the shape, and even in my semi-conscious state I groan. They're back. My nightly visitors, right on cue.

I open my eyes and see a shape in the doorway at the entrance to my bedroom. I sit up slightly, as the shape comes into view. It is a tall black man, covered in what appears to be war paint. He is different from the usual figures.

And then, the peace comes over me, in waves. 'It's okay,' a voice says, from inside my head. 'It's him, like he said. He's just checking they're gone.'

I don't remember falling back asleep. When I wake up the sun is streaming across the red dirt through my window. I stare at the doorway. There is nothing there.

A week goes by with no dreams. My patient comes in for his results, which show he probably has a mild chest infection, and

I give him antibiotics to treat it and tell him if it gets no better we can repeat the X-ray. Just before he gets up to leave, I stop.

'Hey, I haven't had any more dreams,' I tell him. He smiles very slightly.

'And there's just one more thing . . .' I feel foolish, but I have to ask him. 'That night, like you said . . . did you come by? To check they were gone?'

He chuckles. 'They were stubborn, with eyes like yours. I had to clean the whole place out. Took a bit of effort too, having to do the full-body tribal paint.'

My heart leaps.

'It *was* you!' I whisper. 'I saw the paint! But it's not possible, the doors were locked, and you weren't really here, but you were there, because I saw you?'

He smiles.

'You won't have any more bad dreams, doc,' he says kindly. 'But be careful when you go home. They might follow you there, and I won't be there to tell them to go.'

'I don't know where my home is at the moment,' I say honestly.

'They always know where your home is,' he tells me. 'Even when you don't.'

I am speechless.

'Oh, and can I have a medical certificate?' he asks.

I try not to laugh as I print it out. The mundane and the magic.

'You should try and get to Shark Bay on your travels,' he says, 'I think you'll like it there.'

I put the enormous stretch of water, which sits at the westernmost point of Australia, on the mental list growing in my head. I like the sound of it. Shark Bay. A good place.

'You know, maybe one day I will,' I tell him.

For the rest of my time in the Pilbara, I don't have one more bad dream.

The next afternoon when I finish work, I decide to breach the twenty-minute on-call radius and take myself on a scenic drive into the middle of nowhere. I am nineteen minutes down a dirt road, feeling delightfully naughty, with nothing in front of me except horizon and heat, when Holly sends me a photo of a snake crawling through her car vent. I open the message just as I'm stepping outside to snap some photos. I see the photo, jump in the car, slam every single air vent shut, then hightail it back to Q Block. After a few moments spent internally screaming, I let out a loud, long, real scream. I let my lungs fill with air again before letting out another one.

'Can you believe that?' I say to Jennifer, one of my patients, the next day. 'A snake, crawling through her bloody car vent. INTO her car. While she was driving. And there I was, taking myself on a little afternoon drive, in the middle of a place that's full of the ten deadliest snakes in the world, all probably just waiting to leap through my vent and on to me.'

Jennifer is shaking her head.

'Two months ago, I was sitting in Kings Cross drinking white wine. What am I doing here?' I hear a voice saying, desperately. It's mine.

Luckily, Jennifer is understanding, and I do regularly listen to her tell me about how much she hates working for the mining companies. She's also wise.

'You're putting your feet in the dirt, girl,' she says. 'That's what you're doing. Most people wouldn't have the guts.'

'And what happens now?' I ask in a panicked tone. 'Now that my feet are in the dirt? What happens now? And what happens next?'

'That's between your feet and the dirt,' she says to me. 'Don't question it. Just let your feet connect with the dirt. Then, one day, you'll know what to do next.'

'And even if I don't, my feet might,' I say, feeling slightly better and simultaneously, somehow, slightly worse. 'Anyway, speaking of body parts, how's the back? Did they end up switching you over to the digger?'

For weeks, Jennifer has been explaining the loader versus digger situation to me. Considering I don't know the difference between most cars, I feel quite impressed with myself for becoming well-versed in the different kinds of machinery used on large mine sites.

She looks at me bitterly. 'They've given the digger to Phil.'

Phil is Jennifer's supervisor, who has been making her life difficult since day dot, apparently.

'What?' I cry.

'I know,' she says. 'You know how much I wanted that fucken digger. And he knew it too. Four years I did on that fucken loader, doc. Four years on that big fucken tank. I more than proved myself. My back and neck are stuffed. And what do I get in return?'

We look at each other.

'Yep. A life on that fucken massive loader. Fuck that,' she says with meaning. 'Fuck them. They've taken enough from me. Have your big fucken loader. I'm out.'

Jennifer explains she is leaving Desert Town for the bright lights of Paraburdoo. She's had enough. 'I need change,' she says. 'I've been in this tiny town for so long. But I need to leave. I'm getting depressed. I hide in my house. There's more to life—there has to be.'

'There is, Jennifer,' I say with feeling. 'Maybe you need to put your feet in the dirt, too—different dirt, you know. Not the kind from here.'

'Well, I know one place my feet aren't going,' she says, a grin breaking through. 'They're not going anywhere near the pedals of that—'

'—big fucken loader!' we chorus together.

For a second, I forget about my ridiculous life and Jennifer forgets about the loader. We grin at each other: two women on the precipice of change. Two sets of fresh footprints, next to one another, in new dirt, on new horizons.

That night, the son of the cattle station comes over to Q Block, where we drink whiskey and watch the sun go down. We talk about everything and nothing as we sit there staring at the never-ending sky.

I watch my glass anxiously as he pours me a Jameson but then give up: I figure one or two hard liquors never hurt doctors like the real Doc Holliday (well, he was a dentist, but I figure it's almost the same). Really, I was just joining a long tradition of remote general practitioners. Whiskey is essentially an anti-biotic out here, after all.

'How long are you going to stay out here?' he asks me.

It's a good question. 'I don't know. I have to go back at some point. I'm nearly 35. I have to, you know, buy a house, have a baby, or . . .'

*Or something.*

'I don't want to have kids,' the cowboy says, slugging back his whiskey. 'I just want to focus on the rodeos.'

I look at him in disbelief. 'Surely you want kids?'

'Why?' he asks. 'Because you think I'm a country hick?'

Fair point. Maybe I'm pigeonholing him as much as I'm pigeonholing myself.

'Surely you *don't* want kids?' he says, offering the converse.

'Maybe I actually don't,' I admit.

'Why say you do then?'

It's a hard thing, admitting when our decisions are driven by other people's expectations, rather than what we really want. It gets very confusing, thinking you can have it all, and then realising you don't really know what 'it all' is. I let out a big groan and lie backwards so my head rests on the hard dirt of my backyard. I stare up at the big moon.

'I had a bad experience,' I say to the moon, 'and it's made me think that maybe having a baby will give me some kind of peace, some kind of answer. That's what it seems to do for other women. The way they make it out, having a baby is how you know you've really made it.'

He looks at me.

'I think my bad experience changed how I see the world, a bit,' I continue. 'How I see people. I guess I always thought most people were pretty okay. Like, I'm not perfect, not at all. But then you realise there are people who actually will just lie to you and take from you and have no remorse. And it really does alter your view of humanity. That's why I came here, I guess,' I say, gesturing at the red dirt around us and the night sky above us. 'I just wanted to be in a place where I'm surrounded by something that doesn't lie.'

'The mining companies lie all the time,' he says bluntly. 'All the fucking time.'

'Nothing is as it seems in this damn country,' I agree. 'Not even out here, in this place that feels so untouchable. Because it isn't untouchable, is it? Otherwise, those big bombs wouldn't be set off to take out the iron ore for the cold hard dollars.'

'I dunno,' he says, looking at the sun, still just peeking over the red mounds far in the distance. 'Even knowing all of that, it feels pretty real when you look at it now.'

We watch the sun as it slowly sets. The darkness settles. And we sit there, sipping on our whiskey, listening, together, to the silence of everything and nothing.

I have so many depressed patients I'm starting to feel like a psychologist. I don't mind, because the closest psychologist is 350 kilometres away and their wait time is months. I can also relate to feeling depressed, and am honest with my patients about what has helped me.

'Listen, I know it sounds trite,' I explain to Ben, a school-teacher who's stuck out here for the foreseeable future, 'but exercise is actually really helpful. And I'm not even just saying that. I'm often quite low of a morning, but swimming in the pool really helps.' I mentally correct that to gym—I avoid the pool now so as not to incur the wrath of the bloke I didn't give the 50,000 repeats of Viagra to.

I have the same conversation with another three people that day. In the evening, I walk into the gym and look up to see all my patients using a variety of machines with looks of determination. We all politely pretend we don't see each other.

Everyone is making so much money out here. The iron ore is an endless pit of riches. And yet we're all lost, depressed boozers who don't quite know what to do next. Why is it, I ask myself as I pound the black synthetic floor of the treadmill—avoiding eye contact with all my patients, who feel as lost as me as they sweat out their own anxieties and pain—that human beings have done themselves the great disservice of turning unhappiness into coins that they can actually touch? Because even though we need money to survive, at some point, when you're just constantly chasing the dollar at the expense of everything else, those mounds of gold coins may as well just be mountains of misery.

Holly has finally properly quit, in a blaze of glory. I text her asking what's happened to the four weeks' notice when I get to work to see Nurse Lime and Danielle staffing the clinic, sans Holly.

Holly texts back a diatribe—something about her feelings not being acknowledged, she's sick of their shit, and she wants a holiday anyway. I say fair enough, and I'll see her at her place for lunch.

'Sometimes you just have to be true to yourself, you know,' Holly says, looking up at me almost desperately as we eat lunch. 'In the end, I just couldn't handle management acting like I'm just a receptionist and paying me like one when I'm actually running the whole clinic. It wasn't fair, and it was making me feel so bad. I tried to fight back, but it just didn't work, you know?'

I tell Holly that one of life's great lessons is learning where our boundaries are and then acknowledging them: putting ourselves, rather than expectations or fear, first. Holly looks relieved that I'm agreeing with her, and thanks me for not saying she was stupid to quit, or that she's letting the team down.

'No way, mate,' I genuinely mean it. 'Sometimes you don't even know you have any limits. I think being women, and you especially, being a mum, it's like we are limitless, or told we have to be—or not even told, we just silently feel the pressure. Until one day, it happens: oh! There's a limit! A point I can no longer walk past! This is it! And then you have to act. And that's just what's happened with you.'

Holly tells me I am wise. I roll my eyes and tell her I wish I could learn my own boundaries. I haven't really hit my limits—often, doctors have very high thresholds for bullshit—all I've done is come to the desert to widen the fence's parameters.

'But one day you'll find your fence,' Holly says. 'I think you're getting pretty close now.'

Maybe she's right. Maybe I have been walking along the fence this entire time and I didn't even realise.

My next weekend off call, I drive to Dampier. Holly tells me I'm wasting my time seeing its Red Dog statue because it's well known in the Pilbara the real Red Dog was 'a bit of a dickhead'. I point out that dogs aren't dickheads and say I'll be paying my respects anyway.

'The Mermaid Hotel is pretty fun,' she offers, as a concession.

On the way to Dampier, I feel the freedom of the open road. The fear I'd had weeks ago on the drive into Desert Town has melted away. I stop to get fuel at the Fortescue roadhouse, which I'd previously sped past because of my fear of its appearance, and as I pull in, I get a text from Max saying hi and asking where I am. I reply that I am at the Fortescue roadhouse. He googles it and I receive a series of exclamation remarks.

I go in to pay for the petrol, and consider buying a singlet that says *I survived the Fortescue roadhouse*.

'So this is the place, huh,' I say to the lady behind the counter. I want to point out that the map says *Fortescue* as if it's a town, but in reality it's just . . . a roadhouse. I will come to realise that a lot of Western Australia is like that and, later, I'll find the same is true of the Territory. You think you're hitting civilisation—instead, there's one roadhouse.

'Yep,' she says. 'Where you from?'

'Sydney,' I say.

Her eyes nearly pop out of her head.

'What are you doing here? How'd you get here? I thought the borders were shut.'

'They are,' I say. 'But where you're meant to be, you're meant to be.'

I almost get lost on the road into Dampier but then see the dog statue and turn the car around. I stop to take a photo, and see a small child urinating behind Red Dog.

'Sorry.' The boy's father appears, looking apologetic. 'Do you want me to get a snap of you with the dog? I'll make sure junior has finished his business.'

I stand next to Red Dog, trying to ignore the vague smell of child wee. I swear, looking at the photo later, Red Dog and I are both slightly grimacing.

Before I leave Red Dog I pat his head and take a photo of the plaque underneath him.

*Red Dog*, I read. *The Pilbara wanderer. Died Nov 21st 1979. Erected by the many friends he made during his travels.*

'You and me have more in common than you'd think, doggy,' I say to him.

Me and Red Dog. Pilbara wanderers, meeting at last.

I go swimming in Dampier. It's just me and three young First Nations boys. They wave at me and I wave back. We all jump in at the same time. The water is cool and fresh, reminding me of home. Not just Sydney, but my childhood home on the coast. The home I grew up in.

I couldn't wait to get to the big city, to take on Sydney, to see the world. My whole life I'd been waiting for the next step. Mum always said that if you grow up in the country it's always part of you, deep in your heart, which I didn't believe. The city was where it all happened, and the country town where my life began was just a stepping stone to greater things. But now, swimming in Dampier, swallowed up by that great blue swell that curves around me, so different from the red dust, I think of home. My body and mind calm down, with no phone to fear ringing or medical clinic in the middle of the dirt to rush into. In the water, I relax completely.

'Salt water cures everything,' I hear my mother telling me. And I, her daughter, as she predicted, have made it back to the country, all the way to the remotest part of the earth.

I never did like to do things by halves.

I wander up to the Mermaid Hotel and I stare at the sign. *Dampier Mermaid—Hotel and Motel. 'An icon of the Pilbara for over 50 years.' Home of Pilbara's Red Dog. Great PUB* [sic]. *Great atmosphere. Great ocean views. Great food, lunch and dinner.*

Sounds bloody great, I think. A pub with a capital PUB. As I walk in, I suddenly appreciate the significance of the capitals. This isn't just a pub, it's a PUB. It's a huge building with a giant wooden veranda, a menu the size of your arm and about every beer a person can dream of. It also has the true vibe of Western Australia—laid back, and not trying to dress itself up too much. It's there for a beverage and a feed and a bit of a yarn with your mates.

There's also a slight hint of danger in the air: a sense that, at any time, a bunch of FIFO workers in orange vests could come in and really set the place on fire (potentially literally).

I order a steak and a schooner of Hahn SuperDry (low carb— I have my idiosyncrasies, even at the Dampier Mermaid Hotel) and go and sit on the balcony. I am the only solo woman for miles and miles. I eat my steak and drink my beer, ignoring the curious glances of the men folk. I look out at the ocean. I post a photo on my fledgling @sonnie_h Instagram page of me at the PUB. A friend of mine I haven't seen for years who used to live in WA responds almost immediately.

*You're gutsy, Sonnie! The Mermaid is a wild place!!*

But I don't feel gutsy. I sip my beer, and eat my steak. Sitting there at the Dampier Mermaid Hotel, totally alone, I just feel pretty okay.

Everyone, at some point in their lives, should go to the Dampier Mermaid Hotel and sit there, having a schooner and looking out at the sea. You have not lived if you haven't been to the Dampier Mermaid Hotel. Pub with a capital PUB. Ha ha ha.

One night I come back to Q Block and open my door to see a man in a cowboy hat sitting on my couch. For a split second, I consider whether I should rush at him with a kitchen knife or call the police. Then I realise it's the son of the station.

'Are you trying to kill me?!' I say when I've stopped having a heart attack.

'I came by to see if you wanted a whiskey and your door was open,' he says, 'so I figured I'd clear the area for ya.'

I remember Holly telling me that if I ever left my door open I'd be sharing my bed with a snake, no pun intended—snakes do enter any place as soon as a door's even slightly ajar—so I feel a sense of gratitude. I've heard the rumours of a resident snake near Q Block, and I curse myself for leaving the door open.

'No snakes,' he clarifies.

I do a cursory walk around my tiny apartment, jumping up and down to scare off any unwanted visitors. When I am mostly convinced it's snake-free, I look over at my unexpected guest. 'I really have to get myself a cowboy hat,' I say after a moment, looking enviously at his headwear.

'Well, if you do, make sure you don't leave it on the bed,' he says ominously.

'Why not?'

'Very bad luck,' he says. 'Like, a lifetime of bad luck. Death. Terrible injury.'

'Fuck.' I make a mental note to keep all hats away from all beds at all times.

I must be feeling better, I think. If I'm starting to fear bad things happening that means I'm hoping for good things to happen instead. If that means keeping hats away from beds, then so be it.

The phone wakes me up and I feel a sense of immediate dread when I realise what the sound is. I look at the digital clock next to the bed: 1.28 am.

There are three big mines surrounding Desert Town, and the sites operate 24/7. There are hundreds of people working there with very heavy machinery, including loaders, saws, and bombs for drill blasts. But from the patients I've seen the last few months—a lot of them with high cholesterol and fatty livers— what the 1.30 am call really tells me is: HEART ATTACK. SICK PERSON. VERY SICK PERSON. IN THE MIDDLE OF FUCKING NOWHERE.

I stare at my ringing phone for a moment, willing it to stop. It doesn't.

'Hello?' I say, the dread already starting to kick in.

It's Nurse Lime. She's panicked, I can hear it in her voice. She is saying things like 'chest pain' and 'strange heart rhythm'. It is clearly as bad as I'd feared, but she's speaking so quickly I can barely understand her.

'Just tell me the name of the patient, their age, and what the problem is,' I finally interrupt.

'It's Wolff Parkinson White Syndrome,' she says.

'The patient has known Wolff Parkinson White?'

I try to stay very calm. It's Colm. *The patient is Colm.*

At that moment, a memory of studying for my fellowship exams with heartdoc_82 embeds itself in my brain.

We are studying over FaceTime, covering unusual and dangerous cardiac arrhythmias. I can hear his voice, as if he is right next to me.

'What's the main thing to remember about Wolff Parkinson White Syndrome?'

'The delta wave on the ECG?'

'No, like, the main complication.'

'I don't know. Dizziness? Fainting?' I feel defensive, the way I usually do when we study together.

'Sometimes, the main complication of Wolff Parkinson White Syndrome, Sunny,' he says, saying my nickname in the way only he says it, 'can be death.'

'Geez, no need to take it there!'

'No, I mean it,' he says seriously. 'It's rare, but it happens, and you don't want it to happen in front of you.'

Then we are laughing and he is telling me that helping me study actually isn't as bad as he'd thought; now all we needed was the ultimate study lubricant, wine, to make it easier . . . he says that my laughter is his favourite thing to hear in the world, and that making me happy is all he wants, because it makes him so happy too . . .

'Doctor?'

I snap out of the memory immediately. I am not studying, and I am not in Sydney, and I am not laughing.

I am in a town 5000 kilometres from home, and I am the only doctor for miles and miles and miles, with nothing to help me except red dirt and a seriously under-resourced Royal Flying Doctor Service that usually takes at least five hours to get anywhere. It is 1.29 am and, medically speaking, I am it.

I feel sick.

'Death,' is all I can hear. 'The main complication of Wolff Parkinson White Syndrome can be death. It's rare, but it happens, and you don't want it to happen in front of you.'

Nurse Lime doesn't offer much more information aside from the fact the patient isn't too well, an ECG has already been done and they've sent it to the mining company doctor in Perth, who has instructed us to get the patient to the clinic immediately.

'Who's the patient?' I ask Nurse Lime, already knowing the answer but hoping to hear something else.

'Colm Calhoon,' she says, after a split-second of hesitation, which I experience as an abyss of dread. I mumble that I'll get dressed and head into the clinic. My stomach feels like it's inside my head, and then my throat. I take deep breaths. I need help, I think to myself. I need help.

I am desperate.

My hands do what my brain is screaming at me not to do, and text the person who, deep down, I blame for this entire situation. If it wasn't for heartdoc-fucking-82 and all his filthy lies I wouldn't even be here. I wouldn't know and like Colm Calhoon, I wouldn't be close friends with his damn wife, and I wouldn't be the person who everyone is relying on to save the day.

I text him, and he doesn't reply. I call him, and he doesn't answer.

I hear his voice again, one of the last things he said to me. 'I'll always help you when you need it. Doesn't matter what time of the day or night. I'll always answer the phone if you need help. Always. I know you don't believe anything I say, and I get it. But Sunny, I promise you.'

I call him again. It rings out.

I get dressed and walk out of Q Block. I look up at the stars. They are bright and clear as I stand there under that big sky. And for a moment, for the first time since I think I was a child, I pray.

It's dark when I get to the medical clinic. They must still be coming from the mine site. I go to the crash trolley and check that everything is there in case—I try not to think about it too deeply—he arrests.

I walk into the emergency section of the 'pharmacy' (drug room).

Adenosine. Amiodarone.

Hmm.

There's no point calling the flying doctors or Royal Perth until I have the patient in front of me, so I try, once more, from the clinic phone, to call heartdoc_82. No joy. I harden myself to the situation and ring Roy, who thankfully is on a night shift. Roy did a year of intensive care and anaesthetics and is calm and collected. Just hearing his voice soothes me.

'Do you have a blood gas machine out there? Telemetry?' he asks.

'No blood gas machine, and everything else is pretty basic,' I say.

Roy sighs. 'Fuck. Okay, well, you can only do what you can do. Just do what we'd normally do. Bang in a cannula, pull some bloods.'

'The bloods take three days to even be processed,' I tell him.

'Whatever, just do it, it'll get the ball rolling. Then try the vagal manoeuvres. Put the defib on him. Draw up some adrenaline. Worst case is he arrests.'

I agree.

'You can call the flying doctors, right?'

'Yeah,' I say, 'but they take ages. If they're busy with something else they might not be here until morning, at the very earliest.'

'Jesus.' Roy sounds reflective. 'It sounds like you've got nothing. Call me anytime, not that I can do much.'

'I'll call the cardio in Perth as soon as the patient comes in,' I say. 'Although I doubt they're going to say much different.'

'Good luck, mate,' Roy says, sounding sorry for me. I hear a pager going off and for a moment, crazily, I think it's mine.

Then I realise I'm hearing it over the phone, as Roy is called by a nurse.

'Gotta go,' he says. 'Just stay calm. You can only do your best.'

True friendship, that. A call to arms from 5000 kilometres away. I might fail and the patient might die but I am in no doubt as to the solidity of my friendship with Roy. Sometimes, at the worst of times, even doctors just need the backup of a bloody good mate.

Colm is brought in on a stretcher. His heart rate is through the roof, close to 200 and his blood pressure is hovering on the cusp of too low. He keeps saying he doesn't have chest pain but his slight grimace makes me think otherwise. The volunteers hand me the ECG strip, which looks like a dog's breakfast.

'Colm.' I speak urgently, walking quickly alongside him as he's wheeled into the little emergency department. 'This must have happened before. You told me you knew you had this—what do you normally do?'

He looks at me. 'It normally stops on its own.'

'Do you ever hold your nose and blow out your cheeks?' I'm referring to something called vagal manoeuvres, a series of 'tricks' that can, if you're lucky, cause a nerve reflex to slow the heart rate. These tricks include things like blowing hard against resistance (like with your mouth and nose closed), or using a facial ice pack.

'Maybe once? I can't remember. Anyway, I'll try.' He holds his nose and fills his cheeks with air. Nothing seems to change.

'It doesn't work. That's why I called the first aid guys.' Colm is tough as nails, so the fact that he called for help is a very bad sign. He works as a drill blaster, on his own, about a half an hour's drive from the buildings on the mine site, which is half an hour again from the medical clinic. So he's been in this heart rhythm for at least an hour already, with no change.

'What about the cardiologist you saw the last time you were in hospital? What did he say? Surely he would have sent you for an ablation if you needed one? Or told you what to do if this happened?'

He looks, if possible, even worse. 'I never went to the appointment,' he finally says. 'He was too expensive.'

Something in me kicks in and I go straight into autopilot. Cannula, bloods, fluids, is there any magnesium lying around? I tell Nurse Lime to get another ECG, and, just in case, put the defib pads on Colm and draw up some adrenaline.

I call the flying doctors. The bloke on the other end of the phone sounds strangely cheerful as he explains there are no planes and the best they can do is 6 am.

'What should I do, do you reckon?' I ask instead, my tone blunt.

I can almost hear his shrug on the other end of the line.

'Try some amiodarone,' he says, 'or if he's unstable, just shock him.'

I feel like rolling my eyes: as if 'just' shocking him is as easy as giving him some Panadol.

'Sorry to say it,' he says, sounding only vaguely apologetic, 'but you're on your own.'

'Thanks,' I say.

'I just spoke to the cardio AT in Perth,' he says. 'He's awake, and he's pretty all right. I'd give him a call.'

I call the cardio AT. He asks for the ECG. I send him photo after photo, none of which is that clear because our ECG machine isn't that crash-hot, but from the pause as he considers the images I know things aren't good.

'Is he stable?' he asks.

I look at Colm; he's covered in sweat.

'His blood pressure is hanging on, and his oxygen sats and stuff are okay,' I say, motioning at Nurse Lime to squeeze another bag of fluid through his IV, as fast as she can. 'But his heart rate is so high, and he doesn't look very good. I thought I might give the vagal manoeuvres a go.'

The cardio AT starts speaking quite fast, saying words like 'the ECG isn't very clear' and 'pre-excitation' and 'this isn't a standard supraventricular tachycardia, you've got to be careful you don't throw him into atrial fibrillation'. This is all ringing a bell from my Advanced Life Support 2 course. With this exact scenario, I suddenly remember, the advice was to 'seek expert cardiologist opinion'.

Atrial fibrillation, or AF, is essentially a fast, irregular heartbeat, and if a patient is experiencing it in the context of Wolff Parkinson White, and in a place like this, they're essentially—in non-doctor speak—fucked.

'So what should I do then?' I ask the AT. The panic is sitting in my gut, slowly rising. I can't believe how steady my voice sounds. 'Like I said, the flying doctor guy said to give amiodarone.'

'Amiodarone can send him into VF,' he says gloomily. VF is ventricular fibrillation—contractions of the heart that can lead to death within minutes. 'You don't want that. Especially not out there, with no support, no ICU.'

'So all the drugs that work, I shouldn't give him?' I hear the desperation in my voice, and the start of something even more concerning. Resignation.

'Yeah. If he becomes unstable, you're going to have to shock him.'

'I don't have, um, much here,' I finally say. 'No way of checking his electrolytes, no good cardiac monitoring. I mean, yeah, there's a defib . . .'

'I feel really sorry for you,' the AT says, quite kindly. There's noise behind him, loud voices and beeps, and he says he has to go. 'Something's come up,' he says hurriedly. 'I'll call you back. Give me your number.'

I quickly tell him my mobile, and his voice, my only source of comfort, vanishes. Don't go! I want to shout. Don't leave me!

Never before have I understood extreme isolation so well.

Colm doesn't look good at all. The way he's got his arms tightly folded over his chest belie the 'no' he gives to my repeated question of 'do you have chest pain?' I watch Nurse Lime nervously pat down on one of the defib pads. I know D-Day is coming. If his heart continues like this, he's probably going to go into VF and arrest anyway. I stare at the ECG. Is it AF? By now I'm so panicked my thoughts are becoming jumbled. Is it something else? Maybe I could just try the amiodarone? *But he said that might make it worse.* The vagal manoeuvres? I know that one type of arrythmia means the manoeuvres could be a good idea, while another means they could be a really bad idea, and I can't tell the difference: the ECG is so all over the place that it's difficult to make sense of it.

Nurse Lime takes Colm's blood pressure. It's not terrible but it's also not really, I admit, that magical word: stable.

As if reading my mind, Colm closes his eyes and says, 'You can save me, right doc?'

I don't respond. My brain is trying to organise itself. If he gets worse, I'm going to have to shock him, which may or may not work. How old is the defib? Has it ever been serviced? If it doesn't work, he might go into VF. Then he'll arrest. Then I'm going to have to try adrenaline, and the whole shebang of the Advanced Life Support protocol. I can't tube him, so even if he somehow survives all of this, we're going to have to insert a half-baked airway and just keep calling the flying doctors in the hope they can somehow get here earlier.

I feel like I am driving a car at around 300 kilometres an hour into a wall with an airbag that may or may not work, and it's all going in slow motion. It's like a bad medical TV show only it's actually happening.

*How am I going to tell Holly?*

That's when it happens. The image of Holly sitting in her backyard with her kids as Colm serves up smoked fish does something to me. His blood pressure is still okay and the registrar didn't say not to try the vagal manoeuvres. I make a decision.

'Mate.' I clear my throat, addressing Colm as I look at his pale face. 'I'm going to get you a very cold tub of water, and I want you to put your face into it. If that doesn't work I'm going to get you to do the weird cheek-blowing thing again, as hard as you can, and I'm going to very firmly massage your neck. All of these things stimulate a nerve in your body that, if done in the right way, can throw your heart back into its normal rhythm.'

*Or throw you into full-blown atrial fibrillation then ventricular fibrillation that will kill you,* I add silently.

'And if that fails,' I continue, 'and you get worse, I'll have to shock you with these pads. Okay?'

Colm looks terrified but manages half a laugh. Nurse Lime brings over the freezing water and I start massaging Colm's neck. He blows his cheeks out. And then, after what feels like decades, I see his face change. 'I think it's stopped,' he says, looking up at me, almost childlike.

Nurse Lime does another ECG. She hands me the printout, wordlessly. Sinus Rhythm. Normal.

Somewhere in the green hills of Tipperary, a group of leprechauns is standing up with their pints of Guinness and cheering.

Maybe Colm was saved by the stimulation of the vagus nerve coursing through him that night, throwing his heart back into a stable rhythm, giving his cells and brain and soul oxygen and life. Or maybe the underlying arrythmia wasn't as bad as we thought and there was always a chance it would revert—who knows? Whatever it was, the leprechauns and I are both celebrating the grace of blind luck. Because in a place like the Pilbara, sometimes that's all you have. From the relative safety of a giant hospital, it's easy to say it wasn't that bad. But when you're alone, and far from help, all your brain can think is: what if it gets worse, or I make it worse, and I can't fix it?

My phone rings. It's my friend, the cardiology AT from Royal Perth. 'He's reverted,' I say.

'Okay, great.' He's all business. 'But still get him down here. We'll accept care.'

'Colm,' I say when I hang up, 'you're going to see the fucking cardiologist. If you don't get on that plane when it arrives, I'll kill you.'

When Colm is less grey in the face, and three more ECGs look normal, I call Holly, who races into the clinic. As she is scolding him for not going to the cardiologist and drinking too much, and crying and thanking me, I slip out the back door. The lights are dim, but I can just make out the flat tabletops of the mountains in the distance. Soon it will be daylight, and the plane will be here to take Colm to the safety and civilisation of a big teaching hospital.

But, for now, it is just me, looking out over the red, waiting for the sun to come up.

By the time heartdoc_82 texts me back, Colm is well on his way to the city and I'm in bed, trying to sleep.

*Sorry—missed this. Wolff Parkinson White, that's a really tough one. Love to hear about it.*

Part of me wants to feel infuriated at the casual throwaway tone, at the lack of care from someone who promised me they would never let me down. But all I feel is really tired, and really old.

That night I'm so stressed I decide to risk Viagra man and go back to the pool, but even the water can't calm me. I stare down at the black line painted on the bottom of the pool but I can't quite shake the endless stream of images of Colm Calhoon's grey face that flash through my mind, or the question, what if it hadn't turned out as well as it had? I swim half a kilometre then give up and drive home. But when I arrive, I don't want to get out of the car; I want to go somewhere, anywhere—I'm filled with a sudden, mad desire to speed away from Desert Town, out down the red dirt road to where there's no phone reception, no people, no anything. And just keep driving, forever.

It's still dark when I drive out to the tiny airstrip, which you wouldn't even know is an airstrip if it weren't for the flags that delineate the runway. I don't know why, considering there are probably snakes and scorpions and god knows what else hiding in the dust, but I get out of the car. I look up.

The sky is a giant quilt, dotted with the lights of stars that have already died. It covers the world, and me, completely. Underneath my bare feet I can feel sandy dirt, dry because it hasn't rained for many months. I am nothing except a dot. A tiny mass of cells and emotions that may as well not exist because they are not seen or touched, not like the sky and the earth.

What am I doing here, I wonder. But when I say 'here' I don't think I mean here, in the desert, in the centre of Western Australia.

The most basic premise of medicine is to do no harm. But out here it just feels I'm practising harm minimisation. Being a human means you will be harmed or cause harm, and the good country GP can only do her best, or worst, with that.

What am I doing here?

*You're putting your feet in the dirt, girl.*

What happens then? When my feet are in the dirt?

*That's between your feet and the dirt.*

As my patients sleep in the houses around me, and the mines operate 24/7, and the spirits of the land interrupt the sleep of women with light eyes who are out of time and place, I lie down next to the car and spread my fingers into the earth.

I feel it against my back, warm on my skin even though it's night—out here there is never a winter. I dig my heels into the ground underneath me, and feel small ants gently exploring my strange human skin, which has interrupted their work under the cover of darkness. I try to count the stars but only get to nineteen before realising there are so many I will never know them all. Some things are not meant to be quantified, not in a place like this. Time is an abstract concept made up by humans that in the Pilbara means almost nothing.

Lying there, I silently tell the dirt everything that I usually pretend I don't feel or know. I talk about my fears and losses and stupid worries, and about the pain that feels selfish and gratuitous, but is mine. Between me and the dirt, there is no one and nothing here to judge me. I talk about what happened with Colm Calhoon, and my deep feeling it was just blind luck that saved him. I talk about my sometimes regret over becoming a doctor, about my wondering if perhaps there'd been another life for me, a different life, an easier life. I talk about my lost colleagues, the people who slipped into the darkness of the terrible pressure of the job, and I touch that red earth and thank it that I'm here now, feeling it beneath me.

I tell it everything, without saying a single word. I don't know how long I lie there for. At one point, I feel the dirt near my cheek turning to soft mud. I think it must be raining but then I realise it's my tears, streaming down my face and into the red dust.

If anyone had looked down from above, they would have seen the figure of a woman lying on her back in the centre of nothing, talking to nothing, saying nothing, hearing nothing, and yet ...

*That's between your feet and the dirt, girl.*

It's inexplicable but something in me touches something else, that gives me a sense of understanding of what Jennifer, with her years on the loader and her strange, ancient wisdom, was trying to tell me.

Long after I leave, the imprint of my shape will stay here. Some part of me, a shadow on the dirt that waits, silently, for me to return.

Everything after that night feels simultaneously easy and hard.

I love the land more every day and hate the job double that. I love the patients but fear them getting very sick and my not being able to help them. I miss Sydney at the same time as never wanting to live there again now that I've seen the vastness and mystery of the desert.

My contract is coming to an end. I know they want me to stay, but being on call every night is exhausting me and I feel like it might be time to move on. I also have a strange instinct that one night I won't have the luck I had with Colm Calhoon. I'm playing with fire, working out here alone, and I don't want myself, or my patients, to be burnt by the lack of resources or the lack of planes or the lack of everything else.

I peruse other contracts, but don't accept any. I remain in limbo, but I am resolute that it's time to go somewhere else.

My final weeks are wonderful and painful. I spend any spare moments swimming in the river on the cattle station with the station's son and shooting with the Calhoons. Colm assures me he is now recovered and will see the cardiologist as arranged ('if he's not going to charge me through the fucken roof'), and he takes me out into the desert to shoot fire extinguishers and cans. I hate guns but grow accustomed to the power inside the little machine almost too quickly for my own comfort.

'We'll make a Pilbara girl of you yet, doctor,' he says to me in that marvellous accent.

But maybe I always was. Who knows what home is? Maybe

it's just a place where you feel like you belong. I don't know how, but I feel like I belong here.

Holly is organising a farewell for me at the sports club. I have now lived in Desert Town for three months, three days, eleven hours and 44 minutes. All the patients are filing in, one by one, and asking me to stay. Nurse Lime says nothing, but I reckon she might miss me. Sam is still in Perth, where she's now a permanent resident of one of the private hospitals, as her medical team fights not to amputate part of her leg.

Linus the masochistic ringer swings by the clinic to offer me a chopper ride, under the proviso I don't tell anyone, but I'm too scared of dying in a low-flying helicopter with no doors, so politely decline.

'You heading back east? Back to Sydney?'

'I don't know,' I tell him as we stand out the back of the medical clinic.

'Don't go back there yet,' he says. 'You're not ready.'

I don't ask him how he knows that, but his words reflect my own fears when I picture Sydney. He's right. I'm not ready.

I invite him to my farewell drinks but he tells me he's off the grog due to a series of poorly executed, booze-fuelled decisions. I can relate, so don't press him.

Hank and Arthur come in to whinge about the mining company, but also to give me a fishing shirt and rodeo tee and say goodbye. I ask Hank about Broome, which I've heard good things about.

'Can you swim up there?' I ask.

Hank gives me a glance. He informs me he was a chopper pilot for some years (everyone in WA seems to have flown helicopters at some point) and says that after a few trips over Roebuck Bay and Cable Beach he never swam there again.

'Some big bastards in Broome waters,' he tells me sagely. '28-foot tiger sharks. Big fish.'

'Can't be any bigger than the bastards I've already met,' I say.

Arthur tells me I'll be right: just poke the sharks in the eye and Bob's your uncle. 'There's a good croc park up there too,' he advises. 'I reckon you should take a look at the place.'

I google it on my last day in the medical clinic. It's sand and water and sky. Famous for its pearling industry and white lattice houses, and even further from Sydney than where I am now. Even the name I like.

I say it out loud: 'Broome.'

It sounds like the wind, or a gust of water and sand that floats gently along a warm breeze.

Broome.

Maybe I will find myself in Broome. Without thinking, I book a stupidly expensive flight and a week's accommodation on the beach.

*Broome.*

Maybe it's because I've been thinking about Broome, and thoughts about the sun and the air and the sea call out to other people who crave that kind of living, but on my second-to-last morning in Desert Town I run into The Sailor from Fremantle.

We say hello warmly when we spot each other at the only

café in town. She looks surprised when I invite her to farewell drinks. I effuse about Broome and the sea; we talk about Sardinia and boats. I scold her for not coming back into the clinic for a follow-up, but she assures me she caught up with her GP down south. I am relieved.

'I wrote down that conversation we had,' I tell her. 'I hope you don't mind. But it was just amazing, hearing someone who had gone on to Algarve and the Costa Smeralda, all the way from a shed in Freo. What a story.'

The Sailor tells me she doesn't mind at all, and will tell her twin brother he may well one day feature in a book, if he ever gets time to read it between hobnobbing with yachting types in the Med. She says she hopes I will cure my writer's block and write it, and that she will get to build boats with her brother.

'Next time we meet it'll be like we said,' I tell her. 'On the Costa Smeralda, far from here.'

She says she'll hold me to it. Then our coffees arrive, and we part ways. I didn't know at the time that this would be one of the last conversations she would ever have. The Sailor never made it to Sardinia to build boats. Instead, she died in a hospital in Perth six weeks later, blood wilfully seeping into her wonderful brain. She was 28.

When I found out, I remember sitting at my kitchen bench, staring into nothing. The Sailor, my patient but also my almost-friend. The girl who had a twin brother from Fremantle, Western Australia, with whom she built boats out of a shed. Who worked in a mine to make money while her literal other half was floating around the Algarve, Sardinia, Spain, France, building yachts for the rich and famous. I had, so many times, imagined the shed in Freo and the aquamarine water of

Sardinia. I saw her too, away from the chains of the mines and the mining companies, free, and covered in salt and air.

I sat there and asked myself all the pointless questions. How had it happened? How long had it taken to get her flown out? The clinic was tiny, with no CT scanner, no instant bloods, a dodgy ECG machine. Nothing at all, really, except iron ore and money.

I think about Sydney. I think about the hospital where I trained, four minutes' walk from where I lived. I think about some of the more entitled patients who demanded this, that and the other: the best specialist, the best care, the best of the best of the best.

Australia is a country that survives largely on what is under the ground. And there I was, and there The Sailor was, living and working in that place where all the money is, and where did it get us? Absolutely nowhere. Meanwhile, the same night she died, there would have been an 80-year-old man or woman going into St Vincent's hospital in Sydney with exactly the same condition, or close to it, and they would still be alive today. By sheer virtue of the fact that the money made in places like the Pilbara was funnelled into places very far away.

It's a simplistic way of looking at it, but it's not wrong. The truth, if you don't try to dress it up with city-person seasoning, tastes very bitter indeed.

And now she was dead. My almost-friend, The Sailor, the boat-builder from Freo, was dead, very possibly for no other reason than her being stuck out in the middle of godforsaken nowhere, and also by sheer virtue of the fact she was much more likely to suffer a catastrophic event due to genetic tendencies at least partially developed thanks to white people systematically destroying her ancestors' way of life.

I don't know the ins and outs of it, but I can say with some confidence that The Sailor didn't need to die that night. She shouldn't have died. And since I got that phone call, the injustice of this has not left me. If anything, it burns hotter the more time passes.

Had I known she was going to die when we stood there outside the only café in town and exchanged our goodbyes, what else would I have said? The thing is I can't think of anything better we could have discussed. Boats and water and freedom and life. We promised one another we would meet there, and perhaps we already had, just in a plane and a time our small human minds didn't quite understand.

After living in the desert and feeling the power of the earth—and the lack of power of my phone clock—I believe in these concepts far more, and with some conviction. Unusual for a doctor, perhaps, but then again, science just began as an idea and a dream.

Back in Desert Town, with no foreknowledge of this terrible event, I am drinking and dancing. My farewell party is brilliant. It feels like the whole town comes. I wear the Akubra I own by now, and everyone puts songs on the jukebox and we drink and dance and sing for hours. There's no Covid in Desert Town and any concerns about social distancing feel foreign and long-ago. Time, as it has often done for me in the desert, happily stops.

The next day I cry saying goodbye to Holly, who is as hung-over as me. I also cry saying goodbye to Jacqui and Queen Lauren, and sitting with the station's son outside the shop I cry again.

'It's been good for me, this bloody place,' I say, telling him as much as telling myself. He looks thoughtful, and then his eyes light up.

'I've got something for you!' he says. 'It's from Linus, actually.'

I look down. It's a book, an old book, obviously well read and well loved.

'*A Day in the Life of Ivan Denisovich,*' I read aloud. One of the classics.

'Typical Linus,' the son of the station says, rolling his eyes. 'He said it was a good book for a Ukrainian.'

I try very hard not to smile.

I leave Desert Town with one suitcase, and two additions: an Akubra hat and a well-worn copy of *A Day in the Life of Ivan Denisovich.* Before I start the car, I open the cover.

*Till next time—Linus.*

The flight into Broome is like no other flight I've taken. The country beneath me is red and blue, and brighter blue, and green and white and every other colour, all at maximum vibrancy. I stare out the window.

'Wow,' I hear a voice say. It takes a second for me to recognise it as my own.

I do all the Broome things. I go to the croc park, the bird park and Matso's Brewery. I swim, battling against vague feelings of anxiety as I remember Hank's words, at Cable Beach. I wander around Chinatown.

Something strange happens: I realise I really, really, really like the town of Broome. It is old and new. There are black people and white people and Asian people and European people, and people of all four backgrounds mixed together. Everyone is friendly. Time doesn't stop like it does in the desert, it just meanders along more slowly. *Broome time.*

Broome is incredible but has a dark history. After it was bombed by the Japanese, every Japanese person who had come to Broome to work in the pearling industry was put into a POW camp, even if they'd lived there for 40 years. I learnt that pearlers preferred their female First Nations divers to be pregnant, because this increased their oxygen capacity, so they were sent into the depths of that croc- and shark- and Irukandji-infested water to collect pearls for white people to buy, sell and wear.

Great beauty and terrible suffering. Australia.

On my last night in Broome, I go to the Mangrove Hotel to see the phenomenon they call the 'staircase to the moon'. When the moon starts to rise behind the ocean, it's like a sun. I am absolutely blown away. I stand there, my mouth hanging open like a startled dog.

How does that happen? The moon, somehow, is rising from behind the water, blazing red, a giant orb reflecting on the water.

'I can't believe it!' I say to the people standing next to me. 'The moon has become the sun!'

I look down at the mangroves underneath the balcony of the hotel we are sitting in, drinking cocktails and staring at the light in front of us. For a second I imagine a time when there were no hotels and no cocktails and no markers of white people on this stretch of coastline. I read once to stand in moonlight is to be bathed in God's grace, but now I think God, or whatever that concept represents, is also in the land, the sun, the stars, the dirt, the sea.

'Bloody wow,' I say. The two people standing next to me look over again and nod in agreement. We end up sitting down together to finish our cocktail. One of them is a teacher who, as she tells me, came to Broome for a ten-day holiday after a break-up.

'That was eight years ago,' she says.

They ask me where I'm from and I tell them Sydney. Like everyone does up in these parts, they look vaguely surprised.

'So you're escaping to Broome too,' the teacher grins at me. 'You'll be back. Everyone who is meant to come to Broome always does. It's the way Broome is. For some people it's just a beach town, a convenient stop and a nice holiday. But for other people, Broome is something else entirely.'

My last morning in Broome, I lie by the pool and finish *A Day in the Life of Ivan Denisovich*. I text Linus, thanking him.

He asks where I am and I tell him Broome.

*Bit bloody better than the conditions Ivan had to put up with!* he replies.

# part 2

# new south wales

She was born
In the river land

Born to her mother, into her mother's hands
She was free, as the river was wild
She was so innocent
Such a beautiful child

Then they took her away
From paradise
Where everything was beautiful
And very nice.

Archie Roach, 'From Paradise'

I fly back to Sydney and, many months after I was meant to leave for the bright lights of Europe, finally move out of the apartment I share with Roy.

Roy asks me what my plans are, whether I'm going to get a job, like Max has done, at a nice private-billing practice in the eastern suburbs and, you know, ease back into Sydney life.

I think about it. My friends are here. My parents are close by. I could make good money, and return to my old life. It's no doubt the sensible thing to do.

I hear a little voice in my brain: 'Sorry—missed this. Wolff Parkinson White, that's a really tough one. Love to hear about it.'

Four days later I call my locum agent again. Getting back into WA is too hard because of the border restrictions. But there's a job in a town a few hundred kilometres west of Dubbo, and then after that I can spend a few months in a place an hour from Lightning Ridge that has a population of around 700 people.

'I'll come back after that,' I say to Roy.

I put all my things—mainly just overpriced clothes I bought when I was depressed and a series of artworks—into a storage shed in the middle of the city. I think about my frozen eggs, sitting in their cryogenic palace. At nearly 35 years old, my entire life is in storage, including my reproductive system.

It's a relief to get back to the airport.

I fly into Dubbo, where a car is waiting for me. But it turns out the battery is flat, so I ring the NRMA, who take an hour to get there. It's 250 kilometres to the town I'm working in, and I'm not interested in driving in the dark. I call the clinic contact and tell her I'll be staying in Dubbo for the night.

Thankfully, there's someone in Dubbo I haven't seen for years but who I know like a sister. I immediately jump on the blower, internally grinning.

Dr Nina Dowling is a salt-of-the-earth country girl I met nearly ten years ago, on my first day of medical school. She's the kind of mate you don't see or speak to for months and then when you do, it's like no time has passed at all. Nina works as a GP in Dubbo, and has an English sheepdog called Kip, and a personal life that mirrors mine.

We waste no time cracking into some Aperol spritzes in her backyard (we may as well try to pretend we're in Italy), and I throw Kip a saliva-covered tennis ball.

'Didn't think I'd see you in Dubbo, mate,' Nina says, sipping her drink. 'But then I saw you disappeared into the middle of the fucken Pilbara of all places! One thing I'll say about you, Sonnie, you're very adaptable.'

'Thanks, mate,' I say. 'You do know I haven't left the inner city of Sydney for about two decades.'

'See, adaptable,' Nina says as we clink glasses. 'How long you out here in the great central west for?'

'Dunno,' I say cheerfully. 'A month, maybe more.'

'You can come back to Dubbo on the weekends,' she tells me. 'We can go to the pub. I pashed the publican last weekend, actually.'

I'm impressed. 'The local GP and the local publican is a great combo,' I say. 'Both VIPs in the town, stewards of the rural community making a difference.'

Nina laughs so hard she nearly chokes. Kip barks, although maybe he's just laughing too.

I am lucky, I think, to have friends like Nina and Kip.

On the drive to my new home, I go through a variety of tiny towns, a particular highlight being Narromine with its Glen McGrath statue, and a town called Nevertire, which I can't help but smile at the name of. NSW has towns like this everywhere: Nevertire, Come by Chance—who the hell comes up with this stuff?

When I reach the town where I'll be working, I note multiple shops on the main street and a few pubs—compared to Desert Town, this feels positively metropolitan. The main street stops fairly abruptly, leading to another road that goes for another few hundred kilometres further into the outback.

So, not too much happening here then. That being said, there's a nice river and, importantly, in a neighbouring town, a giant statue of a bogan called the Big Bogan. The tourist brochures show off the Big Bogan, who has an Akubra hat and a Southern Cross tattoo. Very whimsical.

I start work the next morning, and it's busy busy busy. There's a huge shortage of doctors and they've been advertising my arrival in the town for weeks. The line to see me is literally stretching out the door. I skip lunch but make up for it at the end of the day by driving to the next town, which features not only the Big Bogan but a good takeaway burger joint. I buy a burger with the lot, and then walk across the road to eat it underneath the Big Bogan, munching away. It isn't as relaxing as I'd hoped—I end up getting roped into taking photos of tourists passing through, wanting their taste of rural NSW.

'Everyone say "Big Bogan"!' I shout as I snap away at group after group.

'Do you want a photo?' one of the tourists asks me.

I say sure, why not. Me and the Big Bogan actually, I think as I peruse the photo after he takes it, look rather good together.

My new patients are friendly, and ask, with a hint of desperation, how long I am staying.

'Just two weeks,' I explain.

'No doctors want to stay out here,' they say mournfully. 'There was one guy who stayed for a year, and he was going to stay another year.'

'That's great!' I say. It's almost impossible to get regular doctors in towns like this so for a doctor to stay two years, for the community, is pretty incredible. 'What happened?'

'Management didn't like something he said,' the patient whispers, nervously looking over her shoulder as if management is about to rush into the room and arrest both of us. 'One day he was here, and the next day he walked out. It was such a pity, because he was a really good doctor and a really nice bloke.'

'Well, that's fucked,' I say, bluntly. 'I can't believe the politics in these tiny places. As if things aren't hard enough.'

She laughs. 'I wish you would stay. We need doctors who care. And swear.'

Sometimes, even as a doctor, particularly in rural Australia, to swear is to care.

One day I get back from lunch to see a tall man, dressed in an unusually expensive suit for these parts, having a stand-off with a very angry-looking lady. They are standing in the corridor outside my consult room.

'I paid for your fucking Lamborghini, Albert!' yells the lady. 'Me and half the patients in this town!! You're a shyster and a thief, and I'm not going to forget it!'

She turns to me as I, accidentally caught in the crossfire, try to open my door.

'Are you the new doctor?!'

'Ah, yes,' I say, trying to avoid eye contact with both of them and slip in.

She suddenly smiles.

'Great. I'm Wendy. I have an appointment with you now, I just had to have a few words with . . .' She turns to the man in the suit, who is spluttering and red in the face. 'This arsehole!'

She opens my door and flounces in.

'This is defamation!' the man in the suit blusters from the corridor, looking at me as if I can somehow do something.

I look at him semi-apologetically and shut the door to find myself face to face with Wendy, a woman in her late sixties who has peroxide-blonde hair, like Dolly Parton, and a firmly set mouth.

'I've got cancer,' she tells me, 'so I don't have time for these money-grabbing pricks. This is a small community, we're already struggling enough, and we don't need to be ripped off by dickhead specialists like him who use us to pay for his Aston Martins.'

'I thought it was a Lamborghini,' I can't help saying.

She raises one eyebrow at me.

'Whatever,' she says. 'Imagine having such a small penis you have to drive around, in a place like this, in a bloody Lamborghini.'

I am trying very hard not to laugh but can't hold it back. When I get myself together I appraise Wendy.

'I own the hairdressers on the main street,' she informs me. 'We do champagne and hair. You must come in one day. It might not be Dubbo but I think we do great hair, if I can be so bold.'

'How's the champagne?' I ask.

'It's prosecco,' she whispers, leaning in conspiratorially, 'but only wankers really care about that.'

'Cheers to that!' I agree.

After half an hour with Wendy I realise she's actually the best. I learn the reasons behind her beef with Dr Albert across the hall: apparently, he did a bunch of procedures no one needed and lost his accreditation at some big hospital in Queensland, before coming out here and suggesting patients have tests for which he charges them 'about five times what you'd pay anywhere else. Do we look rich to you out here? The biggest attraction near us is the Big Bogan, and people even lost interest in that when the drought was on and the river dried up.'

'I heard the drought was pretty bad,' I say.

She shakes her head. 'Terrible thing. Terrible. You know, sometimes we can spend years just waiting for the damn rain. Your days are totally defined by it. Just sitting there, waiting for the rain.'

I've gained some appreciation for the impact of the drought from a patient who came in this morning. He needed a shoulder reconstruction and had already seen the surgeon, but his referral had lapsed. He was in a lot of pain. I look at his MRI—his shoulder really was 'buggered', as he described it.

'Anyway, I can afford to see the specialist now,' he'd explained. 'It's been raining.'

I gave him a new referral, and pray the next drought holds off long enough for him to get his new shoulder.

Wendy tells me it was the worst drought they'd seen for years. Drought, she explains, doesn't just mean no crops and no money: it means more car accidents and more deaths, because all the kangaroos come out onto the road in search of water.

'Teenagers driving at night, you know,' she say. 'There were three dead in three months.'

135

After half an hour of talking, Wendy clears her throat and tells me she's here because, with the cancer, she knows she's 'going to cark it' and she wants me to help her write up an advanced care directive.

As we do the paperwork I start to realise Wendy hasn't actually had her specialist appointment yet, and doesn't even know if they're going to treat her or palliate her. I look at her scans, which are similar to those of a patient I had in Sydney, and read the letters she's brought. I tell her that there's a chance they might want to treat her.

'We can certainly be clear about whether or not you'd want to be tubed in intensive care or that sort of thing, in the event you were in hospital and did have a cardiac arrest,' I explain. 'But to be at the point when you're deciding how much morphine you want at home, might be a little ... pre-emptive? I mean, are you in pain now?'

'I just want to get on with it and be palliated,' she tells me firmly.

I look at Wendy. She's wearing her hairdressing apron over a smart linen shirt and pants. Her phone rings. It's the building guy. I tell her to take the call, and she shouts down the phone about a dodgy job he did on her roof.

When she hangs up, apologising, I gingerly try again.

'Wendy, when you say you want to be palliated, well, we can't really do that until you're sort of ... you know ...'

She looks at me.

'Well, dying,' I finally say. 'Like in pain, needing morphine infusions, that sort of thing.'

'Yes, but I've got cancer,' she says, looking at me like I'm mad. 'I *am* dying. So can't you palliate me?'

'But you might find the specialist says they can treat you,' I point out. 'I don't think I can send you home with your morphine pack just yet, although I certainly can make all these wishes clear in the directive, if and when it comes to that.'

I realise, as I sit there semi-arguing that Wendy isn't at death's door quite yet, what's going on. Wendy is afraid. I know she is because I would be afraid. Once when I was a medical student, I got viral meningitis and ended up in hospital for ten days. At the time, my blood results started doing weird things and my platelet count dropped to be undetectable. I remember being so terrified of having some kind of incurable blood cancer that I didn't want to get any more results: I just wanted to leave the hospital and die quietly, in peace. At least by going home and palliating herself, even if it's too early, Wendy will have an ounce of control.

I tell her about my platelets and how in the end it was treated and turned out okay—I'm still in the land of the living, at least. I say that while I know it isn't the same situation, could she just promise me she'll go to the appointment, and then I'll happily revisit the palliative care plan?

As Wendy leaves, the practice manager rings to tell me I'm running very late for my next appointment. I ignore her and stay sitting there, thinking about what just transpired.

Being a GP is a funny sort of job. Sometimes it's endless coughs and colds, other times it's endless complications. Some hospital doctors turn their noses up at GPs—we aren't there doing all of the dramatic and wild things they do, with the prestige and status that they have. The tasks GPs perform aren't heroic, lifesaving acts like heartdoc_82's putting knife to skin.

But other times, as a GP, I see and feel humanity in a way that I don't think I could in any other job. This humanity, initially, is cloaked by the dynamic of the doctor–patient relationship, the 1-metre chasm between us as I sit in my chair and as the patient sits in theirs. But then, something happens, and even as our roles remain clear, the humanity appears. The bond is palpable, when you feel and realise it. I am a person, and so are you, and for this moment, here, we are in this together.

Status, money and power means very little when you are in a small town 250 kilometres west of Dubbo, realising your dying patient has exactly the same fears, thoughts and needs as your own, and that you can meet her, for half an hour, and be honest with each other about it.

After that, I stop eating at the Big Bogan and swing by Wendy's salon every day for a coffee and a yarn. A few times, I pop in after work, and the 'champagne' is, as she promised, excellent.

The patient has a long beard, nearly down to his knees. He tells me he lives in a shack and has done since he 'got out'.

'How long were you in the . . . ah . . .'

'The clink?' A few years, he tells me. One unlicenced firearm . . . it does all seem a little unfair.

'It's because of the way I look, doc,' he explains. 'They think I'm a druggie, and I know I look like one. But I'm not a druggie, I just identify as a nonconformist.'

'Oh, so do I,' I tell him.

'You don't look like me, though,' he says.

'See? People assume things about me from the way I look too. But even if I look like anyone else, I still identify as a nonconformist.'

'Guess it's harder for you to grow a beard,' he says, generously.

'Maybe one day,' I say. A girl can dream.

He needs his left ear syringed, because he is deaf from a total wax blockage. I syringe it with success.

'That's the most pleasure a female has given me in about 30 years,' he tells me.

The patients come out with some great pearlers. Sometimes I can't believe my ears. One day Margaret, who is in her sixties and comes in for a new referral to the neurologist because her cat ate the other one, tells me the story of her stroke, which led to a long admission in Dubbo. It sounds like things were a bit touch and go for a while.

'So you just waited ages to call the ambulance?' I ask.

'Well, yeah, I mean I found out when I woke up that I'd had a bit of a stroke but at the time I just thought I was cold. It was bloody freezing that day.'

I appraise the CT scan of Margaret's brain done at the time, and marvel at her ability to euphemise: 'a bit of a stroke' when half her brain was drowning in blood.

Friday comes. Dennis, a patient I've seen a few times who has a weird cheek abscess I've been arguing with the hospital about, offers me some good wishes.

'Have a good weekend, doc,' he says. 'Don't drink too much.'

'I won't,' I say, but we both know I'm lying.

Monday must be loud T-shirt day. One patient comes in with a shirt reading *Truth is the new hate speech*, and stares at me while demanding I give him painkillers. He is closely followed by a bloke with a T-shirt featuring a giant rooster and the accompanying line, *Stop staring at my cock.*

I can't help myself. 'That's quite the T-shirt,' I say to him.

He glows with pride. 'It's my favourite.' Then, rather generously, 'I can get you one, if you want.'

On my final day I go past Wendy's salon for one last champagne. She sees me and rushes over. 'Doc! I have to tell you!'

Wendy looks so overjoyed for a second I think she's going to tell me she's won the lotto. And it turns out, in health terms, she sort of has.

'They're going to do it!' she says, tears forming. 'They're going to zap the bastard. We got the phone call driving home from the appointment. And I pulled the car over with my daughter, and we sat there on the road, and we both just started crying.'

We both give in, and stand there, outside the salon, sobbing into each other's arms.

'That's great,' I manage to squeeze out. 'Maybe we won't need to organise the palliative care plan just yet after all.'

We are laughing through our tears. She tells me to stay in touch and gives me het card and a champagne on the house. She thanks me for listening.

I drive back to Dubbo, the green, rained-on grass stretching out on either side of me, thinking not just about Wendy, but also about my other patient, my almost-friend from the Pilbara.

Wendy may now live, thanks to the decision of a specialist team hundreds of kilometres from her home, but I can't help thinking about The Sailor, who didn't. Instead, she died hundreds of kilometres from home, in the sterility of a big teaching hospital. Far away from the land her ancestors touched. The coins were flipped, but they were always going to land the way they fell. Years and time and distance—the invisible strings that determine when it's the end.

I'd like to say the sight of the land, as I drive alone and silent into the setting sun, gives me hope. But all I really feel underneath all that beauty is a vast sense of isolation, the bitterness of blind luck, sadness and fury.

It's a relief to get back to Nina and Kip in Dubbo.

'So when you off, mate?' she asks me as we sit in the backyard, throwing the tennis ball for Kip. 'You're going out somewhere near Bourke next, right?'

'Yeah, fly out on Monday morning,' I say.

'Those little towns on the river are interesting places,' she says, looking a little worried for me. 'I worked in Coonamble for six months, but where you're going is further away. And smaller.'

'Hmm,' I say.

'But I guess you worked in the Pilbara—you can handle anything,' she says, which doesn't inspire much confidence in me.

'I hear from my patients in the last place that there's a hospital there and heaps of visiting specialists. It sounds like it's actually pretty well serviced. And there's another doctor there too,' I say, pointing out all the positives.

Nina looks unconvinced.

'Can I just say,' she offers, 'considering you lived in Kings Cross for years, to hear you say how great it is there's a tiny hospital and one other doctor in a town in the middle of nowhere . . . you've really changed your tune.'

'Change, my friend,' I tell her, as Kip slobbers all over my leg. 'It's as good as a holiday.'

'I don't know about this,' I say uncertainly, as I stand out the back of Dubbo's airport the next day and stare at the tiny plane in front of me. 'It's kind of small. Can I get a lift out there instead, maybe?'

I'm not great with big planes either, but very, very small planes really give me the willies.

The pilot looks at me. 'It's about five hours by road, if you speed. Do you get plane-sick?'

'It's more . . . it's just really, ah, small.'

'Well, I haven't killed anyone yet,' he says cheerfully.

I look again at the tiny tin can with wings, across to Bob, the pilot. He doesn't seem fazed.

'Why don't you sit next to me in the cockpit?' he suggests. 'It's less bumpy that way. You can co-pilot.'

'Ha ha,' I reply.

'It's like being in a car,' he says. 'Honestly, you'll barely know you're in the air.'

Bob's right. It wouldn't even feel like I was in the air, if it wasn't for the view that stretches across northwestern NSW.

We chat about the small plane business being a far better bet these days, with international travel grounded. We agree that, with both of us being Australia-hoppers, going from one place to another in the air, we haven't felt the sting of Covid-19 too painfully.

Bob tells me he lived in Western Australia for nine years and only left because his wife made him.

'Amazing country,' he says wistfully.

'Haven't seen Australia until you've seen the west,' I agree.

I joke that the plane feels like it's on autopilot—it'd probably be easy enough to miss the town we're flying to. Bob agrees, then tells an amusing story of being so relaxed one trip that he forgot to land in Walgett, and kept on going until he was nearly halfway to Dubbo.

I laugh and laugh, sitting there in that tiny plane.

'I bet you've got some top stories,' I tell him.

'Sounds like you do too. So you're just working around the country?'

'Yeah,' I say. 'Putting my feet in the dirt, you know.'

'Only way to do it,' he says, pointing down as the earth suddenly goes from white to red. 'There's some of the Pilbara-red dirt for you—the NSW version.'

It is comforting to see the red again and I go silent, staring down at the ground below. Then I ask Bob about the land out there, what they farm, what the history is. We talk about cattle stations and cotton and the river and the drought.

'River is running again in these parts, so I hear,' he says, gesturing below us. 'They've got a beautiful river out there. Even though they funnel all the water out to service the cotton farms.'

'That's a bit unfair, isn't it? What about the fish? And the people who fish?'

He shrugs. 'Cotton means money.'

I wonder to myself again, how can I have lived in this country for nearly 35 years and never really asked myself these questions?

We start the descent into the tiny town by the river I am working in. From the desert to the river, I think. Desert Town to River Town. All I can see is a tiny red airstrip, but I am used to this by now. Then, I see a car slowly pulling in underneath us.

When we land, Bob pops the front of the plane open and lugs out my suitcase. 'See you in a month!' he says cheerfully.

I stand there, in the red dirt, and watch him slowly turn the plane around on the runway. For a moment, there is nothing but heat, dust and silence.

A man with red hair and dark brown eyes rolls down the window of the car.

'Dr Sonia?'

'That's me.'

He helps me drag my suitcase into the car.

'My name's Charlie,' he says, 'I'm the manager of the clinic. Welcome to town.'

'Thanks.'

'Been out these parts before?'

'I worked out west of Dubbo for a few weeks. Before that I was out in WA, in the Pilbara.'

He looks over at me. 'What you running away from, girl?'

'Everything,' I say.

Charlie grins for a moment, then looks serious. 'Listen, I'm going to tell you now, before we get to the clinic. There was another doc in town, but she's buggered off.'

'When you say "buggered off" . . .?'

'She left last night.' He sounds reflective. 'I think the last thing she said was that she was never coming back here again. Ever.'

I nod. Great.

'I thought there was a pretty good hospital here though?' I say, trying to be positive. 'And heaps of visiting specialists? Apparently there's quite a large First Nations population, which attracts specialists and funding, right? You know, to help out the community?'

He looks apologetic. 'They've shut all that down because of Covid. We haven't had a specialist here for, I don't know, months.'

I breathe in through my nose very slowly, resisting the urge to roll down my car window and start screaming.

'You know,' I say, 'when I worked in the Pilbara, there were these mines out there owned by China, right? This was in the real heart of the pandemic, and they were flying the staff and the CEO, who were all from China, in and out all the time. In a place where there were very vulnerable groups. I guess iron ore is essential. Whereas specialists to a town that's largely Aboriginal? Obviously not so essential.'

'The problem here is that even without Covid the town is dying.'

'Isn't there a doctor at the hospital?'

'There's a GP here, but he's on a working holiday in Bourke,' he explains. 'They're trying to get him to come back.'

'So, just confirming,' I say. 'I'm the only doctor in the whole town. The specialists aren't coming in, so it's really just . . .'

'You,' he agrees.

I must be hardening. Either that or I'm in shock, because all I do is nod.

I go to the doctor's house and get changed, and then decide to bite the bullet and go straight to the clinic. Better to rip the bandaid off.

The main street of River Town is deserted. There are some kids playing on the side of the road who wave as I go past, and I wave back. It's hot. The heat shimmers off the car bonnets. I see one shop and houses that are in varying states of repair, some more well-kept than others. Most of them have large padlocks. It is, aside from the heat wafting through the air, completely silent.

Charlie, thankfully, is there to greet me when I get to the clinic. He drags me through the tiny building, introducing me to a variety of different people. Everyone I meet looks at me with a mix of curiosity, relief and vague suspicion.

'Have you ever worked this computer system before?' Charlie asks.

'No,' I explain.

Charlie sighs. 'I'll try and show ya, and Harry can sort out your printer. He's our Aboriginal Health Worker.'

The computer system is, as I expected, a total nightmare. Finally I tell Charlie to not bother—I'll just learn on the job.

Then Harry comes and sorts out my printer. 'You're the youngest doc we've ever had,' he says. 'What are you doing out here?'

I roll my eyes. 'I'm not that young. I'm nearly 35. I've just had Botox and I've got fat cheeks so all that makes me look younger.'

We both, despite ourselves, grin.

'How old are you?'

'21,' he says.

'Now that's young,' I say to him. 'It's, like, illegal to be that young!'

'Haven't needed the Botox yet, anyway,' he says, reflectively. 'Maybe next year.'

'Touché.' I like this kid already.

'You black?' he asks me.

'Umm, I mean, I don't think so?'

He points at my nose. 'You've got a black nose.'

'I have heard this before, but Dad seems to think we're the Henrys of Irish descent, rather than Aboriginal. And my mum's Ukrainian . . . so probably not?'

'You never know,' Harry says.

Lola, Harry's colleague, comes in to tell me my first patient is *womba*, and to look out.

'Sorry?'

'She's *womba*, doc. Been out bush, now she's back. You let me know if you need a hand in there.'

'*Womba* means crazy,' Harry explains.

Lola's right: the patient is *womba*, that much is obvious. But she also has uncontrolled type 1 diabetes, and she's so, so young to have the medical issues she does. For the life of me I don't know how she's gotten here, because she's been in Victoria and the borders are closed. I decide not to ask, telling myself that her fasting blood sugar of 32 is probably more of a concern than any breaches of Covid protocols, half of which don't make much sense anyway.

I ask Harry and Lola when the endocrinologist is coming back to town. They both shrug. I ask about the diabetes educator, who they report comes in once a week if we're lucky. I try to call the hospital to organise an appointment with the diabetes educator but no one answers. I try again, and it goes to voicemail.

The patient looks up at me. 'I feel sick,' she says, and vomits.

I worry she's going into DKA—diabetic ketoacidosis, a life-threatening complication that happens when a person's blood sugars are too high and they're not getting enough fluid in. DKA is when their body essentially starts to shut down. We don't have any ketone strips at the clinic, which I need because without a ketone reading I have no idea how close she is to full-blown ketoacidosis. Her obs are a bit worrying, too. I try to call the hospital again, before remembering that I'm the only doctor in town anyway.

'So, what's the process?' I ask Harry and Lola. 'Can I just call the flying doctors? Or can I get her transferred to Dubbo maybe? By road?'

No one seems to know. The hospital staff, when they finally pick up, tell me to send her up. They say they're going to call the VR doctor, who is based somewhere very far away.

'Can a doctor really provide the kind of care she needs over the screen?' I ask.

'Probably not. But you don't have admitting rights here. Although,' the nurse says, 'you can come and help if you want.'

'I don't think my insurance covers that,' I say. 'What about if I ring the ambulance? Can't they drive her to Dubbo?'

'No, there's an overnight stop in Nyngan.'

'So what if patients aren't quite sick enough to be flown out, which she probably is anyway, but they're too sick to wait 24 hours to be in hospital?'

'You just have to call and see.' I can hear her shrugging over the phone. 'If there's a plane, they might come.'

In the end, I send the patient up to the hospital, by sheer virtue of the fact at least they can do some blood tests. I ask Harry and Lola if it's always like this. They just look at me. I picture the hospital I trained at back in Sydney. I remember a girl presenting with a mosquito bite one night, and being so confused by this, even though I knew it was just a mosquito bite, I convinced myself I was missing something—she seemed so panicked—and ended up doing a battery of blood tests that were a complete waste of time and money.

I thought River Town being less remote than Desert Town meant there would be more ... things. But now I realise that having a hospital doesn't mean too much at all, if there are no doctors there, and no way of getting an ambulance quickly.

'You right, doc?' Lola asks as I sit in my room, staring into nothing. She appears with a fly swat. 'You might need one of these in here.'

I take the swat. I have learnt to accept such luxuries out in these parts.

'Thanks, Lola,' I say, gratefully.

A week later I have settled into River Town better than I expected to. I have learnt to park my frustrations—or to just yell at Harry and Lola about them in the tearoom—and found there is something about this place that I love.

It's difficult to reconcile the serious, horrific injustices that I am seeing with the fact River Town is beautiful. Take away the grime of poverty, the terrible health outcomes, the results of institutionalised racism—if you see underneath that for a moment, even though the rot is there, there's something else too. The land is different to the Pilbara with its startling red dirt, but it's no less fantastic.

Around a hundred or so kilometres away from River Town is the town of Brewarrina, which is home to the famous Brewarrina fish traps, the oldest human-made structure in the entire world, archaeologists reckon. Harry, who has some family there, tells me about it, and work kindly arranges a 'cultural tour' for me, granting me a half day off to make the drive to Bre.

Before the tour starts, I walk down to the river and stare at the ancient site of the fish traps. There is a small sign informing me of where I am. Aside from that, there is nothing but the sound of the river running over the rocks. Yet again, I am in a place that, if it were in Europe, would be celebrated, preserved, loved, admired—funded. But here, there's just one little sign: *Welcome to the Brewarrina fish traps.* I head to the museum, where Jack, one of the guides, is waiting.

We do a 20-minute tour of 200 years in that tiny little museum. By the end of it, I have a giant lump in my throat and am continuously wiping my eyes.

'Allergies,' I mumble to the woman next to me, who looks horrified by my sniffling.

What else is there to say? When you're living in a place very close to here, seeing patients with family from here, working and making friends with the top-notch people around here, and then you see its history? Photos of little kids rounded up. Remnants of a mission just over the river. A massacre barely anyone knows even happened. To be in this place now, and see the after-effects of that devastation, is stomach-curdling. It's repulsive. It's like swallowing bile you've just thrown up, and then throwing it up again.

In Australia, we learn certain things at school and we are told certain things about our past. The headlines scream about deaths in custody and Invasion Day versus Australia Day. If you sat on the eastern seaboard and read the paper or looked at people's Instagram pages, you'd swear that a lot of people cared, and that change, real, proper change, was afoot.

'We call that faces in places,' Jack tells me, as we stare at a photo of him with our politicians on their day out to the fish traps—doing the rounds. 'They've never been back since.'

When our group heads out to the river, away from the little museum and its catalogue of crimes, we all look out over the fish traps in complete silence.

All I can hear is the river, the water leaping over the rocks. Large pelicans jump along the riverbank, standing on stones, looking up at us with minimal interest. I stare into the formations of rocks in the water, and marvel at the simplicity of the traps.

'Look at that amazing engineering,' I say to Jack. It seems so obvious, to put rocks in a place that would stop the water and act like a reservoir to catch the fish. '40,000 years old. So bloody smart.'

He looks at me. 'My people are smart,' he says, simply. 'We are engineers, architects, environmentalists, artists. Everything we need is here on the land and in the water. Nothing is wasted.'

It's the truth. I turn and look up at the ugly concrete weir, put in a few decades ago, which proceeded to stop the proper flow of water and almost stop the flow of fish, depriving the pelicans of food and almost destroying the whole ecosystem around this part of the river.

Jacks sees me looking. 'A lot of people, when they come here, think the weir is the fish traps,' he explains. 'I don't tell them the weir nearly ruined everything.'

'White-man magic,' I say, more bitterly than I intended.

Jack smiles, but his eyes are sad. 'You're the doc, aren't you?' he asks me. 'Who Harry sent down here? He's a smart boy.'

'He's a very smart boy,' I agree.

'How long you staying in these parts, doc?'

'A month,' I say. 'Maybe more. I'm working just up the river, about 150 kilometres away.'

He knows River Town, and nods.

'How you finding it?'

'I like the river,' I say honestly. 'Even though it's really sad, the health outcomes out here, the deaths, the diabetes—it's been shocking for me, even after a week, to see this. But even with all those really fucking sad things, it's a good place. Like this.' I gesture towards the fish traps. 'This is a beautiful place.'

Jack nods. For a second, I see the flash of pride in his eyes. He knows I can see something that's true. Bre is a good place.

Back in River Town, Friday finally rolls around.

'Harry, want to go for a drink?' I ask him.

'Don't drink, doc.'

'What?'

Lola looks up. 'I bloody do. I'm going home to a nice bottle of white wine.'

'Me too, Lola,' I say, giving Harry a disappointed look. 'What about the pub? Is it safe to go to the pub at night, you reckon?' This is a pretty standard question for any town in remote Australia.

Harry nods. 'Yeah, it's safe. Just use the back door.'

'What if I go in the front?' I demand.

'You don't want to know,' Lola says ominously.

'I'm having a coffee,' Harry informs us. 'I'm actually a bit of a coffee connoisseur.'

'Really?'

'Best coffee machine in this town is at my place,' he tells me.

'I suppose you're also a foodie,' I say to him. 'Michelin star dinner tonight cooked by yours truly?'

He laughs. 'Can't be bothered. Tonight, I'm getting dinner from the servo. They do decent coffee too, actually.'

'Do they?' I look at Lola for confirmation.

She nods. 'Yeah, doc. The Indian guys who own the servo, they do decent coffee, and good fried chicken.'

'Do they do Uber Eats?' I ask, hopefully.

Harry and Lola just stare at me.

'Doc . . .' Harry says, looking pained.

The weekend comes and, with nothing else to do, I find the pool. The River Town pool is fantastic. It's Olympic-sized, surrounded by green grass and a giant pergola. I jump in and begin to swim, spending half an hour staring at my old friend, the black line.

If the line is my life, then I find it everywhere. Every town I go to, I find the line and I follow it. Then I get out of the pool, and leave it for a while. Sometimes I go off the line altogether, but I always find it again. Call it my true north. Maybe it gives me the ability to live completely in the moment. We forget, we get lost, we divert, we make mistakes, but then, there it is— that straight black line. I could be thousands of kilometres from home. Lost in the desert. Far away in the Central North West, surrounded by nothing. But then, there it is again. The water, and the line.

In the pool, I am present.

My first patient on Monday is one of the more elderly people I've seen in River Town. She's over 50, which is incredibly rare around here. After seeing her, I finally ask Harry why everyone in this place is so young.

'No one gets old here,' he explains. 'We all die before we get the chance.'

I cringe. 'God.'

'Five funerals a month here. Even more in Wilcannia, I reckon,' Lola says as she wanders into my room with a cup. 'Doc, you want a Berocca? You look a bit sad. Berocca might cheer you up a bit.'

'Thanks, Lola.' I tend to agree with this, actually. Berocca is really the cure for all ailments.

I tell them how lovely my patient was, and express my shock at how messed up it is that there's barely any technically old people in River Town.

'That's all true,' Lola agrees, then looks thoughtful. 'Harry,' she says, 'is that Elsa's cousin? Haven't seen Elsa for ages.'

Harry nods. 'Elsa must be what, nearly 70 now? Good genes in that family, they all get old. Last I heard, she'd gone down South Australia way.

'Who's Elsa?' I ask.

'She's an ice dealer,' Lola says casually, 'Like Elsa from *Frozen*. You seen *Frozen*?'

'Nah, Lola. I never know about movies.' It's true—these days I almost exclusively watch BBC crime dramas, meaning I'm often out of touch with recent pop culture references. 'Harry, is that nice older lady's cousin actually an ice dealer?' I demand.

Harry nods. 'Yeah.'

'Bloody hell,' I say.

'Yeah, she uses her pension as her super fund, doc.'

'So the ice dealing is . . .?'

'Her streamline account,' Lola says.

'Guys, this isn't funny!' I manage to squeeze out, as we all howl with laugher inside the clinic, 250 kilometres from nowhere, with nothing but people dying too young, a beautiful river, the pain of history, and Elsa the geriatric ice dealer swirling around us.

But among all of that, there is something else. As I berate myself, and Harry and Lola, for laughing, and sip Lola's Berocca,

155

I feel it. The warm glow, in the midst of total chaos, of new friendship.

'Your cholesterol is pretty bad, Jim,' I am saying to the man in front of me, concerned. 'And I'm pretty sure, because your stent wasn't put in that long ago, that you're meant to be on more medication than you're on now.'

'The doctors in the hospital didn't say anything, though,' he tells me.

'Yeah, I know, they want your GP to follow it up. I guess they don't realise out these parts there are often different GPs and these things sort of get lost in translation.'

Jim looks confused, which is fair enough—I'm also confused.

I call the chemist, who works across the road, and we go through Jim's old Webster-pak together. I tell Jim he can start his new (well, old, but newly resolved) medication regime after the appointment.

'What's your diet like?' I ask.

'Good,' he says.

'Good, as in, what do you eat most of?'

'I like the fried chicken at the servo.'

I sigh. 'Yes, I've heard about that.'

'It's really good,' he tells me, looking brighter.

I hear myself droning on about the Mediterranean diet and decreasing intakes of simple carbs. How can I tell the patients to eat more tomatoes when there's one shop in River Town and tomatoes cost an arm and a leg?

Even I, I remind myself, have started going to the servo for the fried chicken. It's cheap, and it tastes pretty good.

Every Tuesday, Annette the dietician comes down from Lightning Ridge to work in River Town for two days. I ask her about the fried chicken conundrum and she agrees it's totally impossible. The food in River Town is ridiculously expensive. The old ways, hunting emu and turtle, are pretty well banned. She says it's just easier to . . .

'Get the fried chicken from the servo,' I finish.

'Annette's from the Ridge,' Harry tells me. 'You been to the Ridge, doc?'

I reply in the negative. 'I've heard of it, I think. Is that the place everyone goes to . . . I dunno, go off the grid?'

Annette cheerfully tells us that most people who live in the Ridge are referred to only by their nicknames. If anyone asks what their real name is and what they're doing there, she says, everyone goes deathly silent, as if that person has crossed a line that should never, ever be crossed.

'If you ask too many questions, you'll end up down a hole in the Ridge,' Lola adds. 'Never to be seen again.'

'Wow, you're really selling it,' I say.

'It's *Mad Max* land out there,' Harry says, with the air of an expert. 'You should go and see it.'

Lightning Ridge. I love the name. Sounds like a band, or a dream.

That weekend I ask Annette if she minds me inviting myself to her place. She says no worries, it would be nice to have a colleague over, so I drive the 200 kilometres to Lightning Ridge.

The Ridge is, as Harry promised, pretty wild. I drive past the sign saying *Welcome to Lightning Ridge* where only a question mark sits in the place the population number is meant to be. The dot at the bottom of the question mark is an opal, the Ridge being home to and famous for its rare black opal.

I drive to Annette and her partner Burkey's place. After a quick introduction to the ways of the town, Burkey takes me out to see his opal claim. His eyes glint with the fever of someone who hunts for opal. 'Lightning Ridge bank in the nineties held more cash than any other bank in Australia,' he tells me. 'That's how much those black opals sell for.'

Out at the claim, we are somewhere near the QLD border. We climb down a rope ladder, until we are more than 10 metres under the ground. We stare at each other with our mining hats on, looking into the gloom.

'So in here, there could be a huge black opal?' I ask him.

'Yep,' he says, looking excited.

Just imagine, we both think as we stand there in the dark: one lucky find, and your life is changed forever.

'Although,' Burkey says when we come back above ground, 'most people who find good opal, they don't sell it. They just hang onto it, and keep mining for more.'

Maybe it's not really about the money then, I think as I take one last look at the hole in the ground where potential riches lie in wait. Maybe it's about the discovery, and the magic.

That night we have drinks around a fire out the back of Annette and Burkey's house. There's a full moon, and I sit there counting the stars. A few locals drop over, each bringing a story about Lightning Ridge wilder than the last. I ask rather hesitantly about the dummy set up at the entrance to town, hanging from a tree with a noose around its neck and a sign saying *Ratters beware*. I learn that ratters are people who sneak into other people's opal claims after dark and steal their opal. The punishment, if the hanging dummy is anything to go by, seems to be capital. 'No ratting from me,' I assure the group, unnerved.

Towards the end of the evening I find myself sitting by the fire next to a man who hasn't spoken much during the night. Now it's just the two of us, under the stars with the heat of the flames and the now open whiskey, conversation flows.

'You know, doc,' he says to me—I've found in the bush that once people realise you're a doctor, they fall into the habit of calling you doc, even in more social settings. I look at him over my whiskey. I must have my GP face on even here, because he leans in as if to confide in me—'about five years ago, when I was in Andamooka, I fell down a mine shaft.'

I stare at him. 'Christ.'

It happened when he was on his way to a friend's place, and he had spent three days alone, 12 metres below the earth. The police hadn't believed his friend when he'd said he hadn't shown up; they just thought he was out getting drunk somewhere in the outback. When they did finally find him, he was nearly dead.

Half a decade later, as he sits across from me in that backyard under the moon and stars, he says, with the sheen of unfallen tears in his eyes, 'Doc, it's been years. But sometimes when I wake up, I'm still down that fucking hole.'

There's a silence that burrows into the earth, stretching through the endless opal claims.

'Some people never get out of their holes, I guess,' I say, looking at him. 'I mean, metaphorically speaking. But you were actually down one.' Metres below the earth, alone, for three entire days, waiting to die.

I have the feeling, as we sit there nursing our whiskeys staring into the fire, that I have just been witness to something extraordinarily tragic, and deeply profound.

In the Pilbara, my knowledge about Australia grew tenfold and my feelings were like the arrow on a compass, spinning wildly. Here in River Town, the arrow is spinning again.

In these parts, there is a lot of syphilis, and not just new cases: tertiary syphilis. There are people dying in local hospitals all along the river from the disease, and one of my patients tells me she's sure her grandmother died only last year because of 'that whitefella teacher out here in the seventies'.

'What do you mean by that?' I ask. 'Like, what did they say in the hospital your gran died from?'

Not that that the hospital could offer much of a medical explanation, I think to myself, because there probably hadn't been a doctor there for months when she died. The supposedly regular GP keeps extending his working holiday in Bourke, so all of his patients are now coming into the clinic to see me. Lola vaguely assures me she's heard he'll be back 'soon' but no one has heard from him for days, from what I gather.

'Gran went mad,' my patient tells me, ignoring my question about the hospital's explanation. 'And my other cousins, they the same about their aunties, and they all had, you know, with that whitefella teacher. And the rumour was he had syphilis.'

Later that week I have to call an infectious diseases specialist in Sydney, who apparently used to take calls from my catchment, although no one at work can remember if he still does, or ever actually did, cover River Town. There's no one else, though, so I ask Nina for his number. There's a bit of an awkward pause when he answers, so I stumble into the conversation with, 'Is this the infectious diseases specialist on call for the Central North West?'

'Am I ever,' he replies, adding after a second, 'I'll be on call for the Central North West till the day I die, and then possibly after that too.'

I ask about the most recent syphilis result I've seen, which is a bit confusing, and he clears it up. Just before I'm about to say goodbye, I decide to ask him about my patient's theory.

'Also, while I've got you,' I say, hesitating slightly. 'I've been hearing some stories out here that some of the slightly older ladies in the town are dying of complications from what really does sound like tertiary syphilis. Apparently there was this teacher? Back in the seventies . . .'

'That wouldn't surprise me,' he says grimly. 'That, and the leprosy. You see it all out there.'

'Leprosy?'

'The things I've seen in that part of Australia, and into the Territory,' he tells me, 'are equivalent to or worse than the things I was seeing when I did a stint in sub-Saharan Africa.'

'But no one knows! Or they don't talk about it!' I spew into the phone, anger suddenly striking me. 'Don't you think that's just wrong?'

'Where are you from?' he asks me.

'Sydney,' I say.

'Well, that's how you learn this stuff,' he says. 'You go out there and see it. I didn't know anything until I did that. So you're helping, by doing that.'

It's nice of him to say, but he's wrong. I am one person, an individual, a humble GP. The difference I can make is so minimal. I can stay here for a month and get paid for the pleasure then vanish off back into my life—that would be easy enough. Nothing would change, though.

River Town isn't very far from Sydney when you think about it. It's a three-hour plane flight, maybe ten hours in a car. Half that to Dubbo. It wouldn't be hard to have regular cover by regular doctors. It actually wouldn't be hard.

But that would mean we would have to admit what I am starting to realise: that Australia is not one country, with everyone having the same access to and quality of care. It's two countries, or three, or millions of different countries.

Certainly, my First Nations mates describe Australia as being around 500 different countries. But from my doctor perspective, it is quite obvious where the line is. My entire career I've focused on practising *good medicine*, meaning the thorough, research-based and careful assessment and treatment of patients. I think every Australian-trained doctor is the same. Some of the best doctors I've met cover regional and remote areas, and I understand the passion they feel for the job because I'm now one of them.

But you can be the best doctor in the world, and you still can't practise the kind of medicine you'd like to if the resources aren't there. While in a city there's a hospital packed with specialists, in the areas I've been working, there's a hospital with a video doctor and maybe the odd locum, and that's it.

What I'm starting to realise is that when you leave the boundaries of a big city, then as soon as something bad happens, health-wise, there's a good chance you're pretty screwed. During my time in River Town, a woman bleeds to death in the emergency department of a regional hospital about an hour from Mudgee. There are no doctors on the floor with her—they only appear over video. The media makes a fuss about it for a few days, acting like it's a big surprise that a doctor hasn't physically stepped foot inside the hospital the woman dies in for four and a half months.

What about the flying doctors, people ask. They can only come if there are planes available. Visiting specialists? They stopped coming during Covid, and even in normal times there were barely any of them. The infrastructure for them also isn't there in a lot of cases, so you can't really blame them—it's pretty hard to do a procedure you need equipment for when that equipment isn't available for a few hundred kilometres.

And my favourite: what about the GPs? Well, what GPs? There's currently such an acute shortage of GPs in remote NSW there's barely one to be found along the entirety of the Murray Darling. But there are nurses, right? Sometimes, but is it fair to make nurses run a hospital, dealing with people on death's door, with just a virtual doctor or a locum to support them? Is that *good medicine?* Is that fair, on the patients or on the health professionals? Can it change? Will it change? The answers to these questions depend not just on how much people know or how much they care. They depend on how much people want to know, and how much they want to care.

'You should go and speak to Brad,' Harry says to me, as we wrestle with VCAT to transfer a diabetic man who has a festering foot ulcer so bad I can see his bone, who is febrile and likely about to turn septic—meaning the infection will spread into his blood stream and possibly kill him—and who already has lost some of his fingers as well as part of his other leg, and all of his other foot.

'Brad knows a lot of stuff, about . . . well, everything there is to know about the river, and us blackfellas. He lives in Bre, does work at the museum.'

'Harry, can I just ask,' I say. 'Everywhere I've been, people talk about "blackfellas" and "whitefellas". Is that, like, offensive? Can I say that?'

Harry looks at me. 'I'm a blackfella, you're a whitefella. What's the problem?'

'Fred?' I ask, turning to the man whose foot is hanging in the balance.

Fred shrugs, and nods towards Harry. 'Like he said, doc.'

'Right.'

'Do you think I'm going to lose this foot too, doc?' Fred asks me. I return to the medical and stare with dread at his ulcer as the air team tells me he isn't sick enough for a flying doctor. Road transport isn't an option, so he might have to get someone to drive him to Dubbo.

'I hope not, Fred, but maybe,' I say. 'Can anyone drive you to Dubbo?'

He looks so anxious I want to cry. Fred lives in a little house near the river, and his only son works full time at the caravan park. Fred is so worried he'll get in trouble for taking any time off, and he's so proud of his son's job, that he doesn't wat to tell him he's sick and needs to go to Dubbo.

'I'm sure he wouldn't mind,' I say, but Fred refuses.

'I'll just wait at home,' he says to me.

In the end, I call the renal physician in Dubbo. He says to keep Fred in River Town, at least for a few days. We decide on a regime of antibiotics, which is a bit tricky because Fred's kidneys are stuffed.

'What if he gets worse?' I ask. 'He's febrile, and his ulcer is ...' I look at the gaping, oozing hole on the sole of Fred's foot, which is so deep I can see through the fascia to the dull grey white of bone. 'Yeah, it's pretty bad,' I say, swallowing.

'He'll have to be flown, I guess,' the renal bloke says.

'There won't be any planes,' Harry mumbles, fiddling around with a dressing pack as I say thanks and hang up.

'Fred, we'll pop you in hospital here,' I say. 'I'll organise it. Maybe the antibiotics will settle things down. But then you need to go to Dubbo.'

As I speak, though, I wonder if Fred ever will make it to Dubbo.

Later, Harry comes into my room, where I'm sitting with my head on the desk. I've been going through my blood results. One is for a 29-year-old woman with a haemoglobin of 42. I can't phone her, because she doesn't have a phone, and no one knows where she is. The rest of them show blood sugars well into life-threatening territory, and a variety of other numbers so alarming if I was back in Sydney they'd all already be admitted to hospital.

'This isn't right, Harry,' I say to him. 'This isn't right.'

He shrugs. 'At least you're seeing it,' he says. 'They talk about closing the gap. They say the Welcome to Country in the cities, and people talk about Invasion Day and Australia Day. They put those black squares up on their social media, have you seen those?'

'Yeah, I've seen them.'

'You only know how bad things are when you come out here,' he says. 'We're dying out here. The gap is getting wider and wider and wider. But, hey, if you say "Welcome to Country" in Sydney or Brisbane, then you must care about the blackfellas.'

As a doctor I have felt lots of feelings. Stress, guilt, fear, joy, deep sadness, bone-crushing fatigue and the full gamut of total misery. There, sitting in that little consult room in a town about three hours from the NSW–QLD border, listening to Harry, is the first time when all I have felt is shame.

'I'm going to drive back to Bre this weekend and find Brad at the museum,' I tell him.

On Saturday morning back at the museum in Brewarrina, Brad eyes me with vague suspicion until I tell him that Harry sent me down. I explain I've met the museum guide but not anyone else really, besides my patients, although I am thinking of asking Harry's cousin Billie if she wouldn't mind taking me fishing. I've heard some good tales about her fishing adventures.

'Where you from, doc?' he asks me.

'Nowhere,' I say, and smile. 'Not really; I'm from Sydney. But I've been working out in the Pilbara, in WA, for a few months, then out near Dubbo, now here. For a month, maybe longer.'

'You going to come back?'

'I might,' I say.

'You like working out bush?'

'To be totally honest, I, ah, sort of had a bit of a personal . . . crisis,' I explain, as one does, 'and I was actually trying to move to Europe, but then the pandemic and stuff . . . so I decided to go as far away as possible. But then I found out all these things that . . .'

Brad takes all this in his stride.

'That you didn't know,' he says.

'That I didn't know,' I agree. 'And, like Harry says, until you know, you don't know. But when you know you can't un-know.'

'So you're not a white person come here to rescue us poor blackfellas,' he says.

'No,' I say. 'I'm just an idiot who didn't know shit, trying to escape, and here I am, talking to you.'

For the first time, Brad almost smiles. Two people wander inside the museum at that moment and ask when the next tour is. Brad says half an hour. They look at me.

'I've just come to ask Brad some questions,' I explain.

They're on a caravan tour of Australia, they explain, trying to get to Victoria. When the border closed they accidentally ended up in Bre, and decided to see the fish traps.

'Oldest human-made structure on the planet, apparently,' the man says.

We all nod.

'I'm doing some work in a town near here as a doctor,' I explain. 'I came here to see if Brad could teach me things about the history of Bre, about the health outcomes in the towns along the river.'

'What do you think, doc?' Brad asks me. 'What do you think about the things you're seeing?'

Old me would have ummed and ahhed and crapped on for half an hour. But in River Town I am learning something. It only took me a few days of chatting to Harry and Lola to realise how much I overdo it with words. They have a straightforward way of explaining extremely nuanced concepts. It's like a language in itself. 'Shame', 'sorry business'; someone very sick being simply 'no good'. Even the fish traps are the same. Simplicity. Absolutely genius.

In medicine we always say to use the least intervention or lowest dose of medication possible to treat the patient for the best results. In other words, don't overcomplicate it if you don't need to. First Nations peoples knew this tens of thousands of years ago: I can see that in the land. The genius is in the simplicity: nothing is wasted. Not fish, not stones and not words. All I needed to do to learn that was come out here.

I decide not to insult Brad by lying to him. So I speak the truth and hope he isn't offended.

'Brad, it's totally fucked,' I say, a feeling of relief starting to enter my chest. 'I haven't seen anything like it. The blood results, the diabetes, the young kids, the mental health . . . but not just that stuff. It's almost like there's something in the water, but it isn't that. It's weird things like disproportionate numbers of blood clots. Really low ferritin with extremely high haemoglobin—stuff like that should be impossible. But it isn't. And I'm starting to realise . . . I think this is because of what happened back when white people first came. That there's been this physiological response to being taken from the land, and to the food, and to the chronic stress of displacement. I knew First Nations health was bad but this is like nothing I've seen. I'm not a professor, or an epidemiologist or whatever. But this stuff, these things I'm seeing, I can't fix them. We need something else.'

I am speaking very loudly and my cheeks are going red.

'Sorry, sorry,' I say to everyone. 'I get a bit carried away.'

Brad isn't particularly tall, and he's dressed very casually. You'd walk past him in the street and wouldn't think twice. But when he starts to speak, and then, for the next 40 minutes, I—along with the two people who have found themselves waiting for a tour of the fish traps in that tiny little museum in Brewarrina—am in the presence of one of the greatest orators I have ever heard, and, I believe to this day, will ever hear. Brad isn't in front of the Brandenburg Gates. He is standing inside a museum that documents the terrible history of what happened in Brewarrina, just outside a river where his ancestors achieved an incredible feat of engineering.

'Do you think the people out here are living, doc?' he asks, turning to me after he finishes speaking to the little audience. 'Honestly?'

'No,' I say. 'They're dying.'

He looks at me, his eyes burning with something I am coming slightly closer to understanding.

'All we are doing now is smoothing the pillow for the dying race,' continues Brad. 'With our CTG and our Black Lives Matter and our funding. The problem was that the race was supposed to just die out. But we didn't.'

The lady with us coughs uncomfortably.

'We talk about the gap,' Brad says. 'What do you think about the gap? Is it closing?'

'No,' I reply.

'And you know what the problem is, when people talk about closing the gap, those big politicians in Canberra who visit us once and take a few photos? The problem with closing the gap is that no one talks about what is inside the gap. And what is inside the gap, you ask, this gap we all seem to love waxing lyrical about? Inside the gap is—it's jam-packed full of—history. The gap can't close because inside, surrounding that history, is complete silence, and total denial. The silence is pernicious. "They can't fix themselves so we fix them," and what do we fix them with?'

I don't answer because I nothing to say.

'The Intervention Act. People talk about "communities", living "in community". What does that mean? Missions, reserves. We just don't call them that anymore. Do you know what the Intervention Act is?'

I shake my head. I look at the people next to me, who look as blank as I feel. I google it and Brad turns to me. 'What does it say, doc?'

'*The Intervention Act was directed at addressing the disproportionate levels of violence in Indigenous communities in the Northern Territory,*' I read aloud, '*as well as the systemic disadvantage of Indigenous people, characterised by economic deprivation, unemployment, social marginalisation, inadequate housing and poor health and justice outcomes. The intervention was enacted by the Howard government just two months after the report was released to the public, allowing little time for consultation with Indigenous communities.*'

Brad nods. 'So they draft up this piece of legislation with the idea it will help us, the poor black people. There's no alcohol, this and that control, no self-determination at all. It's the same sort of thing as the missions, just presented better. In the end the human rights groups had a look at it, and made them change it, but nothing really did change.'

There's a silence in the museum. The man coughs, a bit uncomfortably.

*How can I have not known about this?* That in this country, in this century, we had something called the Intervention Act, which controlled the way people existed, and took away their agency completely? It ended in 2012, technically, but most of the last vestiges of it didn't end till 2022, and its after-effects will last even longer.

'They say they put this in place to save people,' Brad says. 'To make things better.'

'Well, did it make things better?' the lady asks.

'You ever been to an Indigenous community in the Territory, doc? You ever lived there, worked there?' Brad asks me.

I shake my head.

'If you ever go,' he says, 'you let me know what you think, and you tell me what you see.'

Over the next few weeks, Brad's words echo through my head. It's like a constant playback, never quite turning off. I hear him when I sit with my patients, staring at their blood sugars, their haemoglobin, talking with them about how expensive the food is in River Town. Even Harry, my young mate, has persistently deranged white cells, and he's only 21.

'Do you reckon I've got leukaemia?' he asks me, too casually.

'No!' I say, too quickly.

'Why'd you refer me to the haematologist then?' he says, suspiciously.

'I just don't want to ignore it,' I say, 'because I'm a psycho and, you know, I just want you to get properly checked out. Just because we're out here doesn't mean you can't access the same bloody specialist as everyone else in this damn country.'

Harry must appreciate this a bit because he finally arranges for his cousin Billie to take me fishing on the weekend.

'Can you fish?' Harry asks me.

'Me? No,' I say, cheerfully.

I see Harry and Lola glance at each other.

In the meantime, Brad's words continue on, a low buzz in the back of my mind, and in my soul. Once you hear, you can never unhear. Once you know, and I mean really know, you can't un-know.

A patient comes in, on his way through River Town back to Lightning Ridge, needing a script. He tells me he used to live in Sydney, had some high-up corporate job, but then the divorce and the melanoma and all the other joys of life rather did him in.

'I just had to get out,' he explains. 'I realised my life had just stalled, it was going nowhere. And the years were speeding by, you know?'

'Only thing you can't get back is time,' I say briskly.

'Yeah,' he says. 'That's bloody right. And time was bloody ticking. So I got out the map, and I thought, right.'

'Right,' I say, leaning in.

'I've got two options,' he tells me seriously, remembering. 'I can either go to Lightning Ridge, or Broome.'

There's a short silence.

'I've been to both of those places,' I say.

He looks at me.

'What the fuck happened to you, then?!'

There's another pause, and then we both sit there, howling with laughter. Two lost people, travelling the same road, fighting against the inevitability of time.

Kristina calls me from Copenhagen when I get home from work. I sink into a glorious bottle of rosé and listen to her tales of life in Denmark.

'How's work?' I ask her as I walk into the kitchen to pour myself another glass. She is launching into a description of how cool her office is, because, well, everything in Copers is pretty cool, when I notice something outside the back screen door.

I think it's a bird at first, but as I inch closer I see two big brown eyes looking up at me.

I jump, nearly throwing the wine on the ground, as I and the little dog outside the screen door eye each other.

'Sorry, mate,' I say. 'There's this very small dog outside my back door.'

'Cute!' Kristina effuses. 'Maybe it's meant to come to you! It could hear me! It's a wanderer, like us!'

This is not good. I peer through the door, and see no collar. I end the call with Kristina and ring Harry.

'I think the neighbour's dog might have wandered into my yard,' I say before he even says 'hello'.

'What kind of dog?'

'Little black and white pup, I think a cattle dog, with a short stumpy tail.'

'It's a pup?'

'Yeah.'

Harry sighs. 'Doesn't sound like any of your neighbours—round here there's lots of litters. Might have been dumped. Hard to know. Just see if it goes back to where it came from.'

I press end, and stare at the little dog, which is staring back at me. Something about its eyes make me think it is looking for a home, rather than having one.

I am no position for a dog. Or a cat. Or a bird. Or a lizard. I can't even look after fish. I have no car and no home, and everything I own is in storage. A dog is not on my radar.

The dog starts whining and scratching at the door. It is tiny. It has two black patches over both eyes, like the lone ranger, and a little stump of a tail, which is wagging furiously.

We stare at each other.

'No, no,' I say to the dog. 'You have to go home. I am not your daddy. I don't have a house. This isn't even my house. I'm more lost than you. Just run back to where you came from.'

I take a deep breath and shut the glass door. I call Kristina back. Just before I turn the kitchen light off and go to hide in the living room, I look back.

The dog is staring at me through the glass.

'What's going on?' Kristina asks. 'Is it a boy or a girl dog?'

I go into the living room and explain to her that I have left the dog outside in the hope it will return to where it came from.

I drink my rosé and wait for an hour. I silently tiptoe back into the kitchen, and sigh: there is no dog in sight. Then, as I move towards the door, I see it. The little black-and-white body, asleep next to the door.

'Hmmm.'

It's getting dark. It's now or never. I scoop the little body up into my arms and walk to the shop, two doors down.

'Do you know who owns this dog?' I ask the ladies I find there. 'It just came into my backyard.'

The dog is trying to lick me and bite me. Her little body is furry and warm. But I have hardened my heart. I cannot have a dog. No dog for me.

They don't know. I wander around the neighbourhood. No one knows.

By now, it is dark. The dog is licking my face. I return to my backyard and let her run around. I notice she has a slight limp, and is dragging her leg around.

I run back to the shop.

'Found the owner?'

'No, I'll just get some food,' I say. 'Just one can. I'll have found the owner by tomorrow.'

The shop ladies look at me.

'And some milk,' I add. 'Dogs like milk, right?'

The dog and I sit outside the back door. She laps up the milk and eats the puppy Chum. I sit there drinking the rosé. She climbs into my lap, and puts her head on my leg. Then, a small ladybeetle appears, landing on her ear. It's weird to see a ladybeetle in the dark. My mum always told me that lady-beetles are a sign of good fortune, but I can't listen to signs.

I cannot have a dog. I don't even have a home myself. Tomorrow I will find the dog a home. A better home, with someone less lost than me.

I put up signs around the town and on Facebook, and continue asking at the shop. Charlie suggests, considering the dog has a limp, he take her home and shoot her.

'NO!' I bellow at him. 'You guys are crazy out here,' I say stuffily, as I race home at lunchtime to check on my little buddy, for whom I've made a house out of towels and a milk crate on the back porch.

Annette tells me her dogs like sardines, which is why they have such silky coats.

'It's the Omega 3s,' she explains.

I get my little buddy, who I'm now referring to as Buddy, some sardines. They are wolfed down. Buddy smells like a giant fish after that. I decide sardines will only be for treats.

The patients ask if I have found Buddy's owner. The people at the café ask if I have found Buddy's owner. Everyone looks slightly amused, as if there's a joke that I'm part of but don't understand.

'The doctor has a puppy,' the lady at the café explains to the bemused patrons.

'Just until I find the owner,' I explain.

'Owner's long gone or not interested,' one of the other regulars says.

'It's a stumpy tail cattle dog,' the café lady says. 'Good breeding. Someone must know.'

But there is a wall of silence from the town. No one knows. So it's just me and Buddy, lost together.

'It's all right, Buddy,' I say that night, as she and I sit inside on the recliner chair, and she shakes with horror in a towel after I decide to practise some tough love and wash her in the laundry sink, which she pays me back for by doing a sloppy poo on the bedroom carpet. 'I'll figure something out.'

I go fishing with Billie, Harry's cousin. Buddy stays home, sleeping in the milk crate, her bowl filled with enough Chum and sardines to feed an entire ocean.

'So, you got a dog?'

'I'm trying to find the owner,' I say half-heartedly. 'But it's been over a week. You don't want a dog, do you Billie?' I ask, a small part of me hoping she says no.

'I've got Rex,' she explains. 'He's a good dog. Wolfhound.'

'Wow. Does Rex eat sardines?'

Billie laughs. 'Nah, doc. Rex eats real meat.'

We go down to the river and Harry drives down to join us later. I have three beers, everyone else sticks to water. We sit there, with our lines and fold-out chairs, staring over the water. To our right are the mud and the trees, flopping up and over us, creating their mirror image in the river. It's so still, I could feel an ant cough.

'This looks like an Arthur Streeton painting,' I say.

Billie shrugs. 'Dunno who that is. It's my river, that's all I know.'

She gets a bit of hope with a few bites, which creates much excitement on the riverbank, but my line remains untouched.

'Even the fish know I can't fish,' I say.

Harry and Billie, kindly, only laugh for a few minutes.

Billie and I become friends. She's a fit, active sort of person with a keen sense of observation: she can see emus running through the scrub before my eyes have even adjusted to the time of day. She's a straight shooter. This might be partly her job—she works in family and community services in Dubbo so has seen the best and worst of humanity. She's back in River Town on leave seeing relatives, and is happy to show me around. She takes me all over, showing me parts of the area I would never have seen otherwise.

We drive for hours until we reach the mission, driving past the site of Hospital Creek Massacre. 'Most people don't like coming out here,' Billie gestures to a large expanse of land on my left. I can't see anything except yellow grass stretching for miles.

'See that rock?' I look and see the simple rock formation. Without her pointing it out I would have missed it. 'That's the monument for the people who died at Hospital Creek,' she says, after a pause. '300 people murdered.'

I swallow. At school we studied Myall Creek. All we knew about was this one massacre: we read about it and wrote essays about it and felt bad about. Then we grew up and left school and forgot about it.

But now I've come here, to the Central North West, I see the massacres aren't forgotten. They are as alive as the people who were killed in them are dead. They permeate the history of any town or land where they took place, and of every family. There are people in River Town who had relatives who were murdered at Hospital Creek back in 1859. Depending on who you talk to, there are varying versions of what happened. The story that I believe, now lost and muddied through history, goes that a white man from one of the stations went missing after a night out at the pub, and the local white men blamed one of the Aboriginal people living at Hospital Creek for his disappearance. Drunk, and looking to make the blackfellas pay, a group of them went to Hospital Creek with guns and murdered hundreds of people.

'Just let off a bit of steam, you know, cuz,' Billie says.

I am silent, trying, again, to swallow the lump in my throat.

They found the missing white man a few days later, drunk in another pub. And very much alive.

'At night, weird things happen out here,' Billie tells me as we drive away from the pile of rocks.

I believe her. The dead can't rest. How could they, when they know their families are still suffering?

We go to see the remnants of the old mission. There's hardly anything there aside from a few stone plaques, barely visible in among the scrub. The building burnt down, Billie tells me, so that's all gone.

Part of me feels a strange sense of satisfaction that the mission has been razed to the ground. In my mind's eye I see the photographs of the young First Nations children from the museum, dressed head to toe in white with matching white bonnets.

I walk up to one of the plaques and put my hand on it. The rock is cold. '*The manager's house was always called the big house,*' I read aloud.

'Yep,' Billie says. 'The whitefellas lived in there, and the blackfellas' kids got trained to be domestic servants.'

'To the white people,' I say.

'Yeah'.

'And this is all that sits here? Remembering this?'

I turn around. There's nothing. Just grass, trees and the river. There isn't a sign. There isn't a big plaque under laminated glass with the names of the children who were there and information about where they are now. There's pretty much just ... nothing. No tourists, and no pamphlets. Just the stone plaques in the grass, and me, standing there, a person floating through history, not even knowing where I am in the present or where I will be in the future.

When you see something like that, I tell you what, you think about Australia a bit differently. You don't see the land of the fair go or Bondi Beach or beers with your mates. All you see is a very strange place, where history is barely remembered, and places like this mission are fading before our eyes.

I am standing not only on the site of the old mission—I am standing in the middle of the gap. That mission and these cracked plaques are what's inside the gap. The history of abuse and dispossession and displacement. The denial, the ignorance, the best-just-leave-it-out-there-in-the-middle-of-nothing attitude. This is a place where no one goes—where people don't just forget, they forget because no one really wants them to remember. This is what's inside the gap, and it has never been reflected to me so clearly as now, standing here, these old plaques around me, with a friend, and the river.

They took the children away, they took the children away.

'You know Archie Roach, this singer we've been listening to

on the drive, he was taken away,' Billie says. 'Government policy, back in the seventies. Not so long ago, when you think about it.'

I can't even respond. I just stare out the window. Billie sees the tears seeping down my face. I open the window, and we both pretend it's just the wind.

One month passes, then another. The days meander along, and the patients begin to trust me. River Town becomes, for a time, my home.

One weekend Harry, Billie and I go to the river for a fish, and see a turtle wandering in the dust and heat. I ask them if it will ever find water, and they say no, that the little brother has gone too far.

We stop, lift the turtle into the back of the ute and drive out to the 4-mile jetty. Billie gently pushes the turtle in and we stay there watching until he swims away. His initial hesitation, and then delight that he is safe, back in the water, is amazing to see. His little head flicks out once as he swims away, as if he is saying thanks. Then he is gone, disappearing under the surface.

'Figure you've already got your doggy,' Billie says generously.

Harry agrees. 'Best return the turtle to his proper home.'

I'm getting used to living in the little town by the river. I go to the local markets, and meet the newspaper editor. I write an article about the pool for the local newsletter. Harry becomes my surgical assistant and we start removing all sorts of skin lesions so the patients don't have to wait months to see a dermatologist. For someone as risk-averse as me, I'm happy to find that they all go surprisingly well.

It's funny, I tell Annette as we sit in my backyard with Buddy one day, drinking red wine—even though it's probably too hot for it—it wasn't like I didn't fit in back in Sydney. I did. I love (loved?) that city. It gave me some great opportunities, and by the grace of God I bloody ran with them. But now, somehow, I've ended up here, sitting by the river in a tiny town about 200 kilometres from Bourke, and finding that I can be myself—the most myself I've been in months, maybe years.

'I'm really glad you came,' Annette says, as Buddy tries to chew off her left arm. 'It's been great.'

On the weekend I drive nearly 500 kilometres to meet Loretta at a town near Dubbo. I barely notice the drive, which is how used to I've become to these sorts of distances. She's driven from Sydney, in need of a rural getaway, and wants to meet Buddy.

'Other women our age are introducing their friends to their kids,' she points out, 'and here we are with your dog.'

The best thing about the weekend is the pub on the main street, called, like a lot of pubs in these sorts of towns, the Royal. The publican is a bloke called Pricey, who lets Buddy sit inside without any complaints, and we decide to make it our local for the weekend.

Pricey explains they've only just reopened after shutting down due to Covid, so he welcomes Loretta, Buddy and me with open arms. Buddy is wearing a new collar, a blue leather strip dotted with silver scotty dogs I got for two dollars at the shop—a total bargain for something with a bit of bling. I figure she may as well show it off.

Pricey asks me about Buddy's origins. I explain Buddy shouldn't really be alive, appearing as a tiny black and white speck in my backyard, walking with a limp which has since proven to be nothing (we stopped in at the vet in Forbes on the way here). If I hadn't taken her in, I tell him, she would likely have been shot, impounded or lost—or died from parvovirus.

'The dog who lived, hey,' Pricey says, offering Buddy a bowl of water. 'Bit like this pub actually. Although, if Buddy is the dog who lived, the Royal is more the pub that won't die.'

Pricey tells us that he had been manager of the pub, then left. Then he'd bought it, went broke, and sold it. The new owner then had to close it because of Covid and then *they* needed to sell it, and were willing to let it go for a song. So Pricey bought it back. Then he left and got someone else to manage it— but that person died. 'So now I'm back,' he explains. 'Owner and manager. I can't get away from the place.'

'Amazing,' I say, looking around me with admiration. Buddy lets out a little bark. We lift our glasses in cheers to the pub.

Buddy does a wee on the carpet and I clean it up. Pricey doesn't seem too fazed. He comes over with some chalk and draws around the wet patch. *Buddy was here*, he writes.

Buddy, memorialised on the floor of the Royal Hotel, Condobolin. The dog who lived, marking her spot on the carpet of the pub that wouldn't die.

Back in River Town, on one of my final mornings there, I take Buddy for a walk around the edge of the riverbank. It's early, still, and the sun is just beginning to be warm when two kangaroos hop past us. Buddy yelps at them, trying to chase them, until I grab her and we let them hop away in peace.

I watch the fur-covered roos with their little pointy ears and bright eyes hop lazily away. I see Buddy, her little blue cattle dog face straining after them. I think about the fish traps in Brewarrina, and the friends I have made here. I think about the mission, about Billie and I standing there in the silence, looking at those falling-down plaques.

I see the blood results on the computer, and the total lack of access, not just for First Nations patients but for nearly anyone living in remote parts of Australia. I think of the hospitals staffed only by nurses, with doctors phoning in via telehealth from thousands of kilometres away, sitting behind a laptop somewhere in a city.

What is Australia, I ask myself as I watch Buddy try to lick the grass. This enormous place, of vastness and mystery: what is it, where is it, and—like I had to answer in that speech I gave in a Year 6 public speaking contest—what does it mean to me?

I'm being honest when I say that, since that speech, I've never asked myself this question again, and if I hadn't gone into the desert I don't think I would have.

Australia is a place with a dependence on mining companies, with a health system that works best if you're living in a city on the coast and you're white, and even better if you're rich. Small museums in places like Brewarrina entertain prime ministers and premiers once in a while, or even just the once. Faces in places, gaps that continue to widen.

Is that fair? Underneath the startling red dirt of the Pilbara, swimming next to the pelicans at the Brewarrina fish traps, inside the opal claims of Lightning Ridge, I see one thing happening. The land is bleeding, bleeding like an artery that needs to be clamped with strong surgical forceps, only instead we're using a pair of child-sized tweezers.

First Nations Australians, whether you admit it to yourself or not, are the heart and soul of Australia, and they are suffering in ways I can't eloquently describe.

I don't want to be a white person telling First Nations stories. But as a doctor working out in the places I've been, I have no choice but to acknowledge the suffering. It's impossible to disregard, even for the worthy reason that this is a story better told by First Nations writers or doctors, both of which Australia needs more of. But to write a book about this land and ignore this aspect of what I've seen, for the sake of not wanting to overstep, would make me a very poor doctor and writer. So I've had to, at times uncomfortably, try to explain the things I've seen and the ways I've responded to them from my prism of privilege, of which now I am painfully, acutely aware.

I have spoken to many First Nations friends about this book and the perspectives I'm sharing, and not one has said not to write it—rather, I have been encouraged generously, because they already knew what I now know, too: the suffering in the places away from the public eye, if not acknowledged, if not spoken or written about, will continue to be either partially recognised at best, or totally ignored. And nothing will change.

It's funny, I think, as I drag Buddy home from the river, and she resists me by smelling and trying to roll in kangaroo poo, I never really felt particularly Australian. Or a better way of putting it is I didn't really think much about what being Australian really meant. I don't really know how I identified, actually, which I guess is also a throwback to being of Ukrainian stock.

The traumas of displacement and war filter through and shape our identity, or our lack of it, even in the most privileged of lives. Australia was the place my grandparents came to, the place that offered them a new life, and a good life, so they became Australian. Conversely, I was born Australian, and yet, somehow, never really thought too much about it. My Year 6 speech on the topic talked a lot about 'Waltzing Matilda' and the ANZACs, damper, the Dreamtime, and how for me being Australian meant being at the intersection of cultures, as it did for the many children who had at least half of their family move out here after the horrors of WWII. But it was just a speech, and they were just words.

Now, in River Town, I feel much more of a kinship with the country of my birth—overwhelming love and gratitude that I am allowed to stand in a place that is so magnificent, sorrow for the people who lived on this land that was taken from them, and then equally, overwhelming shame at how it was done, the joy I experience mitigated by the reality I see now.

If I feel this contradiction of emotions and this lack of firm identity, I think, then others must too, even if they don't realise it. Brad told me that Australia's white people are equally displaced, and I think I understand now what he meant.

Despite white people having far better health outcomes, a lot of us are overmedicated, anxious, depressed—and maybe a big part of that is not understanding the country we live in, stand on. As a result, maybe, we don't understand a big part of ourselves. Without a home, you can't flourish—without knowing exactly where your home is, and what it stands for, you remain lost in the darkness.

And that is not good for anyone.

Even writing this, I miss River Town. I knew as soon as I got there that it was a good place. But I also knew it was a place where there were five funerals a month, where not far off there was a massacre, a mission, and a river that was ravaged for cotton farms. Should 800 people need eight full-time dialysis machines?

No. They shouldn't. What are we going to do about it?

My patients all knew, when I asked them. They want cheaper food, farmers markets, the freedom to hunt emu; some of the old ways mixed with the new. Better education, city-person health opportunities. Rotating regular specialists who can provide ongoing healthcare, not just the occasional FIFO doctor once every few months. They had lots of ideas, effective ideas. But as long as Australia consists of metropolitan life being 'in here' and remote life being 'out there', nothing will change. Somehow, we need to bridge the chasm.

A lot happened while I was away. Black Lives Matter. The ongoing #MeToo fallout. The sexual assault crisis in parliament. All I hear is that change is afoot, and things are happening. But out here, little changes, and little happens. There are flashes of hope, and then they trickle into nothing.

Before I leave River Town, I make the drive back to Bre to and say goodbye to Brad at the museum.

'Where you off to next, Sonia?' he asks me.

'I dunno, Brad,' I say. 'Sometimes I think I'll never know.'

'You just keep talking to the land,' he says. 'Remember, if you can't connect to the outside you can't connect to the inside.'

I see in my mind's eye those ancient fish traps, and the red dirt of the Pilbara.

'Don't forget the land,' he continues. 'The land offers us every day and every night an opportunity to learn. All we have to do is pay attention, but nobody wants to. Instead, people today want to be paid to give attention. Remember that the land doesn't ask you for money or anything. All it does is grant you opportunity. All you have to do is engage, engage by paying attention to the land.'

I stand there silently. The feelings I have are reflected in his words. For a brief, almost unsettling moment, I have a sense that Brad is much, much older than the 50 or so years his birth certificate would indicate.

'People come to Brewarrina to find themselves,' he says, catching my eye. 'But no matter where you go in the world you're just looking for yourself. Brewarrina is the ancient part of yourself. You keep coming back here, and you come back to yourself, because you are ancient, and Brewarrina shows you that.'

'I am looking for myself. Or something anyway,' I admit ruefully.

'You'll be okay, Sonia,' he says. 'Letting yourself connect with the land, it's all just part of us all learning we're all on our way home.'

I don't know what to say to that, so I promise him that one day I'll come back and hand over the draft of my book, if I ever finish it, to see what he thinks.

Brad smiles, and says it'd be his pleasure.

Buddy Shark Sardine Henry of Central North West NSW, a dog that wandered into the doctor's backyard, a dog that was

never meant to leave that little town by the river, a dog that
came from nowhere and was owned by no one, leaves River
Town on a private plane, in a milk crate lined with dog nappies
kindly provided by her uncle Harry.

'I've only ever been on one plane,' Harry says, awed, 'and
Buddy's first trip ever is on a private plane. See, that's why she
came to you, doc, to live the good life.'

'I dunno if Buddy is going to see the plane quite like that,
Harry,' I say apprehensively. I look at Buddy, her little stumpy
tail wagging, panting as I prepare to heave her into her crate.

'Do you reckon the pilot has dog earmuffs?' I ask Lola, who's
helping me lift my suitcase into the car.

We stare at Buddy, who is oblivious to what's coming. 'Maybe
just wrap her head in a towel,' Lola suggests. We go to the dirt
airstrip. Bob appears and hops out of his tiny plane.

'I told my wife when you asked if you could bring the
dog,' he says, looking amused, '"the doc has accumulated some
extra luggage!" But maybe hide her when we land. Technically
I'm meant to ask for permission to have a dog in the air, but
I couldn't be bothered.'

I hoist the crate into the plane, but Buddy jumps out. Bob says
not to worry. Apparently the noise doesn't bother his dogs, who
tend to just go to sleep. Buddy sits on her seat and I fasten her
seatbelt, which she immediately crawls out of and comes to sit on
my lap. I give up, put my earmuffs on, and cover her in a towel.

We survive the flight, both our bladders intact. Buddy is so
shell-shocked that she goes completely silent, staring at me with
big brown eyes. She only comes to life as we start to descend.

'Sorry, Buddy, sorry, sorry,' I keep saying, as I wrap her in my
arms.

Aunt Nina greets us at the other end. She scoops Buddy up with glee.

'I can't believe you came back with a dog,' she says, laughing as Buddy tries to bite her on the nose.

Buddy whimpers and does a wee on the grass outside Dubbo airport. 'She held on the whole flight!' I say, crowing like a proud parent. 'What a clever doggy!'

Nina and I stand there, proudly congratulating the tiny, furry dog with a short stumpy tail and black eyepatches for managing to urinate on the grass.

Buddy, the dog who weed.

I have been away for nearly eight months, going from east to west and back again. After flying into Sydney, I immediately take the three-hour trip to my parents' house on the south coast of NSW.

Dad picks me up at Kiama train station and we drive to the farm I spent my childhood on, along the same road my dad has been driving me down since I was six years old. The familiarity of this place, after having been everywhere and nowhere, is comforting. Buddy licks my face. We turn up the long drive to my parents' farm, and I see Mum walking down the front steps.

I spend the next two weeks on the couch watching BBC crime dramas with Buddy. It's a quiet Christmas. Dad wants me to stay, maybe get a job at the new family practice in town down the road. It wouldn't be too bad, I think. For a moment, in my mind, I choose the crossroad that leads me back to the tiny country town I grew up in, a place that is as familiar as my skin but also unknown to me now, having been away so long. I could stay here, working as the local GP: the prodigal daughter and her doggy returns. Maybe have a baby and settle down, in comfort and safety.

But Mum knows better.

'You're getting depressed,' she tells me. 'It's time to go.'

She's right. But where?

I think about Sardinia, and twin siblings who built boats out of a garage in Freo. I think about an expanse of red dirt, the startling turquoise of the ocean, and all the freedom I have. Freedom that The Sailor, my patient and almost-friend, will never experience, at least in this world, ever again.

Broome, I think to myself, I need to go back to Broome.

After negotiations regarding a custody arrangement for the newest member of the Henry family, Buddy has a temporary new home. 'This is just for the next few months when you're in WA,' Mum warns, 'then your baby is returning to her mummy.'

'I could take her with me,' I say.

Dad, who is trying to pretend he hasn't already found a new best mate in Buddy, looks appalled. 'What? You can't put this poor dog on a plane!'

'She's already been on one,' I point out.

'That was different—that was Buddy's rightful place on a private charted flight inside the aircraft with her own seat,' Dad says, patting Buddy's head. 'She can't be put in an undercarriage!'

Mum, Dad, my brother and Buddy farewell me at the local airport. As the plane takes off I feel it again—the relief of being back on the road. Going somewhere new, with new adventures waiting for me and the past hopefully, finally, in my rear view.

As soon as the plane descends into Brisbane all the old feelings and vague, underlying stresses of life return, of course—Will this next job work out? Will Covid ever really end? Will I ever have children? Will I ever afford to be able to buy a house? Is my medical insurance up to date?—because you can't ever totally escape from yourself, no matter how far you run. But for that little reprieve, the moment when mind and body ascend into the air, you can taste it, that freedom.

My plan is to work in Queensland for two weeks so that I can then be allowed into WA, following the fourteen-day rule. But because there are a few Covid cases in Brisbane, WA slams its borders shut. My two-week job up at Cape York is cancelled because, despite three negative Covid tests, Brisbane, where I have just landed, is now considered a hotspot, depriving yet another remote community of medical care.

Back in the day it would have taken me a four-hour flight to get to WA. Now it's going to take me six weeks: two weeks at Mum and Dad's farm to avoid Sydney, then two weeks in Queensland, and now I'm told that, to avoid quarantine, I will have to spend two weeks in the Northern Territory after that as well.

'The road to Broome is a long one,' I explain to my parents, wondering if I should just fly home.

The Long Road to Broome. It's not a bad title for a book. I google it and find out it's already been taken. Clearly, I'm not the only who has felt the need to go north. What will happen when I make it to Broome, I wonder, feeling a bit desperate.

But at least it's a destination. With a destination in mind, there's a goal and a road, and challenges and hurdles and life to be lived on the way.

Broome. I will find myself in Broome.

It's ridiculous but, at the moment, it's all I've got.

Loretta's friend Luc, a Frenchman living in Noosa, says I can stay with him to make up the fourteen days. I haven't left the airport hotel since arriving in Brisbane, so haven't been exposed to any 'hotspots'. Besides, multiple tests have shown that I'm Covid-negative. I decide to take him up on it.

Luc is refreshingly honest in the way that only Europeans are. We joke about Noosa being very white and straight, with lots of designer prams and daddies in linen shirts. Luc says all this is a bit of a red herring because most of his Grindr action is with married blokes who strike when their wives are off getting a manicure.

'They want to give me a blow job while their—how do you say? Misses?—is getting her nails done.'

'The old "kill two birds with one stone",' I can't resist saying. 'She gets her pampering, and he gets—well, you get—yours.'

'And everyone stays in their little holiday of denial,' Luc says, cheerfully.

Happy wife, happy life.

We sip the wine, look at each other, and laugh.

I stay in Noosa for two weeks. I do nothing except go swimming, go walking and listen to country music. Loretta flies up, and together we drink low-carb beers and talk shit, as we've done for the last three decades (the talking shit at least).

I decide to treat myself and move from Luc's into an expensive resort, where Loretta and I have breakfast with all the straight white people and their kids. One day, we catch up with some old mates who live further down south, who echo my thoughts about Noosa.

'Yuppieville,' they say.

'Did I used to be a yuppie?' I wonder aloud.

Jules, who has known me since I was nineteen, laughs into her beer.

'Don't worry, Sonnie,' she says. 'You were always too eccentric for that.'

I try to write, but nothing happens. My mind remains frozen. Then, one of the agencies I subscribe to comes up with a job in a remote community 200 kilometres west of Alice Springs. Sitting there in the comfort of a Sunshine Coast resort, I think this seems like a good idea.

'I think Alice is pretty interesting,' Loretta muses. 'My cousin lives there. It's apparently very diverse. It's actually, from memory, the lesbian capital of Australia.'

'Is it?'

'Yeah.'

I google it. The first article I find is about Pine Gap in the seventies, and all the protestors and activists it attracted. A large portion of them stayed on, I learn, and it did indeed end up becoming the lesbian capital of Australia. She's right.

'They've quoted someone with your last name,' I tell her.

Loretta looks at the article. 'Oh my god, that's my cousin! She's a DJ. Her stage name is DJ Faggot Mafia.'

'Shit, wow. Beats married white people and their perfect wives and perfect lives,' I say. Alice Springs, home to diversity, activism, lesbians and DJ Faggot Mafia.

'You might run into her, she does a lot of events there,' Loretta tells me. 'For the last one she dressed up as a boat.'

'Give me people who dress up as boats any day,' I say. 'Next stop: Alice Springs.'

I have a feeling of slight trepidation, just for a second, as I leave Noosa. There's a storm coming, and as I jump into the bus to Brisbane, a crack of lightning illuminates the sky.

'Big storm,' the driver says. It's just me and him on board.

'Where are you going?'

'Alice Springs,' I say.

He turns around to get a better look at me.

'You're based in Alice Springs?'

I explain that to get back to WA, I have had to spend fourteen days in Queensland, and now I'm spending fourteen days in the Territory.

'What a life!' he exclaims, appraisingly me as the wind and rain beat around the bus.

'It's been interesting,' I say.

'Where are you trying to get to?'

'Broome.'

He starts telling me he's always wanted to go to Broome, has heard good things about it, but I am silent, lost in memories of the town by the ocean, the town with white sand, red dirt and a sky that never ends.

Broome. I'm trying to get back to Broome.

# part 3

# the territory

It's no good going on living in the ashes of a dead happiness.

Nevil Shute, *A Town Like Alice*

All I can see from the window as we descend into Alice Springs is more planes. I've heard rumours the desert is being used a storage facility for planes that have been grounded because of Covid, but to see them all is incredible. Rows and rows and rows of huge aeroplanes, sitting next to one another on that red sand. Waiting for Then, I think, feeling an unexpected affinity with those giant hunks of metal with wings, stuck in a holding pattern in the desert until they can take to the skies again.

There's a man standing at the airport holding a sign with *Dr Henry* written on it.

'G'day,' I say. He looks at me.

'Can I help you, love?'

'I'm Sonia,' I say.

He looks confused.

'I was waiting for Henry,' he tells me.

'That's me.'

'No, Dr Henry.'

'Yes, that's me,' I explain again. 'Henry's my surname.'

For a moment, I genuinely don't think he believes me.

'Drop the doctor,' I add. 'You can call me Sonia.'

The driver takes me on a tour of Alice Springs. There's a lot of talk about not going out at night, random assaults and break-ins. A few murders, too, for good measure.

'Just keep the front gate locked, okay, doc?' These are his final words as he leaves me to drag my suitcase inside. 'And remember, don't get around after dark on your own.'

I sit inside my accommodation, staring out the window. I google *is Alice Springs safe*, which leads me down a rabbit hole of concerning links, so I stop. It's the lesbian capital of Australia—surely it can't be that bad. Before I arrived, I was imagining a desert oasis of female empowerment.

I decide to take the 4WD they've provided me with to the bottle shop, just to, you know, take the edge off. A policeman greets me at the drive-through—the only place selling liquor that's open on a Sunday—and I decide to get out for a wander around.

'Excuse me, ma'am,' the policeman says. 'Can I see some ID?'

I fumble around and show my ID to the man, who is now joined by another cop. I look around, expecting to see some kind of large-scale operation. Clearly I've stumbled into something big, if the cops are carding me at the drive-through bottle-o. A sting for one of Australia's most wanted, maybe, hiding out here in Alice.

They ask for another form of ID. I give them my Medicare card. There's a silence, as the first cop compares my licence with real me, standing there.

'What's your address?'

'Well,' I pause. 'I don't really have one.'

He raises his eyebrow.

'I'm from NSW,' I try to explain, which makes him look even more suspicious, probably because of our Covid situation.

'I've been in QLD,' I say hurriedly. 'I've just been travelling around.'

'What address will you be drinking this liquor in, ma'am?'

'I don't know off the top of my head,' I explain. 'I just have to pull it up on my email.'

I fumble through my phone, trying to locate the address of my accommodation. Finally I find it.

'I'm a doctor,' I explain, feeling sort of ashamed about being at the drive-through. 'Just here in the Territory for two weeks. Um, yeah, I'm staying in the doctor's house . . .'

'Who will you be drinking this liquor with, ma'am?'

I look at the two police officers. 'Really?'

'Yes.'

'Um, jeez, well it's just . . . um . . .'

There's a pause.

'Well, it's just me,' I say a tad defensively, feeling my face getting warm. 'That's not a crime, is it?'

I go up to the front counter, where I'm ID'd for a third time, and then asked to scan my licence under a special machine.

'Is this what you do for everyone?' I finally ask.

The bloke looks at me. 'Every bottle-o in the Territory,' he informs me. 'Standard practice.'

'Oh,' I say. 'For a moment I thought it was just me.'

Stevie, a friend I studied medicine with, miraculously happens to be working in the emergency department at Alice Springs Hospital.

I am flustered beyond words after speaking to the police and also keen to have a drinking buddy. It takes me twenty minutes to unlock every gate and padlock at the doctor's accommodation, which is really more of a compound, before I finally get a taxi to Monte's, which is actually a pretty cool bar.

It's very humid in here, and there are fairy lights in the beer garden. There are no masks or social distancing, or anything that even remotely resembles the rest of the post-2020 world.

It's good to see Stevie. After we both remark that we're a long way from Sydney now, she says she enjoyed my book, which for a moment I've forgotten I ever wrote. She asks why the hell I'm in Alice Springs, and I give her the abridged version: heart surgeon, heartbreak, breakdown, and the long road to Broome.

Stevie empathises. 'I'm going on a big camping trip through the desert soon,' she tells me.

We both nod, in understanding and solidarity.

'Someone said to me once, Stevie,' I tell her, 'that the best thing you can do in trying circumstances is to put your feet in the dirt and see what happens after that.'

Stevie, another doctor who has landed in the desert, surrounded by nothing except dirt and the sky, understands.

'So, where are you working in the Territory?' she asks me.

'Oh, you know, a community about 250 kilometres west of Alice,' I say casually.

Stevie looks at me. 'You been out there before?'

Something about her expression, for a moment, worries me.

'No,' I say slowly. 'But I've worked in pretty remote WA . . . like very remote.'

She sips her beer, looking thoughtful. 'The Territory is a bit different to WA,' she finally says. 'I'd be interested to hear what it's like out there.'

'When you say . . . out there?'

'In remote NT.'

'So you haven't been . . . out there?' I ask. 'But you've worked here for a year, right?'

'Yeah,' she says. 'They're closed communities mostly now. And if it rains you can't get back into Alice, so no. If we go out there it's for a retrieval, you know, by air.'

'But there's a road out there?'

She looks thoughtful. 'I think it's dirt, like, unsealed. Somewhere off the Tanami.'

The Tanami Track, I know, stretches for over 1000 kilometres from Halls Creek to Alice Springs. I take a large sip of wine.

'But they're giving you training and stuff, right? So you know what to expect?'

'I think there was an email,' I say.

'No, but like cultural training, and other stuff?'

'The clinic is running a computer training session here in Alice on Monday,' I say, feeling relieved.

Stevie looks equally relieved. 'I'm sure they'll run you through a few things then.'

On Monday I attend computer training in a big, air-conditioned building. There are people everywhere, busy at different tasks.

'So the place you're sending me, there must be a few doctors out there? Considering how many people that are working here?' I ask the trainers.

Everyone assures me there are lots of doctors and nurses and it's enormously *well supported*.

I get a ride with Jim, the manager of the clinic where I'll be working and one of the midwives who is rotating through the outback. We start on the Tanami Track, which soon enough turns into red dirt.

'This used to be a drovers run, all the way through to Western Australia,' Jim tells me.

I stare out the window. Western Australia. Somewhere, along this track, further, is the border between the Territory and that frontier, that great expanse of red earth.

You feel a remoteness in the Territory you don't feel in other places. Even in the Pilbara, the highway is sealed. The mines bleed the land but inject the money. Here it doesn't feel like that. Here I really am in the centre of this ancient continent, seeing places, seeing rock formations and dirt that most people will never see. Almost as if they can hear my thoughts, a pack of wild horses appear in front of us, charging down through the scrub.

The sky is blue, with barely any cloud. The rocks are dark, jutting out of the earth, silhouetted against the sky. The earth is orange, transitioning slowly into a burnt red as we travel further along the Tanami. The two people in the front seats are chattering quietly, but as I watch the horses I don't hear them. All I can see are these four-legged creatures, galloping along the side of this dirt road that once was used to transport people and things all the way to the frontier of the west.

Wild horses, running along the side of the Tanami track, into the desert. It is, like so many things out there, utterly magnificent.

Oh, the places you'll go!

When we arrive in the community I'll be working in, I feel the sun beat down on me. Everywhere I turn, it's there, reflecting off the red dust and the collection of buildings that sit in a giant square in the middle of the Territory, on either side of them only dirt, sun and the shadow of the giant rocks that hover in the distance.

I have been in Desert Town and River Town. Now, I think, I am in Sun Town. Sun Town is a First Nations community that's closed to the general public. Like most of these parts of the Territory, you need a permit to enter. It's a mix of a few different First Nations peoples, who were all relocated here, a place equipped with nothing more than some thrown-together dwellings and a single water bore, after they were forced off their traditional country back in the 1930s.

I read on Wikipedia it's one of the closest areas to the Australian 'continental pole of inaccessibility', a geographical term that, in this case, can be defined as 'the centre of the largest circle that can be drawn within an area of interest without encountering a coast'. Access to Sun Town, in other words, is challenging. And for its residents, access to everything else—medical care, decent food—is nearly impossible.

I am dropped at the accommodation, a small unit surrounded on all sides by a giant 3D metal box.

'You'll be safe with the cage,' the manager assures me. 'Just make sure you lock everything.'

The cage? 'Is it unsafe here?' I ask bluntly. 'The lady in Alice Springs said it was safe for me to be out here.'

He hesitates. 'It's fine at the moment,' he says. 'Just, you know, best to be cautious.'

Cautious about what? I can't help but wonder as I shut the cage, then the screen door, then the main door. Community unrest? The rain, because then we can't get into Alice? Snakes?

There were murmurs on the drive here of recent events in Yuendumu, a community a few hundred kilometres away. I'd heard of Yuendumu because the powers that be in Alice Springs had suggested I work out there. I then heard from Stevie that all the nurses were being pulled out of the community because a cop had shot someone under murky circumstances and riots were likely. This didn't bode well so I declined Yuendumu and chose to come here instead.

My unit is old, and filthy. There are cockroaches and spiders, but at least, I think when I look out the back window as the sun sets, the view is spectacular. The MacDonnell Ranges are silhouetted against the big, big sky, and underneath them, a wonderful expanse of red that shimmers with remnants of heat from the dying sunlight.

I feel it again, the same thing I felt in Desert Town, then River Town, but even more acutely now. It's the sense that despite being in the same country as Sydney, where I lived for so long, I am on another planet. I feel the prickle, again, that something is not quite right—that this amazing land should be lived and breathed in a way that doesn't involve small white communities, designed by white people, and controlled by government legislation. The white people who come here live in battered old units surrounded by metal cages, constantly uneasy. But where does the unease come from? Is it a sense that perhaps we shouldn't be here? That our 'doing the right thing' is the remnant of an invasion that has never been properly acknowledged, even though the people and their country have been bleeding and dying ever since?

There are doctors who have spent years working in First Nations communities. I have deep admiration for the people who devote their service to places so isolated, and so incredibly difficult to work in. One thing that nags at me, though, is when you occasionally hear described, in articles or interviews, 'the interesting medicine' you see in places like this. I understand what this means: out here you see a variety of unusual diseases and presentations, and I guess mentioning this is meant to encourage other doctors to come and experience the 'remote medical presentations'. But the worse the outcomes, the more supposedly 'interesting' the medicine becomes. And kids dying of rheumatic heart disease at twenty isn't interesting medicine: it's just wrong.

I'm not saying doctors shouldn't work in remote areas, not at all. But you should be able to work there at the same time as being honest about how bad things are, instead of terrified of telling the truth for fear of reprisals. Some doctors have, but its pretty rare, and usually because it's forced on them by an inquest, or a death or some other flashpoint that shines a brief spotlight onto the Territory. If awareness is the only thing that will lead to change, why are we so reticent to talk about it? Whatever happens during NAIDOC week, and however many times people in corporate meetings in Sydney or Melbourne say 'we acknowledge the Traditional Owners of the land', the truth is that places like Sun Town are the land *right now.*

And short of the *Beware, Asbestos, Condemned* signs that rather worryingly surround me in my little prison, I'm not seeing much meaningful acknowledgement of that.

'The great thing about the Territory is that culture is really intact out here,' the manager tells me as he drives me to the medical clinic.

I've told him it's such a short distance I could have walked, but he brushes me off. Is it not safe to walk here? I wonder for a second.

I am literally in the middle of Australia, 250 kilometres down a dirt track that, if it rains, will flood, and I'll be living inside a cage that surrounds a small unit riddled with asbestos, completely stranded, surrounded by people I don't know.

What happens if I get sick? Like, really sick? And they can't get a plane to me? Or even if they do, and get me to Alice, what if it's something that can't be dealt with in Alice?

This, I realise, is the experience of every single human being who lives here. This is Australia.

My unease is increasing. I remember all the slideshows I saw at uni on the health of First Nations Australians. I google some keywords and find a presentation called *State of cardiovascular health in the NT* by Dr Marcus Ilton, and sit there in the car reading it. There's one slide that states the clear points: potential factors contributing to worse outcomes for Aboriginal and Torres Strait Islander populations with ischaemic heart disease:

- *increased prevalence at a younger age*
- *inadequate acute treatment*
- *inadequate revascularisation*
- *inadequate long-term treatment/education.*

All the preceding factors are affected by issues related to:

- *cultural issues (language/family access)*
- *access: remote, regional or urban*
- *potential for systemic or institutionalised racism.*

When I first saw them, the words from this slide and others like it didn't have much impact on me, aside from a cursory 'gee that sounds bad'. Sitting in a lecture theatre at uni, I read the slides and felt a sense of this being wrong, and then walked out and went shopping for a new computer charger, to power my laptop so I could memorise the slideshows to pass an exam. But standing in Sun Town, the words jump off the computer and the letters march around me.

I attempt to make sense of the words, but I can't. What does make horrible sense is one of the last slides, which reads, *Coronary artery disease and stroke are the major specific causes of death for Indigenous people, and people aged 25–44 have ten times the death rate of non-Indigenous populations.* There in Sun Town, reading this slide, all I can see is The Sailor, a woman in her prime at 28, with everything in front of her.

'They speak Language out here, not English,' the manager says, dragging me out of the mental rabbit hole I have gone down as we arrive at the clinic. 'Which is great.'

'That is great,' I agree, trying to feel optimistic instead of saying what I'm thinking, which is that all people, whatever their culture, probably *should* be speaking their own language.

Then something strikes me. 'If the patients don't speak English, how do I communicate with them? Is there an interpreter?'

He says that yes there's an interpreter, but some patients can speak a bit of English, and also, I will likely just sort of 'pick up' some words.

'But I'm only here for two weeks,' I point out. 'I don't think I'm going to become fluent in these particular regions' traditional language by then, or even basics.'

He tells me not to worry: it will all be fine and there's a meeting now anyway where I'll meet another doctor, who works out here, who is really experienced and really nice and she will help me, *no worries*.

I can't believe the meeting as I walk in. There are so many people here. A men's health guy, a dietician, the other doctor, a nurse. The manager. For a moment I feel a sense of hope. All this funding and all these people—surely that has to mean something.

After we sit down, everyone begins to talk about the rheumatic heart register. The Territory has a relatively young population compared with the rest of Australia, but it has the highest death rates from coronary artery disease in both males and females. It also has the highest death rates in rheumatic heart disease, in both the Indigenous and non-Indigenous populations.

In the Northern Territory, there are no cardiac surgeons or cardiac operating theatres, and barely any cardiologists, despite heart disease being the most predominant disease in the NT. These days people in cities talk about how much we respect First Nations culture and connection to the land, so why are children needing cardiac operations removed from their homes to be taken into hospitals in entirely different states?

Once, I'd asked heartdoc_82 why there weren't any cardiac surgeons in Darwin. He had looked at me like I was being a

210

bit stupid, and said, incredulously, 'You couldn't have a cardiac operating theatre in Darwin.' I remember thinking, *why not?* It just takes money, and people.

I snap myself out of my musings to hear the others in the meeting discussing their plan to introduce a mobile app for people in the communities that will help them with their diets. The aim is to try to mitigate complications from the type 2 diabetes that's rampant around here.

The dietician is explaining how the app works and how great it will be, and saying she can't wait to roll it out, and I start to wonder how many people here actually have phones, because where I've been previously I haven't seen that many. When I did see them in places like River Town, they were mostly old-school Nokias, not smart phones you could download an app on.

I imagine the minutes of the meeting being emailed back to HQ, where there will be a lot of boxes ticked for the rheumatic heart disease register. There will also be a tick confirming that the type 2 diabetes intervention has commenced, even though it's based around an app when barely any of the patients who are meant to benefit actually own a mobile phone.

I have a mental image of a dirt patch being watered, over and over and over. The dirt isn't the right kind for the climate, and isn't conducive to growth. But we keep going anyway. The water is distributed and politicians espouse how great this is. The flowers never grow, and everyone keeps turning a blind eye, acting like one day they miraculously will.

I hang back after the meeting to talk to the other GP who works out here. I'm wondering how she goes living somewhere so remote for such a long time, but it turns out she's there with a friend, and actually they spend part of every year in the Whitsundays.

Dr Catherine seems nice enough but something feels slightly off, though I can't put my finger on why. She explains that today she'll be busy doing paperwork because she's recently been away, and asks me to start seeing patients.

'Sure,' I say.

I see three patients, none of whom can speak much English. I try to sort out an interpreter, and stay on hold for 40 minutes, only to find out that there's no one servicing this part of the Territory who speaks the patients' language. When I get off the phone, the nurse managing the emergency section of the clinic runs in and tells me a patient is having a seizure. Dr Catherine has disappeared.

Thankfully, the seizure self-truncates. I ring the flying doctor and we arrange a transfer to Alice. In the meantime, I ring about a million other numbers, trying to get onto a neurologist. The relevant notes are all over the place, with the patient living between here and another community. I finally get onto an advanced trainee at Alice Springs Hospital, who is understanding.

'It's so tough out there' she says. 'Well, it's tough here, but out there . . .'

I struggle through the rest of the day, and feel like I am failing constantly. The language barrier is so great and the only advice I get from Dr Catherine and management is 'you pick up a few words' or 'the patients can understand, mostly'.

I try to force people's family members to help me interpret if they speak slightly better English, but they are as in the dark as me.

Dr Catherine tells me the patients love her and welcome her, and that she is so good with language now and health outcomes have really improved.

I am not really seeing that. I am seeing people trying to help, but it still feels like chaos. I am also seeing white people working for an organisation that throws money at them to stay for a while (albeit, there are some very devoted, geniune people who stay for years) and see what they want to see, before leaving. People like me, I guess.

And nothing changes. As the small holes are plugged and boxes are ticked—*doctor present in community: tick*—the gap around us gets wider and wider.

But, I think, staring at my computer and trying to ignore the pounding headache that is starting behind my eyes, we're introducing an app that helps people with their diet. So we're winning, aren't we?

Dr Catherine offers me little help, aside from criticising medication I'm prescribing. She asks me to go and assess her patient and then report back to her, like I am her registrar. I say yes, and describe the patient's chest sounds. I consider reminding her that I am a fellow GP, not a registrar, but I don't want to make things awkward.

I go through old results and try to ask Jim if the high sugars and abnormal results are being followed up on, but the computer system is so old and clunky it's hard to tell. I want to test some people for *H. pylori* but there are no test kits and pathology is only done three times a week. I ask Jim for a speculum to do a pap smear and he looks at me as if I've asked for a new BMW. He rifles through a dusty cupboard and produces an ancient speculum. I say nothing and return to my room.

By the end of the day, as the dietician breezes past me to inform me she's put up some posters about the diabetes app in the one shop in the town, I am close to tears.

All day, Dr Catherine has continued to inform me that everything I have done could have been done better, but she says it in such a saccharine way I am confused about whether I'm being gaslighted or genuinely helped.

She comes into my room at the end of the day to tell me that I've printed a script incorrectly, without the code the pharmacist will recognise when we send it to Alice Springs. No one has explained to me how to use these codes.

I feel tears begin to slide down my face. I want to go home. I feel the thought, rather than hear it. *I want to go home.*

Dr Catherine responds to my tears with words of comfort, and asks if I'd like to come over to her place for a drink.

Every part of me is screaming not to go but I am alone, exhausted and miserable. Against my better judgement, I say yes.

For 40 minutes I sit inside Dr Catherine's mansion—a beautiful old two-storey house on stilts, with a large wraparound veranda—and hear her life story. The ex-husband, the daughters in Adelaide at boarding school, the doctor heroics over the years.

'There's not really anything medical that I can't handle,' she tells me as I sit there, drinking non-alcoholic beer and desperate for a full-strength Hahn SuperDry.

'Do you have any, um, normal beer?' I ask, rather timidly.

She looks at me. 'It's a dry community,' she says, placing the emphasis on dry.

'Oh, right, yep, absolutely,' I say, quickly, terrified she will report me for my transgression.

Dr Catherine takes me around the house, showing me the huge pieces of incredible Aboriginal artwork with which her house is packed. All sourced locally, and for a song, of course.

For a moment, I imagine these pieces on the walls of her big mansion in the Whitsundays, overlooking northern Queensland, as she has friends over and describes her heroic feats in remote Australia.

But Dr Catherine is a hero, a woman who has got out of her comfort zone, made a shit-tonne of money for her troubles, and can go to sleep at night knowing what a difference she has made to people *less fortunate than her.*

'Don't you ever feel a bit uncomfortable about working out in these parts?' I finally ask.

She looks at me. 'We feel very safe here,' she says confidently. 'They'd never hurt me.'

*They?*

'I didn't mean safety-wise,' I say. 'I meant health outcomes. Like, we're really just plugging a haemorrhaging hole, aren't we? And not being paid badly for it. But nothing's really changing.

Like, do you ever feel—with the essentially minimal difference we're making—like a bit of a hypocrite? Do you feel like the government or whoever is in charge needs to make really significant changes, rather than just send solo doctors out here to sort of, I don't know, tick a box? In places this isolated, to me, it feels impossible. Do you ever feel that?'

'No,' she says. 'I wake up every morning and feel so grateful I have this opportunity to *give back*.'

Rather half-heartedly, I thank her for the beer. She walks me home, holding a large stick. 'To beat off the wild dogs with,' she explains. I refrain from saying how surprised I am that the wild doggies don't recognise her and act with the appropriate amount of respect.

I notice she chains her gate, with not one, but two chains.

'Just in case the children try to come in for food,' she says rather breezily.

She walks me back to my tin unit, surrounded by its cage. She eyes the asbestos sign in the window.

'See you tomorrow! I hope it'll be a better day for you. You need to ask me questions, to avoid making the mistakes you made today, okay?'

I let myself inside, feeling more uneasy than ever.

Later that night, as I sit in the one bedroom, I ring Harry. 'I'm in the Territory,' I say. 'It makes River Town look like New York.'

He laughs.

'They keep saying how culturally intact it is out here. The white people keep saying that, because the patients speak traditional languages. But there aren't really any great translators, so it's really hard to, you know, practise decent medicine. But

I guess that's a good thing? The cultural intactness?' I say the words half-heartedly, picturing the horrendous blood results, the seizing patient, the woman who hadn't had a pap smear for twelve years.

Harry laughs again, but there's an edge to it this time.

'Just because the culture is there, that doesn't keep the diseases out,' he says. 'You can die before you hit 50, but why does that matter if you make a bunch of white people feel great because you speak the language that you were always meant to speak anyway?' Harry, with his effortless ability to cut through bullshit, has summed it up instantly. 'You be careful out there, doc. The Territory, that's a wild place.'

I look out the window, at the dying sun, hovering over the McDonnell Ranges.

'I'll try, my friend.'

Jim picks me up the next morning. I slept poorly and there's a pit of anxiety hovering in my stomach that I can't seem to shake. We make small talk as we drive to the medical clinic. Finally, he asks me if something is wrong.

I mumble that everything's good until I see Dr Catherine getting out of her car and walking into the medical clinic. The dread hits me.

'Jim,' I say, 'look, between you and me, I'm finding the other GP a little ... odd.' There's a pause. 'But it's probably just me,' I add. 'And, you know, it's an adjustment, being somewhere this remote ... you said she was really nice, right?'

All I actually want is Jim's reassurance that Dr Catherine isn't a sociopath who will make my life miserable with her passive-aggressive, smiling criticisms as I battle the most diffi-cult environment I've ever worked in.

Jim looks at me. 'She's a total narcissist,' he says bluntly, as we watch Dr Catherine open the door to the clinic. 'She thinks you want her job, I'd say. She's on a nice wicket out here, being able to head to the Whitsundays whenever she likes. But yes. Your instincts are spot-on. She's a complete narcissist so watch your back.'

'But you said on the way here that she was really nice, Jim!'

Jim looks apologetic. 'I didn't want to scare you.'

'So when you say to watch my back, what does that mean? Like, she'll go through my notes? She was already questioning my clinical decisions yesterday over really minor things, things that were actually in accordance with the remote guidelines anyway.'

Jim looks grim. Grim Jim. I almost laugh.

'This happened with the GP who was last out here on a locum. He left after three days because she was doing that to him. She's got the shits because they want more doctors, and they want you to keep working out here. They know you're young, and keen. She wouldn't like that.'

Fucking ace. So, thanks to an accidental stroke of fate that's forced me to spend fourteen days in the Territory to get into WA, I have somehow landed in a place that has more politics than Berlin before the wall fell.

'This doesn't sound that great, Jim,' I say, honestly.

'I mean it,' he says grimly. 'You be careful of her.'

He drags me out of the car into the morning meeting. I say nothing throughout and, as soon as it ends, I walk outside to consider my options.

I make a few calls, and end up on the phone to Mandy, the head of HQ in Alice. I am too tired to be diplomatic and bluntly explain that I'm not, as a locum, going to work in a clinic with a known narcissist. I say that I am meant to be practising medicine, not watching my fucking back.

'I can stay till the end of the week,' I say, 'but that's it.'

In my mind, I'm already gone. The relief is overwhelming. Unfortunately, like a lot of women, I'm starting to realise, I have a hard time saying no when people try to talk me into things. 'Don't let Mandy persuade you into anything,' my locum agent told me before I called HQ. 'She can be quite charming.'

As predicted, Mandy is immediately charming and convincing. 'But you seemed so keen,' she says. 'And then there's the fact you've worked so remotely before! I think this sounds like more of a personality clash. We've had some issues in that department before ...'

'Mmm,' I say.

'Why don't we pull you out of there today?' she suggests. 'And then give another place a go? It was mainly just Catherine that was the issue, right?'

'Well ...' I picture the cage around the tin shed with the asbestos sign, the cockroaches and the spiders.

'It's best to get one of the drivers to come and get you today, if you do want to try somewhere else,' she is saying. 'If the weather changes, it'll be harder.'

I see the red earth turned to mud, and me stranded for days. She's right, mostly. It was just the other doctor. If it worked out, I could get a regular job out here. The Territory is beautiful, after all. I can't proselytise about changing things that need changing if I just give up and leave.

I am a lot of things, but I'm not a quitter. So I say yes. I'll give another job a go.

Before I leave I go and visit the local arts centre. It's incredible. Inside, on the dirt floor, are huge canvases featuring beautiful First Nations art, and the people in there are painting. Their talent is mind-boggling.

I ask the lady who seems to be running the place where the money goes if I buy something. She says that 100 per cent goes to the artist and the arts centre; there's no commission to anyone.

I picture the Art Gallery of NSW in Sydney, where paintings like this are hung and lauded. I picture universities and private art collections and hear the clink of wine glasses and the chink of dollars. A little bit of real Australia for the living room, a touch of the desert, and some authenticity to dress up the house.

I catch the eye of one of the men who is sitting on the floor painting. I look away, not wanting to be rude or appear too curious. It gives me such an unusual feeling, to watch him. On his canvas, where all this beauty is spilled, there are amazing dots and colours and land and water and sky, thrown on with such dexterity and talent. But as I look at him, it's like I have X-ray vision. I see the blood cells inside him, coagulating with sugar almost solely because of displacement, forced intake of the wrong foods, and cruelty. I see the weirdly raised white cell count, and the lack of access to medical care.

Then I look again at his canvas and see that beauty, being painted to be sold to white buyers in galleries around Australia and the rest of the world.

This is where it all begins, I think to myself. We celebrate the art and beauty, and we don't want to see anything else. Not really.

I buy five paintings. They are rolled up and covered in bubble wrap. As I leave I see the man again, looking up at me. I hold my hand up, a tiny wave. He looks at me, and gives a slight nod of his head.

There are so many things I want to say that I almost stop. But there is no way to say them, and my words are absolutely meaningless anyway. So I leave instead, clutching the rolls of canvas, saying nothing. The very definition of Australian hypocrisy: someone who sees things, and says nothing. Or sees nothing, and says everything.

My chariot back to Alice Springs is a white Prado driven by a man with a variety of tattoos and a penchant for pop music.

'Thanks for getting me,' I say, a bit sheepishly, as Taylor Swift's voice resounds around the car. 'I feel a bit stupid. I've only been here two nights.'

'You lasted longer than the nurse I picked up last week,' he says cheerfully. 'She was there for half an hour. She was threatening to walk back to Alice down the Tanami.'

'Really?!'

'Yep, she said it would have taken her a few days but that anything was better than being stuck in that joke of a clinic.'

'Wow,' I say.

'Yeah, she had a fight with the manager,' he explains.

'Right.'

'You know what they say, doc, to be out here there's gotta be something wrong with you.'

I nod. Touché.

'Didn't mean you, mate,' he says apologetically. 'But what's a young doc like you doing out here, anyway? Never seen a doc this young. And alone? You alone?'

'Yes,' I say, sighing. 'I am alone.'

'You had a bad break-up or something?'

'Just tired of life,' I reply.

'Me too,' my chauffer says, as I stare at the thorny rosebush drawn rather artfully across his skin. 'I'm off relationships, they're no fucken good for ya.'

'Preach, sista,' I say.

He starts laughing. 'What's your name, doc?'

'Sonia. But my friends call me Sonnie.'

'My name's Matt. But my mates call me Slam.'

'Where'd Slam come from?'

'You don't want to know, Sonnie,' he tells me, sensibly.

Slam and I travel together across the country. We talk about everything from conspiracy theories and Pine Gap to First Nations health (Slam is, as he tells me, a blackfella) and the bullshit he sees, being the driver for a health organisation.

'They don't give a fuck,' he tells me eloquently. 'They send docs like you with no training out to these really remote places where it's just wild—no one tells you what it's really like, they just dump you in it. Then they wonder why no one wants to work out here.'

I can't believe that after my week dealing with all of this, the truth is being given to me by a driver with rose-thorn tatts called Slam. But I am starting to learn that truth comes from unexpected places and that, actually, often the most honest people are not the ones wearing suits or working for the powers that be.

'I don't know how much some of them really care about the blackfellas,' he tells me. 'I reckon they care about ticking their fucken boxes and sitting there in Alice in the air con.'

I start laughing. 'I noticed the air con!'

We drive through the red dirt, and Slam stops now and again for me to take photos underneath the oddly shaped white fluffy clouds and the huge rocks that suddenly spring from the earth.

'No man's ever set foot on that rock probably,' he says as we drive past one. 'No white man, anyway. How's that for you, doc? You're seeing places no white people have ever touched.'

I can only nod my head, awed.

We drive past the entrance to the Larapinta trail. Slam asks me if I want to go down and see the ochre pits.

'Aren't we meant to be back by a certain time?' I say, hesitating.

He grins. 'I won't tell if you won't.'

I look out the car window, into the never-never. The red, the yellow, the blue, the white. The dirt, the sky, the scrub, the rock. And then this tiny trail, snaking through. The Larapinta Trail.

'Fuck it, Slam,' I say. 'Let's do it.'

It is stinking hot; it must be over 40 degrees. As we wander around the ochre pits, Slam tells me how the ochre is used for ceremonies and for painting. He shows me the different colours. I kneel, and gently rest my hand on the wall of brown and red and white ochre. I close my eyes.

From above, I look down. In my mind, I see a globe, zeroing in on the centre of the Territory. I see a woman I know but don't know at all, kneeling, feeling, with her hand on an ancient bit of ochre, asking for the answers from the land that sees and knows everything.

But the land remains silent. The mysteries remain just out of reach. Maybe one day, further north than here, I will hear the answers.

After a quick stopover in Alice, I specifically request that Slam drives me to my next destination, the job that's meant to win me over to a life spent living and working in the Territory. HQ tries to make me drive myself, but I explain that, because I can't change a tyre and I'll be driving north through 450 kilometres of land, a large portion of which has no phone reception, I'd prefer to go in a big 4WD with a driver who knows what he's doing. I trust Slam more than anyone else I've met so far. Plus, he has a wealth of knowledge about life in Alice, and he's easy to talk to.

The two of us make our way up the Stuart Highway, and I nearly have a heart attack as I realise we will be driving on the stretch where Peter Falconio went missing and Joanne Lees flagged down a truck to take her to Barrow Creek.

'It definitely wasn't the guy they put away,' Slam says with the air of someone in possession of inside info.

'Really?' I look across at him. 'Who was it then?'

'I'm not saying for certain but most of the big hitters in Alice reckon it was a bloke called . . .'

Big hitters in Alice? I think, as Slam says the name of his suspect.

'And the theory behind this is . . .?' I ask sceptically.

Slam launches into an explanation featuring people running drugs between Darwin, Broome, Alice Springs and Adelaide, and drug lords hiding out in Alice, but when I ask for more details he clams up.

'Listen, I know what Alice looks like to an outsider,' he says, 'but take my word for it, doc, there's fucken multimillionaires living in that town.'

I have seen and heard so many wild things on my journey through Australia that these days I'm more inclined to believe things like this. I make Slam calculate exactly where it was that Joanne Lees, bound and covered in blood, was picked up by the unsuspecting truckies in the middle of the night. He dutifully pulls over so I can perform a forensic assessment of the scene.

I paw through the scrub as the occasional truck flies past us. For a second, I imagine Max and Roy sitting in Potts Point, having a beer over lunch and talking about work.

'Found anything, doc?' Slam is lighting a cigarette and watching me with a slightly amused expression.

'Nothing to see here, Slam,' I say with a hint of pride, like I am a detective. 'Like, nothing.' And then I pause. 'Actually, that is kind of weird, isn't it? Like there's kind of nothing here. Where the hell did she hide?'

Slam takes a long drag of his cigarette, and raises an eyebrow at me.

'I'm not saying nothing, doc,' he says, while implying everything.

We both look up the highway. There are no cars or trucks now, just us. The air becomes very still. When you're driving down the highway in a nice, air-conditioned car, listening to music and chatting, you could be anywhere. So sometimes, you actually forget where you are. But when you step out of the car, onto the deserted highway that disappears into the horizon, that's when you suddenly feel it.

I am in the middle of absolutely nowhere. I feel like I am literally the furthest from any town, any landmark, any coastline—anywhere that I could ever really be in this enormous landmass. To the left, to the right, in front, behind, is just the road, and the earth.

I swallow, imagining what it would be like to be here, terrified, alone, in the dark. Right here. In this exact spot.

'I dunno, Slam,' I say as I get back into the car, shuddering. 'Something very fucking weird happened out here, regardless of what the exact details might have been. I don't know anything else, but I know that.'

Slam drives me into the community I'll be working in. We are somewhere to the tune of four or five hundred kilometres north of Alice, and about 60 kilometres east, according to Slam. The nearest 'major town' is Tennant Creek. As we turn down the road, Slam points out two dingoes, sitting in the dust. I am enthralled, and beg him to slow down, which he does, but by then they have scarpered off into the bush. They move so quickly, with their pointed ears and glittering eyes. Dingoes amaze me. I think of Buddy, being pampered by Mum and Dad, and imagine her surviving only on her wits.

'Lot of them out here,' Slam tells me, 'Think you'll be right, it's not such a bad place. The riots were a while ago now,' he continues as we take the turn into Dingo Town.

'Riots?'

'It's all settled down now. They put another cop in town. So there are two cops here.'

'That's good,' I say half-heartedly.

We have phone reception as we get close to the community, so I google the name of the place. Sure enough, all the head-lines relate to major riots. I start to feel slightly sick. I curse myself and my lack of conviction, and curse Mandy in her office in Alice Springs for convincing me to come out here.

Slam tells me not to worry—'she'll be right'—and drops me outside my accommodation, another tin shed surrounded by, worryingly, an even bigger and sturdier-looking metal cage.

'You've got the cage,' he tells me. 'No probs, doc.'

I wonder why I keep finding myself in places where sleeping behind a cage is widely seen as normal, even desirable.

When Slam leaves, part of me wants to run after him, to tell him this was a mistake and I want to go back to Alice Springs. Instead, I sit inside the little tin donga, staring at the metal bars on the windows.

I drive myself to the medical clinic. It's locked. I'm let in only after someone has looked out to see who I am. When I finally get inside, I see two women in there, staring at me. Startling me, one leans in and gives me a hug. 'You're a doctor, you're a doctor!' she keeps saying.

I step back. 'Yep,' I say, uncomfortably. 'I thought you guys always had a doctor out here? And one just recently left? That's what they told me? I'm sort of just filling in?'

'We haven't had a doctor out here for *months*,' one of the women says, looking as if she's overcome with joy. 'The last one stayed only two weeks! That was months and months ago. It's just been us.'

I run my fingers through my hair and try not to let my anxiety overwhelm me.

The women—MJ, a nurse, and Annie, the clinic's manager—show me around the clinic. They are super nice. The clinic is clean and pretty well stocked. They seem to have a good set-up with the air and telehealth doctor, which, I think, they'd have to, considering it's a nurse-run clinic.

The nurse, looking at me slightly desperately, asks if I want to go and meet the policeman, just to get a feel of the place.

'Um, sure,' I say.

As we walk across the road to the police station, I try not to focus on the obvious crime scene set-up around the house next door. All the windows are smashed. There are two burnt out cars sitting next to the front door, and police tape surrounds the property.

The police station is locked and barred. The nurse bangs on the door. Finally, it opens a crack.

'Who is it?' a male voice booms out, so loud and threatening that we both step back quickly; I nearly fall over.

'Um, it's the nurse from the medical clinic,' she says. 'I'm just here to introduce our new doctor.'

The door opens a little wider. I find myself face to face with a giant, bald policeman in a bulletproof vest, holding the leash of a huge Alsatian that's straining and snarling.

'Hi,' I say, 'I'm Sonia.'

'Sorry, but we can't speak to you right now,' the policeman says brusquely as the dog growls at me. 'I'm not even from here. I'm from CIB Tennant Creek.' His accent is so broad I feel like I've stepped into some kind of outback noir horror.

'What's CIB?' I can't help asking.

'Criminal Investigations Branch,' he says bluntly.

'Has there been a crime?'

He looks at me. 'See the tape across the road? A woman was beaten to within an inch of her life last night. That's why I'm here.'

The door slams shut, and we walk back over the road to the clinic.

'How'd the police go?' the manager, Annie, says with forced cheer as I walk past, totally mute.

'Did someone come in last night?' I ask her. 'A woman, badly assaulted?'

She nods. 'I think she was raped, too,' she says sadly. 'I wasn't on but she was flown to Alice. Last I heard she's probably not going to make it.'

How do you react in that situation? I walked to my doctor's room and sit down. I turn on the computer, and log in. My login code isn't working, so I call Alice Springs. They say there's some IT glitch and to just see patients anyway. I try not to think about what I've just heard and seen.

I spend the next few hours seeing some patients. A woman comes in with a gorgeous-looking, three-week-old baby. Thanks to my experience in Sun Town, I have already resigned myself to the language barrier and the lack of translators, but the mother's English isn't too bad. I establish that her baby has bad diarrhoea, which seems worse than just regular newborn bowel changes.

Baby is happy, though. I do some obs: all normal. She is alert, and doesn't look unwell. I ask about breastfeeding, and gather that hasn't been going so well. I wonder about formula— is there even formula out here? Surely there's some kind of midwife who can help with these things?

'What are you feeding Baby?' I ask the woman.

She pulls out a bag. Inside is some old orange Cottee's, packed with sweeteners. She points to it.

'You're feeding baby the orange drink?'

She nods.

I don't know what to say, although I understand completely. Her breast milk isn't coming, formula is too expensive and the midwife who should provide it is likely never here. She wants to feed the baby something it will like, and sweet cordial makes sense. It makes total sense.

She sees my expression.

'No good?'

I want to tell her that part of me gets it, that I am not being nasty and that there is no judgement. I want to tell her she shouldn't be in this situation, living with the archaic Intervention Act that was written by politicians in Sydney or Canberra who didn't even know what was going on out here. But I don't. Too many words.

'No good,' I say, nodding slowly. 'No good.'

I tell her to wait for a moment, and I go and find the nurse. I locate her wrestling with a cannula, trying to help a patient who has appeared in the emergency room.

'Do we have a midwife out here?' I ask her. 'Like, one who goes and visits the newborn kids? Helps the mothers?'

'There was one, but she hasn't been out for ages,' she says uncertainly.

'Well do we have any handouts of formula? Do we have formula we can give patients?'

'The shop should have it, if it's open.'

'Is it expensive?'

She looks at me.

'Sorry, stupid question,' I say as she rummages through a drawer.

'This mum can't breastfeed and she needs some tips on formula,' I explain. 'I need to give her something.'

She finds an actually quite decent factsheet with pictures and straightforward advice on what and what not to feed the baby.

I go back into my room with the pamphlet, feeling like at least I can do something. But the mother and baby have gone.

I run out of the clinic and look around. I see some kids running past, who look at me but don't stop. I look to my right, to where the crime scene tape is fluttering in the breeze. There is nothing but heat, and silence.

I feel my hand drop by my side, and the pamphlet flutter to the ground. I grind my boot on top of it, shoving it into the dust. I move my toe so the paper rips, and keep grinding and grinding. All of my anger is being funnelled through my boot, and into that pointless fucking sheet of paper in the dust. A small dog with golden fur and pointy ears runs towards me. I put my hand out, without thinking.

'No!'

A man is shouting, running towards me. He charges at the dog with a big stick, and the dog slinks off, growling.

'Stop that!' I say, 'Don't hit the dog! Leave him alone!'

'Doctor,' he says, short of breath. 'They're small dingoes— wild, totally wild. You can't pat them. One second later, you wouldn't have had a hand. You have to carry a stick whenever you go outside. And don't walk around, anywhere. You drive to and from work. No jogging. You stay inside, either in the clinic, or your unit. Never pat the dogs. Never.'

I'm so shell-shocked I just stand there, gaping at him. I bend down, and pick up the torn, dirt-covered pamphlet with happy images of Aboriginal women drawn with big smiling photos of formula and breasts. The dirt has ruined it.

'Thank you,' I finally say. 'Sorry, do you work at the medical clinic?'

'I'm the cleaner,' he says, putting out his hand. 'Very pleased to meet you.'

I shake his hand. He is warm and friendly and sturdy and real, not like the unreality of this place or this day.

'Please stay,' he tells me. 'We need good doctors.'

'I don't feel much good anymore,' I say, and walk back inside.

I am dreading the end of the day, knowing that when the sun goes down it will just be me, alone, inside the caged donga.

I ask Annie and MJ if it's safe, at night. One of them looks at the other.

'It's pretty okay at the moment,' Annie says. 'I've been broken into a few times. And when MJ started, she didn't sleep for three months, she was that terrified.'

'Of what?' I ask.

The answers are varied: of riots, which can be caused by tensions between the two sides of the town, or by something that inflames the community, like the death of the boy in Yuendumu, shot by the police officer; of booze getting in, or drugs; of dogs, or severe weather.

'If anything really bad kicks off, we come to the medical clinic,' they tell me. 'It's sturdy. There's a room we hide in, we'll show you.'

I am walked through the clinic to what looks like a large broom cupboard, with a reassuringly large metal door. 'When the riots were happening, we stayed in here,' they tell me.

I stare at the cupboard, trying to imagine hiding in there as chaos rages on around us outside. Something niggles at me.

'When you say things set off unrest . . . hasn't a woman just been badly beaten across the road? And she's probably going to die? Wouldn't that set off some unrest?'

Annie shrugs. 'Possibly.'

I see some more patients. There's a guy who, at twenty, already has a mechanical heart valve, the after-effect of severe rheumatic heart disease.

He hasn't been in for weeks and his INR is well below therapeutic—meaning, for his condition, it's well below what it should be. INR is a ratio that essentially delineates how long it takes your blood to clot. The lower it is, the quicker your blood will clot, basically, and because people with mechanical heart valves have higher risk of clots, they need higher INRs to give them some wiggle room. He's on his way out bush, and wants some warfarin (a drug used to prevent clots). He speaks decent English, and he's friendly and kind. We try to figure out a way to manage his INR without regular checks, which is borderline impossible. But there's a funeral on and he has to go.

It's difficult to know what to do. As it is, a formal INR will take days to get back anyway, having to be driven for processing in Alice, or Darwin. So I ring the cardiologist, and we bash together a half-okay plan.

The cardiologist sighs into the phone: 'It's hard out there, with follow-up. A lot of the people in the community are transient, on their way somewhere else. You can only do your best.'

My best isn't really good enough, I can't help but think as I send him on his way with 10 milligrams of Warfarin a day and a Clexane shot, hoping for the best, or at least something better than the worst.

Before he goes, I ask him where he's travelling to.

'Home,' he says, 'my Country.'

'Isn't this your home?' I ask, genuinely curious.

He shakes his head. I see something in his face but he doesn't elaborate, and I don't ask.

I am transported back to the Brewarrina museum, and Brad's words. That the communities are designed by white people, and all the displaced First Nations peoples are shoved into these areas where they were never meant to be.

'You see Australia as one country, this idea of nationhood,' Brad had said to me. 'But that's not the case. For us there are hundreds of countries, in this one land. So by disregarding that, it's like putting the different fighting sides during a war into the same building, and forcing them to live together. It completely disrespects our systems and our way of life.'

I get in the 4WD and drive the 150 metres to the metal cage. I let myself inside, lock the cage and both the doors. I pull the curtains, and hear, in the distance, barking dogs and the vague sound of glass shattering, like a window being smashed.

My unease intensifies.

Kristina rings me from Denmark, but I don't want to answer the phone. The knot in my stomach is getting larger by the second. As it gets darker outside, I pull a mouldy old doona cover from the cupboard and lie down in the single bed.

I realise I am flinching every time the cage rattles or a dog barks. Sleep is impossible. I get up and rifle through my toiletries. Surely, somewhere in here there has to be a sleeping pill. I find an old Phenergan. As I walk back to the bedroom, there is a loud rattle at the front of the cage. My heart is beating so loudly I can hear it.

I walk to the front door, and peer through a crack in the shutters. There is nothing outside, aside from a large gum tree hitting the cage as the slight wind blows. Out of the corner of my eye I see a dog, wandering around in front of the cage.

It's just the wind.

What am I so afraid of?

Tangibly, I suppose, it's the low-level threat of riots, unrest, wild dingoes, the rain—all those things make sense to worry about. But it isn't just that. I have lived and worked in some very remote places, but never have I felt the isolation I feel on this night, lying wide awake inside the steel cage, somewhere between Tennant Creek and Alice Springs, completely alone.

I am afraid because I am in a place most Australians will never see, and for them it may as well not exist. Except it does exist, this giant crack inside this giant landmass containing a parallel universe with wire fences on either side of it. *Stay Out, Do Not Pass.* I know it exists, because I'm lying at the bottom of it, and inside it, as Brad told me, is not an empty void—it's jam-packed full of history.

There shouldn't be places built solely for the purpose of housing displaced people, the original owners of the land, because they have been taken from where their homes really are. There shouldn't be a place ruled by a government act, controlled and determined by white people. There shouldn't be a place where different tribes are forced to live together, bound by the shared trauma of displacement and abandonment.

There shouldn't be a place where one doctor rolls up every few months, and the nurses beg them to stay, because there hasn't been another one out here for so long. Where near-teenagers have mechanical heart valves, and the nearest place they can be operated on is an entirely different state. Where the quality of living is so appalling that people become desperate and violence ensues. Where women are beaten to death, and the people who come to manage that are big, burly, white policemen, who put the people in prison where they can die in custody and nothing happens, aside from a few headlines and royal commissions that appear to affect minimal or no change.

In the supposedly developed country called Australia, there shouldn't be a place where you are told it is not safe to walk outside and, if you are to spend a day there, you must stay locked inside a cage, staring at the wall, while the bureaucrats sit inside their air-conditioned offices in Canberra and pretend this is normal. *Nothing to see here.*

No one place in the Territory is the same. These were my experiences at the time, so do not, by any means, represent the Territory in its entirety. There is a big chasm between the perception and reality of desert communities. They are often seen as a concepts or news headlines rather than actual places with actual people. Rather than telling the stories of First Nations Australians, which are not mine to tell, I am trying instead to tell of the experiences that led me to dip my toe into the river that divides black and white Australia.

That night, I read an article recommended to me by a friend. I printed it back in Noosa, thinking it might be informative for me as I headed to the Territory. It was published in the *Griffith Review* and written by Kim Mahood. It's called 'Kartiya are like Toyotas', *kartiya* referring to a white person who works in and around First Nations communities in Australia. Mahood took the title from a remark a Western Desert woman made about whitefellas who work in Indigenous communities: 'Kartiya are like Toyotas. When they break down we get another one.'

I lie there in the little donga surrounded by a metal cage, and begin to read.

SINCE THE REVELATIONS about child sexual abuse in remote Indigenous communities scorched the national consciousness a few years ago, conditions in remote communities and towns have been back in the public eye. The flaws ... have been exposed, and it has become possible to speak aloud truths that until recently would have seen the speaker branded a racist, and his or her voice neutralised. That some of the most articulate and influential voices are Aboriginal has made it possible for the private conversations many people have been having for years to enter the public domain.

There is, however, one story that doesn't get much mileage: remote Indigenous Australia has a significant white population that is disproportionately influential while being unequipped, unprepared or unsuitable for the work it does. There are the good people, who are overworked and undervalued; and there are the sociopaths, the borderline criminals, the self-righteous bullies and the mentally unhinged, who gravitate to the positions no one else wants, entrench themselves and contribute in no small degree to the malaise that haunts Indigenous communities.

It is mandatory for anyone wishing to work in Antarctica to undergo a physical and psychological assessment to establish whether they will stand up to the stresses of isolation, the extreme environment and the intense proximity to other people. All the same factors exist in remote Aboriginal communities, along with confronting cross-cultural conditions. Yet there don't appear to be any recognised training programs for people who aspire to work in a community, or screening criteria to weed out the mad, bad and incompetent who prowl the grey zone of Indigenous service delivery . . . The famous quip about mercenaries, missionaries and misfits has a lot of truth in it, and each type covers a spectrum, from highly functional through incompetent to downright destructive.

. . . This desert culture, where the power of family and country encompasses and transcends all other preoccupations, is where the crossed purposes of Indigenous and non-Indigenous expectations are at their most extreme. It's probably the zone of greatest discomfort in Australia, a place where the white noise of the kartiya world and the Babel of Aboriginal voices create a static through which we blunder, grinning and waving like mad people, signalling that we mean each other no harm, though harm frequently occurs.

Me, *kartiya*, inside this place where I should not be, feeling the tides of history, land, culture and a pain that is not mine.

As Mahood writes, and as Brad told me, the zone of greatest discomfort in Australia is really just the gap.

I fall into an uneasy sleep, clutching the printed article, my fingers sweating onto the paper. My dreams are fractured: they skim between the blue ocean of the Mediterranean Sea and fluttering blue-and-white tape around a house with smashed windows and burning cars. I see the Stuart highway, that long stretch of road that cuts through the desert—only one road in or out. There is a baby crying but I am not sure if it is only in my dreams.

The centre of Australia is a place like no other. It would take my mind a long time to reconcile my experience there.

Two days later, MJ asks me if I will come back after spending the weekend in Alice Springs. I have survived so far, so I tell her I will. I tell myself I will.

She asks me if I can buy her some liquorice bullets, because she hasn't had any for months and is craving them. I promise her and myself I will get the liquorice bullets, and that I will return to the cage and the medical clinic.

The relief is overwhelming as we drive into Alice Springs. I marvel at how quickly my perspective changes. When I first landed in Alice, I was scared as hell—now, after where I've been, I feel as if I'm about to arrive in Zurich.

Stevie invites me on a night out with some of the other doctors. I agree, relieved for the distraction. We go back to the same bar, with the fairy lights and music and people and wine. I like the nightlife in Alice. It reminds me, strangely, of Berlin.

Everyone mingles: black people, white people, Asian people, South American people, gay people, straight people and everything in between. This place has a bohemian, cosmopolitan feel that isn't so common anywhere else in Australia. It feels like in Alice Springs, you can be whoever and whatever you want to be. Despite the problems that exist there, it is an amazing place.

It's warm in the bar, and everyone seems to be in a good mood. The normality of Friday drinks is soothing in a way I can't adequately describe. Yet Stevie notices I am uncharacteristically quiet and asks how the week has been.

'Sonia has been out working in some of the communities,' she explains to the other people sitting near us.

One of the guys looks at me. 'Really? By yourself?'

'Yeah,' I say, taking a large sip of wine.

'I was out there for a while,' he says slowly. 'Where were you exactly?'

I explain the week I've had, the places I've been, the leaving, the going.

His eyes are bulging. 'You shouldn't have been out there by yourself. No training, no nothing?'

'Well, there was, like, a nurse and manager and stuff,' I say, hesitantly.

He is shaking his head. 'You're done now, right?'

'I said I'd go back next week,' I say, picturing the packet of unbought liquorice bullets.

I see the cage in my mind's eye. I see the darkness, and hear the dogs barking in the night.

Another girl sits down next to the guy, a nurse, and his girlfriend.

'Bec,' he says, turning to his girlfriend and gesturing to me, 'this is a friend of Stevie's. She was sent out to the communities up north as the only doctor, staying by herself.'

Bec almost chokes on her beer. 'Fuck.'

'So you wouldn't go out there?' I ask.

She looks at me as if I have turned green. 'Are you kidding? As a solo female? With no experience in that kind of medicine? No way in hell.'

'Mate,' the guy says, leaning in. 'My advice to you is to quit, and not go back. They've sent you out there for no other reason than because they can, and they want to say they're putting doctors in places.'

'Faces in places,' I hear Brad say.

'The difference you're going to make is almost negligible,' the guy says, reading my mind. 'Sure, you make a bit of money, but is it really worth it? If something bad happens to you out there, like what happened to that nurse in South Australia, no one is going to care. It'll just be another tragic incident, somewhere in the middle of a place no one else in Australia knows or cares about.'

Later, as we walk to another bar, everyone buoyed by Friday good spirits and the other kind of spirits, I quietly ask Stevie what she thinks. Stevie is like me, a Sydney girl who now finds herself in the desert.

'If I were you I'd cut my losses,' she says bluntly. 'Just tell them it hasn't worked out and that you're leaving.'

I hear Stevie's words, but I decide to forget about my work dilemma as we go into the nightclub. The scene on the dance floor is unbelievable. My time in Alice is complete when I see a girl in sequined red, a girl I recognise, dancing near me. For a split second I think I'm going mad. She sees me looking at her.

'Do I know you?' she shouts, grinning over the music.

I almost can't believe it, but I have to ask. 'Are you DJ Faggot Mafia?'

'I am!' she shouts.

I start laughing and laughing. 'You're Loretta's cousin, right?'

She looks startled. 'Yeah, do you know her?'

'She's one of my best mates,' I say. 'We've known each other since we were eight. She told me about you.'

They say there are no such things as coincidences, and as I stand there, on the dance floor of a nightclub in Alice Springs next to a woman with a moustache, who is dressed head-to-toe in glittering red sequins and goes by the stage name DJ Faggot Mafia, and happens to be the first cousin of my oldest friend who is currently 3000 kilometres away, on the other side of the country, I have to say I agree. I'm not sure of the meaning behind it, but maybe it's the universe's way of telling you that you are not alone, and that friends and connections are never as far away as you might think.

The next day, I ring my locum agent and tell her it hasn't worked out. Mentally, I apologise to the nurse about the liquorice bullets that will never be bought, and my broken promise. There are so many broken promises in this country already, and I have just made another one.

Still, time cannot stop for guilt—if that were the case, Australia would cease to exist—and that evening, in the humidity of the Territory's wet season, I step onto a flight to Darwin.

In my backpack, resting by my feet, sits the now-raggedy-from-being-read-so-many-times article from the *Griffith Review*.

Two sentences from the final paragraph burn a hole into the plane floor: *Kartiya are unpredictable and unreliable. Even the best of them make promises they don't keep.*

I stay in Darwin for nearly two weeks. It rains and rains, and rains a bit more, but I don't mind. Every morning I run in the rain, around the promenade, looking out over the Arafura Sea.

I go to the pub and meet other people like me, stranded on their way into Western Australia. We sip beers in the rain, exchanging stories. I make some friends there, other doctors who are nomads too. Darwin seems to be a town that attracts Peter Pans, but it's so enjoyable and so refreshing to be in a city that feels devoid of expectation and pressure, that I wonder whether being a Peter Pan is such a bad way to live. Everyone I meet in Darwin is either honest about being lost, or close to being found.

Plus, the tales from Darwin's emergency department are so entertaining, although I feel bad laughing: tales of axes thrown at people, a series of booze-related crimes and injuries, not to mention the scooters.

'These fucking scooters,' Charlotte, one of my new-found Darwin mates, is telling me. 'You are literally forbidden to hire one while you're here. They kill people. No one can help themselves from riding pissed, so you can imagine how that ends up.'

'How'd Darwin go during all the Covid lockdowns and stuff?' I ask. It is, I realise with some surprise, 28 January, 2021. For a moment, I feel like I've lost time. I guess that's what travelling does to you. Especially being in Darwin in the wet season—it's like being in a strange dream. My own life aside, Covid is still not really over. The Top End, from what I gather, didn't have it as bad as the eastern states, but they still went into lockdown for a while.

Everyone laughs.

'You know how the bottle shops were considered an essential service? Here, that was because everyone in Darwin drinks so much, the health advice was that if they were shut, we'd be overrun not with Covid, but with people going into full-blown alcohol withdrawals.'

'Relatable,' I say.

Everyone raises their glasses. Who are we to judge?

I meet one of the journalists at the *NT News*, a publication famed for its wild headlines.

'So, the croc stories, they're pretty popular, right?' I ask her.

She sips her beer, and looks mildly stressed. 'Mate,' she says, shaking her head. 'I've had a lot of pressure lately, a lot of pressure.'

'To what, write about crocs?'

'I haven't written a good croc story for weeks,' she says. 'The pressure from above is getting really full on. If I don't pull something out if my arse soon, I'll probably lose my job.'

'Might hurt a bit to pull a croc out of your arse,' I point out.

We grin into our beers.

Things are a little different in Darwin.

Charlotte tells me about Territory Day, the only day of the year you're allowed to set off firecrackers. People make their own, and then blow them up.

'How does that turn out?' I ask Charlotte hesitantly.

She looks at me, and I see the face of a woman who has worked as an emergency doctor in Darwin for possibly too long already.

'How the fuck do you think it turns out?'

On my last few days here, I go to Darwin wharf. I stare over the ocean, and try to imagine what it must have been like when the bombs fell from the air like rain. Darwin is so close to the rest of the world that it feels exposed, vulnerable. If I were to step into the ocean and keep swimming (croc attacks notwithstanding) I would hit Indonesia, then the rest of Asia. Darwin is in the psyche of Australia because of the bombing, and yet, oddly, it doesn't feel as Australian as I would have thought. It feels more like a melting pot of Asia and Australia, almost like another world. I love it.

It starts to rain but I don't feel it: all I can feel is the experience of being here, *in Darwin*.

I can't believe it, but tomorrow morning I am finally flying into Western Australia. It has taken me seven weeks, and I have crossed almost the entire country. But when the sun rises in the morning, I will fly just over the border of the Northern Territory, and spend six weeks working in Kununurra. And after that, finally, I will make it back to Broome.

# part 4

# western australia

Cable Beach with its immense horizon and endless sand is where heaven and earth meet.

Susan Sickert, *Beyond the Lattice: Broome's early years*

Flying into Kununurra is like descending into Costa Rica. Below me are green mountains covered in red soil, lush vegetation and giant waterfalls.

Kununurra airport reminds me of Hawaii. There are palms trees everywhere, their fronds almost eclipsing the sign on the little white building that says Kununurra Airport. A policeman looks up at me when I walk through, holding out my pass to be allowed back into the Kingdom of Western Australia.

'Where have you come from?' he asks me.

'The Territory,' I say.

'And before then?'

'Queensland. Before that, rural NSW.'

'Were you in the Territory for fourteen days?'

'Feels like a lifetime since I left Sydney,' I say, nodding to confirm. 'It's taken me nearly two months to get back here.'

He half smiles. 'Welcome back to WA, and to Kununurra.'

'Thank you,' I say and, absurdly, I realise I am close to tears.

In Kununurra, everything stops. Kununurra is a town in far northern Western Australia, at the eastern extremity of the Kimberley, about 50 kilometres from the border with the Territory. It's famous for the Ord River Dam, Ivanhoe Crossing, crocodiles, huge barramundi, pink diamonds, melons, mangoes, sandalwood, waterfalls and its proximity to Lake Argyle. It's good to land in Kunnas, and not just because of these local attractions—I have been on the move for so long that I've forgotten what it's like to have a house, a job and six weeks of knowing exactly where I'll be coming back to every night. For a while, at least, there will be no more rumbling anxiety about border closures and losing work and money, and being trapped somewhere I don't want to be.

My first night I sit in the backyard of the doctor's accommodation, in the hot, wet humid air of the Kimberley wet season, listening to country music coming from the house next door and watching the blazing red sun fade into pink. Apparently, my little cyclone-proof house is in the dodgiest street in Kununurra but now I know that everything is relative. This is paradise. The heat seeps into my skin. There's no rain, like in Darwin, and I let the humidity pour into my body. My weary bones accept the warmth without question.

The days go by and I go to work, go home and sit in the humidity, watching the sunset and admiring the boab trees. I make good friends with Jade, one of the other GPs at the clinic I've been posted to. I've become so used to working largely solo that it's nice to have other doctors around for a change, especially ones who are all actually really good quality—medically speaking, and as people.

Jade's from Melbourne, and like me she doesn't know to change a tyre, drive a 4WD, or do anything even remotely outdoorsy. She likes designing jewellery and appreciates film noir and fine dining.

'What are you doing here?' I finally ask her one day.

She shrugs. 'I got a bit sick of being in lockdown all the time. My friend from medical school works at the hospital here and she told me they needed GPs, so I applied for the job, and suddenly I've got this ridiculously huge Prado and I've committed to a twelve-month contract living in the middle of the Kimberley.'

'Hey, it's an adventure,' I say, with admiration.

Jade invites me for dinner at the Kimberley Grande with her friend Victoria. I am about to decline, then realise I have nowhere to be and nothing to do except sit alone in the backyard staring at the boabs, so I say yes.

I've always liked a good pub, and the Kimberley Grande soon becomes my new home. It's an old-school country pub with more than a hint of outback swish, a good menu with large wooden outdoor tables and a relaxed sort of vibe. Victoria, Jade's friend, is in a long cotton dress with earrings and jewellery, looking like a glamorous Byron Bay bohemian, but when we start talking about work I realise she's still definitely a doctor.

The small hospital in Kununurra sounds like any other place I have worked around Australia: full of intrigue. Victoria and I discover common ground: it turns out she's come to Kununurra from Perth after having been royally screwed around by a senior consultant at her previous work. The way she describes him, he almost makes heartdoc_82 look like Bambi.

'We reckon he might have been a sex addict,' Jade says, examining her wine glass with interest.

'Honestly,' Victoria says, after telling me the whole story in excruciating detail. 'Can you believe there are people like that in the world? Working in medicine?'

'I can,' I say wryly.

Victoria gives us a few more particularly dire anecdotes from her own sorry tale, which has Jade and I cringing, groaning and laughing simultaneously.

'Goes to show,' I say, feeling strangely cheerful, 'no one is safe!'

'Well, here's to new friends,' Jade says, also sounding positive as she raises her glass.

'And new horizons,' I add with a grin.

We drink another bottle of pink wine and find ourselves being chatted up by two men. They are definitely younger than the three of us, but Victoria has a gleam in her eye and Jade and I have had a fair few pink wines, so we decide to join them for a while.

'If you're new to Kununurra, you have to go to Andy's,' one of them keeps telling us, repeating himself so many times I start to wonder if he's taken some kind of drug. 'It's out of this world.'

'What's Andy's?' Jade asks.

'Andy's Chasm,' his friend tells us. 'There are plenty of waterfalls in the Kimberley but Andy's is on another level.'

'Who's Andy?' I ask.

'I think he died in there,' the first guy says casually.

'Is it dangerous?'

He considers my question. 'Well, it's not just a regular waterfall,' he explains, leaning in. 'It's more like a series of canyons—that's why it's called 'chasm'. You go through these cracks in the rock and you find yourself in this other little world.'

'Cool,' Victoria says, looking interested. To me this screams danger, rather than coolness, but she has lived in the Kimberley a lot longer than I have after all.

'But is it dangerous?' I ask again.

'It is if you go at the wrong time and it rains,' he says. 'The rain fills the chasms up and they basically turn into whirlpools and you can get sucked under and drown.'

'Sounds really fun,' I say pointedly.

'We can take you,' the second guy offers, and pulls a card out of his wallet. 'I'm a tour guide.'

'And you're also a plumber and financial advisor,' Jade says, looking at the card, which lists a variety of credentials.

'So you do banking, plumbing, air-conditioners and tour-guiding,' Victoria says.

He shrugs. 'I like to spread my wings to help people in need,' he says, palms outstretched, Christ-like.

'Are you high?' I can't help asking.

The two guys look at each other.

'I knew you were high!' Jade says.

'We've been at Dick Creek,' Guy 1 finally says, as if this will explain everything. 'You know, in the Territory.'

I look at Victoria, who is, after all, a local. 'What's at Dick Creek?' I ask.

'Mushrooms,' Guy 2 says.

'Like, the hallucinogenic variety?'

They both start laughing, confirming yes.

'Dick Creek is pretty dangerous with the crocs, but the mushies grow best in cow shit,' one of them explains to his audience of three doctors. 'So we went in and grabbed some, but it was pretty scary. And even getting there we had to get through the Covid roadblocks at the border.'

'What did you say to the police?' I ask, interested.

'That we were going fishing,' Guy 1 explains. 'On the way back, they asked us to show them what we caught, and we had to explain we'd caught nothing.'

'But the cops just thought we were shit at fishing,' adds Guy 2.

'Where are the mushrooms now?' Jade asks, looking curious.

'We ate them back in Dick Creek.'

'And you drove?' I say, incredulously. 'All the way from the Territory, high on mushrooms from cow shit in Dick Creek?'

There's a pause, and we all start cracking up.

'Well, when you put it like that it sounds bad,' the plumber/financier/air-conditioner fixer/tour guide says defensively. 'But the Territory is literally like 40 minutes that way.'

'Plus we were stressed out,' Guy 1 says, 'after the crocs, and the cops, you know.'

They ask us if we'd like to go to Dick Creek one weekend in search of more grown-from-cow-shit magic mushrooms. Jade looks like she's seriously contemplating it, and Victoria hasn't said no either.

'There's some closer,' the guys say. 'Near Ord River. We could go there.'

'Maybe,' I say, quite liking the sound of the whole thing.

'We can even go tonight if you like.'

For a moment, I flirt with the idea of saying yes. Of throwing caution completely to the wind, and following these two blokes I don't know down a dark river into some cow shit to pull out hallucinogenic mushrooms before proceeding to get very high, here in Kununurra, in the Kimberley.

'I think I better head home,' I say, 'before this all ends in tears.'

'Or cow shit,' Jade adds.

'Welcome to Kunnas,' Victoria says to me.

I can't help it: I find myself laughing all the way home.

Work is simultaneously interesting and boring, rewarding and frustrating. The clinic is the usual chaos, but the people I work with are nice, and I like the patients. Kununurra at least has a hospital, a few medical clinics, lots of doctors and enough support that it feels like you aren't ever really alone.

Maybe I'm just getting acclimatised, but the issues I'm faced with every day start to affect me less. I argue with the hospital locum about the eighteen year old with a mechanical mitral valve, who has resting tachycardia (high heart rate), a three-month sub-therapeutic INR and signs of overload. I ask if she can be admitted for optimisation of management, or at the very least given a few days' reprieve from her abusive boyfriend.

'What do you think I can do any differently in here to you in the clinic?' the locum says to me, rather belligerently.

'Well, she's a bit tachy and her oxygen sats are a bit low and . . .'

'Her heart rate isn't that high,' he says bluntly. 'Can't you get on top of her INR in there?'

We argue for a bit longer. He brick-walls me to the end. Who knows? He's probably dealing with some catastrophe in there and is in it up to his neck already. So I just say thanks, and hang up the phone.

I ask the patient if she can come in every day for a clexane injection until her numbers improve, and get regular INR checks. She looks at me.

'I have to leave town,' she explains again. 'My boyfriend will kill me if I stay, and I have nowhere else to go. I thought I could go to hospital, but . . .'

'Is there a medical clinic where you're going?' I ask desperately.

She shakes her head, looking almost sorry for me.

I give her a clexane shot and talk her through how to inject herself for another few days, and ask her to come back at the end of the week. I tell her she needs an echo—an ultrasound of her heart—and I book her in with the next visiting cardiologist. I beg her to keep the appointment before she leaves. She says yes, I suspect just to make me feel better. I let her go without a fight. I wonder as I drive home whether this is a sign that I'm giving up.

Outside of work, I'm spending a lot of time hiking through bushland and swimming underneath waterfalls. Being appropriately terrified of crocodiles, I ask everyone and anyone the same question whenever we plan a weekend adventure: 'Is it safe to swim there?' By this I mean, 'Are there saltwater crocodiles that will death-roll and then eat me in there?'

Before I came to Kununurra, I had a healthy fear of all crocs, saltwater and freshwater. To me the difference was negligible. They both looked like crocs and had teeth like crocs. That was until I came here, and realised that freshwater crocs didn't seem to scare anybody.

'Honestly, if they latch onto you, they're more at risk of you breaking their jaw by flailing around a bit,' the local cop tells me one evening as we all sit at the Kimberley Grande having a beer after work. 'Like, honestly.'

'I think freshies only really try to bite you if you step directly on their heads,' one of the doctors from the hospital offers. 'I've seen a few freshie bites, one was pretty bad, the rest were, you know, nips, essentially.'

'When you say "pretty bad" . . .?'

'About fifty stitches,' the doctor says, casually.

Everyone in the Kimberley is extremely gung ho, and it must be starting to rub off on me because every weekend I find myself clambering up rocks and jumping into lakes and standing under waterfalls. I go swimming in Lake Argyle, which is apparently home to 40,000 freshwater crocs, so I mustn't be that scared. Or perhaps I think that what I can't see, can't hurt me.

One Saturday Georgia, one of the doctors I work with at the clinic, 6ffers to take us out in her boat down the lower Ord River. I love that all these Kununurra women regularly just jump in their boats and take on the water (Victoria also has her own boat and skipper's licence), but I still feel a little on edge. Not about the drivers, more the things below the water that aren't quite as obvious to the naked eye. The boat feels worryingly low: this close to the water, I worry that a croc could just leap up into it.

'No salties in here,' Georgia says confidently. 'They can't get over the diversion dam wall, don't worry.'

I'm reassured, until I notice the weird steel cage things dotted here and there along the river's edge. I nudge Jade. 'What are those?'

'Saltie traps,' one of the other girls explains.

Jade and I look at each other. 'If there are no saltwater crocodiles in here, why are there traps?' I demand.

There's a bit of a silence, and the boat whirs along.

'Oh, you know,' Georgia says. 'Just in case.'

'Like, there's *probably* no salties,' the other girl explains, and I look at her as if she's saying 'there's *probably* no Ebola'.

I'm starting to notice that the Kimberley is the land of 'probably'. 'There are probably no salties.' 'You probably won't get stuck in that ravine.' 'You probably won't get the car bogged in the middle of fucking nowhere.'

In the Kimberley, you have to become a glass-half-full sort of person, or you'll probably die.

That night I walk—against everyone's advice that you're not really meant to walk around after dark—to the local tavern. I've been going to the Kimberley Grande so much I've started calling it the 'KG', so figure I may as well diversify and sample the other watering holes in town. I order a glass of pink wine at the bar and just sit there, thinking.

You can only work in remote Australia non-stop for so long before one of two things happens. You either get fatigued and give up, or you become desensitised and accept things as they are. That may not be the case for everyone but I'd say it rings pretty true for most.

I finish my glass and order another one. As I sit there, pondering these grand concepts, a woman appears at my side.

'Do you want to have a drink with me?' she asks, flat out.

I'm a bit startled. 'Well, I was going to make this my last,' I say. 'But sure, I mean, why not?'

'I just noticed you were sitting alone and thought you might want some company,' she says, pulling up the bar stool next to mine.

'It sounds weird, but I actually like drinking at bars alone,' I say.

I realise that I actually spend a lot of time these days doing things alone—although I do make friends wherever I go. Travelling alone, living alone: is this the beginning of knowing myself?

The woman looks at me like I'm mad. 'Are you on a holiday?' she asks.

'I'm working out here.'

'What do you do?'

I sigh. 'I'm a GP.'

'I'm a teacher,' she says. 'I just got here.'

'What brings you to these parts?' I ask.

'My husband of 25 years had an affair,' she says, looking into her glass of white wine. 'Anyway, he lives with her now. And my kids are grown up.'

'Life, huh,' I say, because there isn't really anything else to say.

'You know, I'm nearly 60,' she says. 'We were meant to be spending this time in a van together, seeing Australia. The kids grown up, the house paid off, everything sorted out. We were meant to be on Easy Street.'

'Goes to show,' I say, with surprisingly little bitterness. 'You never know what's going to happen, so you should never take your plans too seriously.'

She shrugs. 'And now I'm here, living in this town in the middle of the Kimberley, alone. And he's in my house, probably having sex with his new girlfriend.'

'Was the sex that great anyway?' I ask.

She laughs. 'It was terrible, actually.'

'Well, there you go, maybe this is your second chance at life.'

'Not sure I'll find what I'm after in the tav,' she says ruefully, as we both survey the other patrons. 'I gave my best years to that guy, raising his kids, and he's left me for a woman half his age. Now all my plans have gone to shit and I'm sitting here drinking with you at a pub in the middle of a place where there are more crocs than people.'

'Actually, that's right,' I say. 'I read that too, there are more crocs than people in the Kimberley. Mad, isn't it?'

She lifts her eyebrows at me as she sips the wine; it's not as mad as anything else she's experienced, clearly.

It is awful, I think, as I sit there with my new friend, the way humans abuse and mistreat one another. And for what? Sex? Money? Power? I now think that, to use someone emotionally, to make them love you and then abuse the privileges that come with that, is a really shocking thing to do, but it's unfortunately really common.

Humans are unreliable, fickle creatures, is the truth of it. As a patient said to me once, most people are okay, some are really great, and then there's a small percentage who are just a pack of absolute stinkers.

After all the croc chasing and a disastrous trip to Andy's Chasm that I think I'm still traumatised by, my next outback adventure is somewhat more civilised. After finding out that one of my colleagues, who doubles as a fishing guide, has just taken Ernie Dingo out on the Keep River—'You could have told me!' I berate him after the morning meeting—Jade promises we will do something fun to make up for it. I say nothing will make up for missing a fishing trip with Ernie Dingo. But when Jade, Victoria, a few others and I get on a small plane to see King George Falls, I have to admit that while it's not Ernie, it's still pretty good.

We land in a place called Faraway Bay, which is, as its name suggests, extremely far away from anywhere. When we walk into our boat, I ask about the chances of getting eaten by a croc if I have a quick dip. The water is crystal-clear, blue-green and enormously inviting.

Georgia looks across at me. 'You can't risk it,' she says. 'They move like lightning. And they're so stealthy you wouldn't even know they were there. But they are, believe me.'

I don't truly believe her until, as we take the boat towards the falls around an hour later, a gigantic saltwater croc appears, totally silent, next to the boat. It lazily flicks its tail, looks up at us with one beady eye, and then, as if it was never there, submerges itself again, leaving barely a ripple.

'Still want to go for a swim, Sonnie?' Georgia asks.

I shift away from the edge of the boat and say no thank you, I will be fine out of the water.

You hear the King George Falls before you see them. The roar is echoing through what feels like the entire world. As we get closer, it gets louder, reverberating through my entire body. I have seen so many waterfalls recently that I thought I'd be a little desensitised, but I have never seen anything like this.

The boat stops at an intersection of rock and we look up. Nature has somehow arranged itself so there are two giant waterfalls with hundreds of thousands of litres of water spilling over them, right next to one another, separated only by rock. Kev, our skipper, takes the boat closer, so we are almost directly underneath the first waterfall. Everyone goes silent, staring above us.

And then, nature speaks.

When that much water is all falling from the same place, it looks less like water and more like whipped cream, cascading down, with steam wafting off it. It's like ribbons of white mist, but with the strength of twenty armies—incredibly delicate, but hugely powerful. It is every feeling I have ever tried to suppress: it's all there, in that organised chaos collapsing into the river below.

'It's all the tears of all the broken hearts,' I say out loud, not even realising I'm speaking. 'All of them, this is where they go.'

For a moment, I catch Victoria's eye. She doesn't say anything, but I know she understands what I mean.

On my last night in Kununurra, the storm comes in. I'm swimming at the local pool as the sky turns grey and blue then dusty pink. I stop at ten laps, fearing the lightning.

I sit in the car in my wet swimmers, watching the flashes pierce the earth. When the storm ends, it's like it never happened, but it lingers, slightly, in the muggy air.

I have breakfast with Jade before I leave, and give her one of the paintings I bought in Sun Town, in the Territory. Jade has become a good friend in the time we've worked together. One minute, I didn't know she existed, and then the next, we were swimming in Lake Argyle at sunset, four-wheel driving through rivers and drinking pink wine at the KG together, while battling with work and all the catastrophes that can come with it. She's from Melbourne, I'm from Sydney and somehow our paths have crossed here, in the Kimberley.

I ask her what her plans are for the future. She shrugs, and smiles.

'I think I'll stay,' she says. 'Why not?'

'Watch out for the crocs,' I say. 'And no more trips to Andy's bloody Chasm.'

We shudder into our coffees.

I make a mental note that Kununurra, now I have friends here, is a place that I can, and will, come back to.

After leaving Kununurra, I go to Perth to see Holly. It's been nearly a year since we sat in her backyard in the Pilbara, talking about life.

'Broome will be great,' she says, as we sit in her new backyard in Perth. It's significantly less dusty here, but we're drinking the same cheap booze. Bongo, now a city dog, appears and licks my hand.

'I keep telling myself I've been waiting to just get back to Broome,' I explain to Holly, 'but now I'm nearly there, what happens?'

Holly looks at me. 'We always end up in the places we should be. It takes a while, sometimes forever. But in the end . . .'

Surely she is right. She has to be.
*I will find myself in Broome.*

The plane ride up the coast of Western Australia is like crossing time and space. This is the closest you can get to seeing infinity, I reckon. You leave the skyscrapers of Perth, the sentinels of flashing metal with the signs of their gods on the top—Fortescue, BHP, Rio Tinto—very quickly, and the next moment you're above a land so red it looks awash with dried blood. Even from the air and after this many months, the earth of the Pilbara astounds me as much as it did the first time.

As the plane crosses the country, I marvel, as always, at how *huge* Western Australia is. One state covers the entire coastline. I look down, amazed that I, a person who has spent the last two decades living in Darlinghurst, have dropped myself into the middle of that red dirt.

I see Broome above the red, even further north, and feel things I don't quite understand, deep inside myself: excitement mixed with joy mixed with grief mixed with something I can't really describe.

Possibly, this is what freedom feels like.

The long road to Broome, the path to some kind of enlightenment: it sounds ridiculous but as we fly towards the tip of Australia, I feel it again. It's the sense that this is the place I was meant to come to, where maybe, I will find peace.

We always search for the magical elixir of happiness, I think as I stare out the window. Achievement or money, or the right relationship or the biggest house. We are a society of me me me me, and then a little bit more me. But maybe all that we're really seeking is peace within ourselves, which can only come from truth. And until we get rid of the background noise, all the things about ourselves that we're told, all the expectations that we're meant to meet, it's very hard to find any truth: our own or otherwise. But maybe it's easier in places like Broome.

Broome is so far away from where I've spent most of my life that the insignificant parts of that life, things that used to hold so much importance for me, seemed here to become as insignificant as they actually *are*. It's like Brad said to me in Brewarrina, if you can't connect to the outside you can't connect to the inside.

As we float through the air, I think about all the people I've met and the stories I've heard as I've travelled across Australia. As if my mind is a loop recorder, I remember the man I met in a backyard in Lightning Ridge, who'd fallen down a mine shaft: 'Doc, it's been years. But sometimes when I wake up, I'm still down that fucking hole.'

People always tell us to get over things and say that time heals everything. But I don't think that's true anymore; it wasn't true for him. What I do think is that we should give ourselves permission to recover only when we're ready, and that in every small step away from pain, something is healed. I think that with all these small steps and small acts of healing, we slowly discover things about ourselves and our strength, and realise we are still standing, despite all that has tried to destroy us. Broken, I guess, but unbowed. And able to see beauty, able to experience it.

Many years ago, when I was a physio, I had as a patient a quiet woman who came in twice a week to work on her ankle, which had been broken. When, one day, I asked her what she was training for, she looked straight at me, and told me quite matter-of-factly that her son had thrown himself off the top of a nearby lookout. He was 21. The only thing the woman wanted to do now was get her ankle in good enough shape to be able to make the trek up there. A pilgrimage of sorts, I guess.

'You'll find as you get older,' she'd said to me, 'that tragedy stalks us all in many forms. It's as unavoidable as the day or night. That's something I've learnt.'

I never forgot that. Life, that giant casino where we are all *playing to lose.* I always liked to joke with my accountant that his office happened to be, unbelievably, between a funeral parlour and a cardiologist. Death, taxes and heartbreak: the three certainties of life all next to each other on a road in suburban Sydney. There's some freedom in knowing these things are inevitable. Even if life is, as Harry used to say to me in River Town, nothing more than an endless state of coming good, at least there *is* some good. The ability to see that good, or to hope for it at the very least, is what makes all the difference.

The plane starts to descend into the sunset. My nose is pressed to the window, and I see them again, those incredible colours. Not the flat, burnt, red dirt of the middle of Western Australia, but all the startling colours of the gateway to the Kimberley; blue, green, red, white, yellow, fading pink, exploding out of the ocean and the sand and the earth and shining straight through the plane window as the sun sparkles all over them.

It has technically taken me twelve weeks of travel across the continent to get here but, really, I have been searching for Broome my whole life. As we land, I know that I am taking another small, healing step of my own. When I climb down the little ladder and see the tiny, humble sign saying *Broome Inter-national Airport*, and feel the heat, that glorious heat, I'm filled with such a deep sense of joy that I want to turn around and hug the person next to me, pull them close, and say, 'I am out of the hole, and under the light, because, finally, I have made it back to Broome.'

The magic lasts up until I drive to the resort the medical clinic where I'll be working has me staying in. I leave the car I've fetched from the clinic and try to find reception, so I can get the keys to the apartment.

A woman appears, looking flustered. 'Are you staying here?' she asks.

'Um, yeah,' I say. 'Do I get the keys from you?'

'No,' she says. 'No, no.'

I look at her. 'It's closed' she says. 'The resort is closed.'

'But I'm meant to be living here for the next two months,' I explain. 'I'm a doctor working here in Broome.'

'A lizard got into the fuse box,' she tells me, 'and it's destroyed the power and electricity to the whole place. So we're shut.'

'What?'

'I know,' she rolls her eyes. 'One bloody lizard has taken down the entire resort.'

'So how long will it take to fix?'

'That's the thing,' she says apologetically. 'We don't know. We're waiting on a part that has to come from over east, so it might take a while.'

'You can't get it in Perth?' I ask.

She shakes her head. 'Nope.'

I stand there, with my bags, letting it sink in that the resort really is shut because of the actions of one lizard.

'Most other people have moved into the Oaks resort next door,' she tells me. 'It's really nice. Just ring your boss and explain. We've emailed them a few times but no one has answered. I'm sure they'll put you up there.'

I call my boss. Her husband answers, and promises he will sort something out. I go and wait by the pool. Could be worse, I think. The day is hot, and the pool is clean and blue. I lie out on a deck chair.

It's a pity about the lizard, resort living wouldn't have been a bad way to start. But soon, I am sent a link to my new accommodation and a text saying to call him if any problems.

I farewell the receptionist. 'Off to the Oaks?' she asks, busily turning away other holidaymakers who have just arrived for a Broome escape.

'Umm, no,' I say. 'They've got me staying at this other place.' I show her on my phone.

Her forehead crinkles. 'You said you're a doctor, right?'

'Yeah?'

'Funny place to make the doctor stay,' she finally says.

'Is it bad?'

'It's not bad. Like, it's clean and there's a pool and stuff.'

'Sounds fine!' I respond, not adding that, considering some of the other places I've stayed in, as long as there aren't any *Asbestos* or *Condemned* signs it'll be an upgrade.

'You'll see what I mean,' she says.

I see what she means as soon as I arrive. I'm staying in a backpackers. An upscale backpackers, to some extent, but still, a backpackers. A flashpackers?

'So, there's plenty to do in Broome,' the girl at the front desk is saying enthusiastically. 'There're tours, and marine life, and the croc park. We have open mic nights at Matsoes on Tuesday, and Thursday night there's the wet T-shirt contest at the Roey, that's always a fun night out.'

'Wet T-shirt contest?'

'Yep, it's a local tradition,' she says. 'If you win it I think there's some money.'

For a moment, I imagine me, the local GP, proudly displaying my trophy when I return to Sydney, telling my family that as well as being a steward of the local community, I have also won a wet T-shirt contest that, by the front desk girl's account, is a real Broome institution.

'Seems a bit sexist,' I point out. 'Is there a wet testicle competition?'

'Oh, yeah, that goes after,' she says, without blinking an eye.

'You're kidding.'

'Nope,' she says. 'But we call it wet balls.'

It's good to know, I muse, that in remote Australia, gender equality—in the form of seedy wet clothing nights at the pub—has not been forgotten.

'Oh, by the way,' she adds, looking a little apologetic. 'Just letting you know there's a school excursion arriving later in the week. So about 40 kids are moving in.'

Me, at the backpackers, with the school excursion.

What was that about finding myself in Broome?

'No worries,' I say.

The next morning before work, I walk to the golden sands of Cable Beach. The backpackers is in a great location, I'll give it that. But it's the tail end of the wet season and, according to my googling, swimming is still a little risky.

'It's risky all year round,' a guy who's now on the front desk guy tells me when I ask him about it. 'But, you know, chances are you'll be right.'

Chances are . . .?

'I mean, everyone's still a bit edgy because of what happened to that guy last year,' he says, lowering his voice. 'A shark got him. Ripped his legs off.'

'Jesus! Where was that?' I ask, not sure if I really want the answer.

'Just in front of the resort,' he says, pursing his lips. 'Pretty bad, you know.'

'I heard he was 40 metres out,' a nearby girl chimes in.

'I heard it was 200,' the bloke says, 'and he was surfing over a bait ball.'

'Well, he was my neighbour and I know he was knee-deep, just left of the rocks. He got taken, just like that,' says a lady, leaning in.

'So I might just go for a bit of a jog along the beach then,' I say.

Everyone shakes their heads. 'You'll be right, it was just bad luck.'

'Last shark attack was 1993,' he says, confidently. 'I mean, aside from that one I just told you about. And there're also the Irukandji . . . watch out for them.'

I wipe sweat from my brow. 'Is there anything that can't kill me in this place?'

Everyone shrugs. 'Hey, you got to go out somehow.'

Even in a paradise like Broome, work is still work. On my first day, the printer breaks, I run late and the receptionist overbooks me even though I've sent some very clear emails about my planned admin breaks.

The patients, like they do everywhere, file in one by one. One looks at me with vague suspicion.

'Are you from here?' she asks.

I explain no.

'Where, then?'

'Sydney,' I say. 'But I've been travelling around a while.'

'You be careful of the other patients,' she half-shouts, half-whispers. She has wild hair and is wearing a loose flowing dress with chunky wooden jewellery.

'Why?'

'There are some very strange people in this town.' She leans in, her eyes widening. 'Don't let them bully a young girl like you. OKAY?!'

'Okay,' I say.

'You know what a doctor in this town did once?'

'What?' I ask, feeling like I'll be told anyway.

'Or maybe she was a nurse.' The patient looks uncertain. 'Anyway, doesn't matter. Her name was Lottie, and she used to do home visits. And my mother, she was on death's door. Then after one visit from Lottie, well, she left.'

'Left?'

'Left! Gone!' She starts pointing frantically at the roof.

'Ah, right.'.

'Lottie was the angel of death! Every old person she went and visited, they left too!'

'So Lottie was killing people with . . .?'

'I don't know! Morphine! Whatever it is they use!'

'Did you share your concerns with the authorities?' I finally ask, because I'm not really sure what else to say.

'Why would I have done that?!' She looks at me like I'm insane. 'Lottie did her a favour. And me,' she adds, looking slightly guilty. 'Mum could be very aggressive at times.'

Every day I have lunch at the same café on Broome's main street. Despite the heat I always sit outside, watching the little world of Broome go past me. Sometimes an old man comes and sits next to me, and we chat about nothing. He asks me the same question every time I see him.

'Where you from?'

I always say Sydney, but by the second week, things are changing.

'I think I live here now,' I tell him. 'I think I live in Broome.'

He doesn't say anything, just sticks out his hand. I shake it.

'We are friends now, sister,' he says.

I accept that, after all the friends I have made on my travels around Australia, in Broome I will largely be alone. I've become so used to such tiny places, where you get to know the other residents immediately, that I feel like it will be harder to meet anyone here. After living in Sydney for so many years, my compass has now spun to the point where a town of 20,000 people seems too big to make friends in, which, I acknowledge to myself, is insane.

But then I meet AJ, and realise that the place where I least expected to make friends is hiding some of the best.

AJ is loosely introduced to me through Georgia in Kununurra. I expect we may meet once for a beer and a stroll along Cable Beach and that'll probably be it. But that's not what happens at all.

Angela Jane looks, I think when I first see her, like how you would expect an Angela Jane to look. She is tall and thin with the kind of hair I've always envied: thick and heavy and capable of being pulled into one of those long, cheerful-looking ponytails, like you'd see on a girl in an American teen horror movie—you know the girl, the one who either outlasts the serial killer and holds on till the end, or, being too beautiful for this world, is murdered at the frat house party in the opening scenes. With hair like that, I imagined, Angela Jane would have a fiancée and be expecting a baby in the next year or so, while playing a lot of netball.

But AJ, I learn, avoids relationships because she just doesn't have the time. After starting another career, she decided to go back and do medicine and now, at nearly 35, is in her final year. While I think she was a keen hockey player once, she's now more into her women's AFL.

Also, she seems to like me. Considering that these days I identify as a bohemian, I would've expected the Angela Jane I created in the movie in my head to be polite but uninterested in a friendship with me. Yet it turns out that the real AJ is a bit of a bohemian herself. Or nonconformist, as we both like to say.

And so it happens that AJ and I become instant friends. We bond in the way that women in their mid-30s who haven't got a mums-and-bubs Instagram page, and like to drink beers on Saturdays in remote towns on the beaches of the Kimberley, bond. It doesn't matter if we all say that, these days, you can be whoever you want to be, if you're a woman my age in a country like Australia you still feel that if you're not 'doing the things'—having the wedding and the house and the baby—then somehow, you're missing out or failing. But hanging out with AJ in Broome, I don't feel any of those things. I just feel happy.

There are no massive highs or crashing lows or self-analysis; there is no uncomfortable sense that as the hours tick away we are meant to be doing something else. We sit at the Broome Surf Club, eating pizza and looking out at the sunset over Cable Beach. And this, I think, is exactly where I am meant to be. I have to say, despite what we all pretend (and do we ever pretend), it's not very often that a person gets to feel this way. When you find that place, you should stay. At least for a while. Maybe forever.

Despite the manager of the medical practice's assurances that I'll be in the resort soon, the elusive electrical part remains, well, elusive and the place remains shut. Meaning I am now a permanent resident of the upscale backpackers.

The main issue I have is that half of my patients also seem to be living here with me, which makes for awkward encounters as I sit at the bar after work drinking the famous Matso's ginger beer, and realise that I've just treated the bloke next to me, who's chatting up the new girl, for chlamydia.

Is there some kind of ethical code, I ask myself as we exchange a wave, to help guide me? As their GP, I am aware at least a third of the residents here have some kind of highly transmissible STI. I have my doubts any of them have listened to my instructions to 'let your partners or potential partners know'. I consider putting a little sign up on the notice board where jobs and tours are advertised, saying, *Forget Covid—there's a chlamydia outbreak on our hands. Stay Home. Don't Fuck. Save Lives.* Or maybe, *Stay Safe—No Sex.*

I text AJ before I retire to bed, and ask her if she wouldn't mind going for a cocktail with me for my 35th birthday on Friday. It's either that or hanging out with my patients at the backpackers, so I figure she'll take pity on me.

The next few mornings, I find myself reflecting as I take my morning run along Cable Beach. This week I turn 35 years old. It's the official entry into midlife, and I find myself homeless because of one lizard, residing in an (upscale) backpackers, where my neighbours are young Spanish girls in crop tops, and half of the residents have chlamydia, for which I am prescribing them antibiotics.

I stand on the water's edge, looking out. I've never seen a horizon like the one in Broome. It is just so unbelievably endless. The ocean is perfectly aqua, and there's no hard line between the water and the sky: they melt into each other. It's like life, I think. Life rarely ever changes overnight, it just progresses and transitions into something else, until suddenly you realise how different things have become.

One Friday morning 35 years ago, I was born. Three and half decades later, I get into work to see that my first patient is a middle-aged man who sits down, looks me in the eye, and says, 'Do you prescribe sex pills?'

'Happy birthday, Sonia!' the receptionist calls as she goes past my door, which is slightly open.

I get up to shut the door and the patient turns around.

'Is it your birthday?'

'Um, yeah,' I say.

There's a silence.

'Happy birthday,' he says.

'Thanks.'

'I mean, that shouldn't affect whether I get the sex pills, right?'

'Yes, you're totally right,' I say. 'It shouldn't. But meaningful days like this do tend to affect whether or not I will offer certain prescriptions, particularly for sex pills.'

'Really?'

I sigh. 'No, but let's talk about why you need the sex pills.'

He starts laughing.

I can't help laughing too, and it ends up being a very good consult.

'Can I make you my regular doctor?' he asks before he leaves.

'Only on special days,' I say, grinning.

Happy birthday, Dr Henry.

'You came here at the right time,' my last patient for the day tells me.

'How's that?'

'The end of the wet,' he says.

The wet season in Broome sends people mad, I've heard. The heat does crazy things to the community. Tensions, quite literally, boil over. When the rain comes, my patient tells me, it's a release of far more than just clouds.

There's something about the way the weather influences everyone in this place. Even I feel it. Being a human being in Broome means you're not made of human flesh alone—everything in you feels connected to the land: you are pulled and pushed by the sun, and the moon, and the rain.

'So when will this bloody thing move?' my patient then asks me, referring to the kidney stone stuck inside the top of his ureter.

'It's pretty small,' I explain. 'Should be in the next few weeks.'

He rolls his eyes. 'So I'll keep taking these damn tablets till then.'

'You know what they say,' I tell him. 'This too shall pass.'

'Sounds like you're not just talking about the stone,' he tells me.

I shrug. 'But it's true, isn't it?'

AJ and I drink cocktails while looking out over Cable Beach. Two other people next to us are having their birthdays too. They tell me I am young at 35: one is 47, the other 63.

We all cheers, these three people who don't know one another, to the day of our birth. AJ and I get admirably drunk then float down to Divers, the pub around the corner. There, we become friends with a bunch of women drinking bottles of white wine, who are all around twenty years older than us, and drink and dance to the live band. Everyone is laughing.

The band is made of teachers from Broome high school, and they play the same set every Friday night. It isn't until the final song that I really let go. They are playing 'Khe Sanh' by Cold Chisel. For the first time I really seem to hear the lyrics as I stand there in the middle of the dance floor, listening to this song about travelling across the country, trying to find somewhere to mend a mixed-up life.

I'm not the only one, I realise, as the bodies and music move around me. The person singing this song felt *the same way as me*. The thought is so comforting that I feel myself grin as I stand there in the middle of Divers Tavern in Broome, at a live music night on the day I turn 35 years old.

As I hear the words I see it, the long path I have taken. I didn't even really know what was happening when it started, and I don't know when it will end. I know now that it began in Sydney, and that I have been running away from that place, and myself, ever since.

But now, standing there in that old pub at the northwest tip of Australia, I feel something close to happiness: I feel the me that was me long before life took over. I touch it, just for a second. I'm not there yet, but I am closer. I am closer.

Then AJ spills a wine, and I am drenched in rosé and laughter.

My routine of swimming at Cable Beach is becoming slightly more stressful every morning. It seems that every day I see another patient, usually a pearl diver, who has been stung by Irukandji, or wrestled sharks or spotted crocodiles—the big, scary ones, saltwater crocs.

'I don't think Irukandji really kill people,' my pearl-diving patient tells me. 'But, fuck, you want to avoid it if you can. I'll never forget being stung by one of them. Got me on my finger. You can still see what it looks like.'

He shows me his thumb, which is deformed and permanently swollen.

'I think it got infected or something,' he says casually. 'Anyway, that one was a few years ago. But it wasn't really my thumb looking fucked that was so bad: it was the doom.'

I've read about this so have some idea of what he's talking about. The toxin released by Irukandji jellyfish, creatures tinier than fingernails, has some neurotoxic effect that causes symptoms so severe and so bizarre there's a name for it: 'Irukandji syndrome'. The worst thing, my patient confirms, is the horrendous sense of impending doom. Apparently no one's quite sure what causes this feeling, but it's been suggested that the venom results in an uptake in adrenaline and noradrenaline, which are connected to anxiety.

'That sounds absolutely horrendous,' I say, feeling a little sick.

He nods at me. 'I was crying on the phone to my mum,' he says. 'It was so awful. I couldn't stop crying. When they got me onto the beach they thought I was crawled up because of the pain, but it wasn't that. It was just this sense that my whole world was collapsing.'

We both shudder.

'So pearl diving's pretty, ah, risky then,' I say.

'The problem is the people who jump onto your line.'

'Your line?'

'When you're diving for pearls you're on a line,' he explains, 'and for every pearl you get there's a financial incentive, so the more you get—'

'The more money you make.'

'Exactly,' he says. 'So sometimes, some fuckers will cross onto your line.'

'What happens then?'

He laughs. 'I've seen guys trying to kill each other.'

'Bloody hell.'

'Pearls mean money,' he points out.

'Money does make people do strange things,' I agree.

When he leaves, I consider what he's told me for a moment. Fighting for that next pearl, for that next dollar. Money to then ... what? Have freedom? The only good thing about money, I am starting to think now, is that it can buy you health and freedom, each of which cannot exist without the other. Without health and freedom, you don't have much at all.

And yet I am living and working in a country where I have met a lot of people who have neither.

A few mornings later I come out of the water with a small, painful red lump on my leg. The water is warm, probably over 26 degrees, so I knew the Irukandji would be about and swam anyway. I've heard it takes around twenty minutes to determine whether it's an Irukandji sting, so I head to the vinegar station, which is essentially just a seedy old bottle of vinegar near the surf club's steps.

I don't have a towel, so use an old leaf I find on the sand to ineffectually rub vinegar onto my leg.

A man comes past, heading down the steps, and stops.

'You right, mate?'

A typical Broome understatement, as we both know what it can mean if a person is throwing vinegar on themselves in a place like Cable Beach.

'Guess I'll know in about fifteen minutes,' I tell him. 'I'm okay now.'

Fifteen minutes later I'm still alive and haven't started crying, so I put it down to sea lice and get ready for work. Another near-death experience narrowly avoided. If I were a cat, I'd be coming very close to nine up here.

A patient comes in terribly depressed. I've seen him a few times already for a variety of relatively benign sorts of things—a tweak in his blood pressure medication, a mild cough. Today, though, he's in tears.

'My wife's left me,' he explains. 'It was a while ago, but I'm just not coping.'

I let him cry. If I've learnt anything, it's that sometimes people crying in the GP's office haven't cried in front of anyone else for a long time. So when they start, the best thing to do is just offer tissues and let them keep going.

When the tears subside a bit, we talk about his feelings: what he feels and why he thinks he feels it.

'The relationship wasn't working,' he tells me. 'It really wasn't.'

'Do you think you're pining after her?' I ask him.

He pauses, considering. 'No,' he says, after a while. 'It's not that.'

'Is it the loss of the marriage, do you think?'

'I think it's just the unknown,' he says. 'And, yeah, maybe it's that I feel like I've failed because the marriage has failed. I don't even think we wanted to be with each other, either of us, but it's just the unknown. Even when we were miserable together, at least I knew what to expect.'

'It's hard, isn't it,' I muse, as the man pats his eyes with the tissues. 'As humans we package everything into these little boxes for reasons I'm not really sure of. Like marriage—even if it's miserable, we feel stuck in this box, right? Or work, jobs we feel we can't leave, it's the same sort of thing. Because there's this sense we can't escape these expectations, even if we are being suffocated by them. They're so drummed into us it's like they've been microchipped into our arms at birth. But I reckon that humans aren't really meant to be boxed like that. It's like trying to box the wind or the rain or the sunlight—you just can't by the sheer virtue of the nature of it. I think people are the same.'

He looks up at me in a way that makes me think he might understand.

'You're right,' I tell him, 'that there's comfort in known misery, even if it's misery. But change is where the joy will return. I can almost assure you of that—change will help.'

'But to change I need to, you know, take the leap,' he tells me.

'In the end, two types of people change,' I say to him. 'Brave people or desperate people.'

'Which are you?' he asks me.

'On good days, a bit of both. The rest of the time, just desperate,' I say.

He smiles.

'But in the end, change is always worth it.' I mean it, too.

'I don't want to feel like this anymore,' he says. 'I know it's for the best the relationship is over. Why am I so fucking depressed?'

There's a short silence. I refer him to a psychologist. We complete the Medicare requirements, the little assessment that will get him the referral. I tick a few bureaucratic boxes and then I sit there and talk to him, doctor to patient but really just human to human.

'Think about it like this,' I say. 'Your marriage and your life before this point, emotionally at least, is a riverbank that's collapsing around you. You've got no choice but to jump, because otherwise you're going to die there, in the mud of that river. Right?'

He looks at me. 'Right. So I'm on the edge of the collapsing river, and I have to jump.'

'Yep, and swim,' I say, leaning in and feeling myself becoming more animated. 'You have to swim to the other side of the river. You don't really know what's over there, but it's on the other side so it has to be different. Right now, you're swimming through this croc-infested river. But then, you finally get to the other side.'

'I get to the other side,' he repeats.

'And there,' I say, 'there, on the other side, as you haul yourself out of that croc-infested river that you've somehow survived, there's a person standing there. And do you know what that person says?'

He looks at me.

'They say, "You know how you were scared of swimming across the river, swimming over to this side of change and new horizons, because of the crocs? Well, there was nothing to fear, because the crocs WERE ONLY FRESHIES ANYWAY!"'

We stare at one another.

'Change is terrifying,' I continue after a silence. 'But usually when we take a big leap, we realise that all the things we feared were nothing except figments of our imagination that, until we changed and grew, we didn't realise meant absolutely nothing. Absolutely nothing at all.'

'What if there was one saltie in the river, though?' the patient asks. He's right to point out the possibility: here in the Kimberley there usually *is* a rogue saltwater croc roaming around.

'He's already eaten that day,' I tell him. 'And you, my friend, have made it to the other side of the river.'

It isn't until the patient leaves that I admit that the person on the other bank was me. I have already swum across that river, and now I am waiting there, on the far side, ready to step into the new world.

The nights AJ doesn't kindly bring me along to dinners with her other friends, who also welcome me with much generosity, I go to restaurants and dine alone. This is something I feel a vague sense of guilt about—shouldn't I be sitting in the kitchen cooking a big roast while the kids run around and Daddy comes home from work?

But I'm not. So I decide to embrace it.

After months of dirt and travel sunlight, I am tanned. I have a constant salt sheen from mornings spent swimming before work. I wear my hair out, because after months of living out of a suitcase I've lost all my hair elastics and given up on ever finding them. I order French rosé (pink wine, as Jade and Victoria would say in Kununurra), and sit there, almost every night, in one of the three restaurants near me.

I order fresh mussels and eat them with my fingers, in a land where everyone else is wearing masks and using hand sanitiser—in Broome, none of that applies. I listen to the music and chat to the bar staff, one of whom is my patient. We talk about how long she's staying in Broome and where she's from and what she's doing here. She's probably ten years younger than me but I don't care and neither does she. I order more fish— it feels like an extravagance and maybe it is, but it also feels good, and I want to feel good.

Women at a certain point in their lives experience this strange subliminal pressure to only do things for other people— doing things just for yourself, after this arbitrary point, means there is something wrong with you. That you're selfish, or you're not quite right in some other way. But as I sit there, eating fresh fish in the warmth of the end of the Broome wet season, I feel so incredibly relaxed and happy. Not happy because of someone or something or happy because of adrenaline driven by a high-intensity situation. Just happy.

I scratch a mosquito bite on my leg and it bleeds. Even the red against the brown of my skin fascinates me. I watch it drip, just before I stop it with a serviette and wonder at it looking so rich, the red. It is a hedonistic shade of red, deep and beautiful.

Broome. So far—even after all that's gone wrong—it surrounds me and holds me in the way that, deep down, I knew it would.

I arrive at work one day to the good news that the lizard scenario has been resolved: I am free to leave the (upscale) backpackers and move into the resort.

The best bit about my new quarters is the outdoor shower, and the fact that there isn't an indoor shower at all.

Ask yourself: in a place that doesn't rain, where it's warm all year and the moon is bright, why would you need to shower inside? See, there's no reason. This shower is surrounded by wood and stone and no one can see in. The night I move in, I stand there for what feels like hours, looking up at the moon as the warm water cascades over my skin.

From now on, I promise myself, I will always live in a place that has an outdoor shower.

Like anywhere you go in the world, even in paradise the cracks will start to show sooner or later. After leaving Kununurra, I laboured under the delusion that Broome, being a bigger place, would have way more facilities. This delusion remains intact until the day I need to, first, send a girl for a medical termination of her pregnancy and, second, refer a bloke who needs a brain MRI.

I ring Marie Stopes to discover it will take three weeks to get the termination drugs up to us. No one in Broome who prescribes them is available, and I beat myself up for not having done the online course that will enable me to prescribe them yet (it's on my growing medical to-do list). At any rate, I am assured by the practice nurse that the local pharmacy hasn't had stock for ages anyway due to some delivery issues. Because the hospital clinic is full, my patient can't be seen until the end of next week.

The girl is crying with frustration and I'm close to tears myself. After making what feels like a billion phone calls, finally, we both accept that the end of next week is the best that can be done.

In Sydney, or Perth, or even a regional centre the same size as Broome in different parts of Australia, this girl would have had those drugs posted to her, and had an ultrasound and bloods done, all in 48 hours.

But not here.

I ring the neurology registrar in Perth to see what they think about the unusual presentation of my next patient. He's a pearl diver who has had such a severe headache he can barely move his eyes. His inflammatory markers are through the roof, but he has no other symptoms besides this horrific pain when he looks to the left or right and up and down. The neurologists consult with infectious diseases and we all wonder if it's some weird tropical bug, as you get a bit of that up here. The patient's brain CT is normal, I've sent him to the local hospital and they can't find anything either, so Perth recommends another panel of bloods and an MRI. I ask where that can be done and they say they don't know. I ring the nurse, who suggests Karratha might have a new MRI machine.

The patient looks a little desperate, but Karratha is only a ten-hour drive away, which in WA speak is semi-doable. It turns out, though, that there's no MRI machine in Karratha, and so he has to fly to Perth.

The man has to take two days off work and fly across half the country, while in Sydney, there is a radiology practice with an MRI in almost every suburb.

I must be close to the edge because when a patient comes in to ask for his blood pressure to be checked I look at him like he's insane. Then I remember that I'm a GP and this is a pretty standard request. I take his blood pressure, which is normal, and he tells me he runs fishing charters off the coast of Broome.

'Gee, that sounds fun,' I say, wistfully. He says it is, and gives me his card.

'Just in case you ever feel the need for a fish, doc,' he tells me, seeing the things that I thought I had hidden. 'It's good for the soul.'

That night, AJ and I go to Divers and play pool with her friend Kat, who's come down from Darwin. We meet some people who are here on holidays from other parts, and talk about the best things to see and do around Broome. Nothing particularly notable or fantastic happens aside from sinking some pool balls and beers and talking. I go home and swim in the resort pool, under the stars, then have an outdoor shower, staring up at the big moon.

I wonder if perhaps, before this time, I have been overcomplicating my life.

At work the next day, a young woman comes in. She's gorgeous and articulate. She's also sobbing. She's being bullied at work and hates her life. We talk.

'I just feel like I'm never good enough,' she says, wiping her nose with the two-ply I managed to find after much apologetic faffing around. 'Every day I wake up and wish that I hadn't.'

Here we are in paradise, and it's the same as anywhere else. I hear these things everywhere I work. It's always the same. Some other human making your life miserable, a job that doesn't need to be as stressful as it is, a relationship that's failing you're too scared to leave, and then this terrible, pervasive sense that you're totally worthless and life is simply too hard to live, or at least to live well.

And this is the lucky country, so they say. It's amazing to me: those colours, that sky, the white sand and the moon that is like the sun—the beauty of Broome is like nowhere I've ever seen and, yet, there is misery everywhere.

Maybe we've got it all wrong. We live in this beautiful land we rape for money, as we work in jobs we don't like, to please people we don't care for, to earn money for things we'll just throw out. We are so caught up in all these things, things that mean really very little, that we can't see the beauty around us.

Not for the first time, I have a strange inkling that perhaps this is the suffering we deserve for what our fellow humans did to this land and the people who understood it the best. We are cursed to stay in our little boxes of expectation and failure, simply because we don't know how to ask for proper forgiveness, how to listen to the silent wisdom of the earth and the sun and the moon.

I have a patient by the name of Spencer Lim Joon. We get on really well. I wonder if he might be descended from 'old Broome' people, being Asian and First Nations.

Broome is fascinating like that. There's the First Nations influence everywhere, but then there's these strong splashes of Asia, a throwback to the Japanese who came for the pearling industry in the late 19th century. There's nowhere else where I've really seen that particular intersection of culture: only in

Broome. A lot of things, I am coming to realise, you will only ever experience in Broome.

I love his name: Spencer Lim Joon. He has a broad Australian accent and I see him at Divers one night in March, wearing a green hat for St Patrick's Day. I want to say hello but think he won't recognise me so don't. I see him in the clinic and ask if he was at Divers the night before. He says yes and then asks why, if I saw him, I didn't say g'day?

'You like the food at Divers?' he asks.

'I do,' I say. 'They do great mussels. They're like mini steaks!'

'I make a really good crab linguine,' Spencer tells me. 'You like cooking?'

'I'm hopeless,' I say.

'What do you think about the restaurants in Broome?'

'I like Divers,' I tell him again.

'That's just a pub!' he says indignantly.

I start laughing. 'Sorry, I didn't realise I was talking to a foodie.'

'Best steak in Broome is out at the roadhouse,' he says. 'They're great.'

He's wearing a T-shirt with a VW Beetle on it. 'I like your shirt,' I say. 'My first car was a VW.'

He looks at me. 'You like VWs?'

'Yeah, the old ones,' I say.

He laughs. 'You must have a bit of hippie in you then.'

'You know what?' I admit to him. 'I'm starting to think that I do.'

Spencer and I talk about a lot of things besides his health, and I appreciate hearing his perspectives. One of the days he comes, the news has been reporting on more First Nations deaths in custody. We talk about it.

'What do you think it is, out here, why this stuff happens?' I ask him.

He shrugs. 'A lot of things. Displacement, crime. Sad people, taken from their land. The mood of the town, which changes like the wind. Dirty cops.'

'So you reckon there's a few dirty cops around?' I ask, hesitating.

'Yeah.' he says. 'Not all of them. Some are really good. But a few are really dirty. You know who to avoid.'

'That's kind of really bad, though, isn't it?' I point out. 'Like, that people just have to accept there are dirty cops, and avoiding them is sort of the only option?'

He shrugs again. 'There's a lot going on up here,' he says. 'Worse than before.'

I sigh and he smiles. 'Don't let it get you down, doc.'

'Hard not to,' I say. 'How do you cope with it, knowing this stuff, seeing it, living it?'

'Me? I just go fishing.'

'You know, you're the second person who's said that to me in as many days,' I tell him.

'Nothing can hurt you fishing, doc,' he says. 'Well, unless a big croc jumps in your boat or something.'

That night I go for a walk along Cable Beach, watching the sunset. I listen to 'Khe Sanh', the song I'd heard so many times without listening to the lyrics until I heard them in Broome.

I google the song, and discover Don Walker wrote it in a few afternoons, sitting at Sweethearts Café in Kings Cross.

It's the story of a jaded, damaged Vietnam vet, crossing Australia looking for something, anything, but not finding it. In an interview, Walker said it was the story of a misspent youth.

I think about Kings Cross, as I curl my feet into the sand. I think about Sydney, and about Rushcutters Bay, the boats bobbing along at the marina. I remember the Spanish café that was open 24 hours a day, where Keno, the owner, let me write my first book sitting at a table drinking orange juice, while he showed me how coffee beans are turned into dust. I see the streets of Darlinghurst, the old apartment blocks, the man who walks around with a parrot on his shoulder. I see the rich people and the poor people, and me, a junior doctor struggling home after a night shift.

Sydney is a city that is expensive and painful and frustrating, but I love it and I always have. It's the jewel of Australia, that bloody town on the harbour. Sydney was as much a part of me as my blood and my skin. Until one day I couldn't be there anymore.

So now I am here instead, thinking about Sydney the way one thinks about an old lover. They take and take and take, but somehow you know that one day, you'll go back for more.

That weekend AJ is busy playing football, so I decide to take myself on an adventure. I drive up the Broome–Cape Leveque Road until I hit a left turn onto an unsealed red dirt road, maybe not the best idea without a 4WD. There are two guys standing next to a car by the road, peering at their tyre. I slow down and unwind my window.

'Am I right to get to Quondong Beach in this car?'

They say yes, telling me the dirt is hard-packed and there's been no rain, so I'll make it.

I fly along the pindan earth, somewhere up the top of the northwest of Western Australia. I finally get to the beach, which is totally deserted, and experience some nerves when I realise that if I encounter a croc or a shark I'll have literally no phone reception, no satellite phone and no fucking idea, as usual.

So I drive back, and decide as I get closer to the highway that I'll go and see Willie Creek Pearl Farm—it's only 8 kilometres down the road and a tourist spot, so I assume I'll be right.

It turns out I'm not right, though. The road is narrow, with scrub on either side, and the sand underneath my tyres is dangerously soft. By the time I realise how tough this will be it's too late: there's no way to turn back. The sand is getting so sketchy now that I know there's probably at least an 80 per cent chance I'll get bogged. By the time my destination comes into view, I am sweating like a pig and cursing my stupidity.

I arrive at the pearl farm, which is all white sand and light-blue water and signs saying *Don't stand under the trees* and *Beware the falling coconuts.*

I immediately order a glass of pink wine from the girl who . . .

Is one of my patients.

'How are you, doc?' she asks me.

'Not great, Maddy,' I say, pointing to the car park. 'See that sedan? I drove that here.'

'Down the sand?'

'Yes,' I sigh.

'You're lucky,' she says, trying not to laugh. 'Another guy did that last week and got bogged, it was really shitty.'

The drive back is terrifying, but when I turn on to the tarred bitumen of Broome Road I picture the beauty of that pearl farm and, for a second, I'm glad I accidentally went down there.

Spencer Lim Joon is my first patient on Monday and as I explain my adventures, and he is laughing so hard he is nearly crying.

'You drove all the way to Quondong without a 4WD?' He is gasping through his laughter. 'Then down the sand turn-off to Willie Creek'

'I know, Spencer,' I say sheepishly. 'Stupid, right?'

'What was your plan? There's no Google Maps out there for Sydney girls like you, doc.'

'Dunno,' I admit. 'I just wanted to see the beach.'

'You were just driving till the road ran out, huh?'

I look at him. 'You know, that's been pretty much what I've been doing the last twelve months,' I say. 'Going and going, until the road runs out.'

I start an anecdotal survey on my patients, questioning them about whether they swim in the ocean in Broome. My own swims turn into quick immersions, as the list of people who say, in no uncertain terms, 'no way' or 'you mean the pool? I swim in the pool?' starts to grow.

The receptionist comes in to try to help me tidy my desk, which is growing messier by the day, and asks me what the weird piece of paper with *Y* and *N* in two different columns with lots of numerals next to them means.

'Is this about patients who do or don't want the Covid vaccine?' she asks me.

'Since we are a medical clinic, yes that would make sense,' I agree. 'But actually it's a small survey to discover whether or not people swim in the ocean. Because, you know, of all the stuff that can kill us in the water up here.'

She looks down. 'Seems about even.'

'Do you?' I ask her.

She looks at me.

'I generally prefer the pool,' she says, vaguely. 'But it's probably fine, most of the time.'

'Hmm.' I say. I've heard 'probably fine' before.

I'm still thinking about the risks of swimming in the ocean when I call in my next patient. He looks at me with suspicion, the kind I get now and again from people who still seem to think GPs should be 60-year-old men with white hair and ties. But I don't say anything, just mildly invite him in and introduce myself.

He sounds aggravated. 'Listen, some other doctor prescribed me these pills for sleep but they're doing nothing. And they said I was depressed, but I'm not bloody depressed, all right? Anyway, I've stopped taking them, okay?'

'Okay,' I say, not really knowing what else to offer. Usually when people have things to get off their chests, I've found it's better to let them go on. It's easier to try to work through things after they've knocked the steam off the top, so to speak.

'I'm just having some trouble sleeping, because I work at night a lot, run my own business, and I've just taken in three small dogs,' he says, glaring at me. 'So I'm not depressed. Life's just shit. Once you accept that, it's a lot easier.'

I like the way he pronounces shit, emphasising the 't' so it sounds really powerful. 'ShiT.' 'Life is ShiT.'

'Well, I actually kind of agree with that,' I say. 'But how's your mood? And if you are depressed, should we try a psychologist?'

'Tried that,' he says bluntly. 'I went to this marriage counsellor. Still got divorced. So that went really well.'

Fair enough.

'Are you suicidal?' I ask him. 'Having thoughts of self-harm?'

He looks at me. 'Of course not! I've got a business to run!'

'That's, ah, good,' I say, for want of anything else. There's a silence. 'What kind of dogs do you have?' I finally ask, just to develop a bit of rapport.

He shows me some photos of his pups and I tell him about Buddy. We talk about our dogs for a while.

'You're not from here, are you?' he asks, looking at me.

'No,' I confirm. 'I'm from Sydney.'

He looks surprised. 'Over east? What the hell are you doing here?'

'Just travelling around,' I say.

'You haven't been here long enough to be affected by the area,' he says directly. 'Which is good. You're obviously escaping something, but that's okay. Escaping's fine. It's the people hiding here, that's the problem.'

'Are you hiding?' I can't help asking.

He looks at me. 'Of course I am! Anyone who lives here this long is!'

I can't help but laugh. I encourage him to try a herbal sleep medication, and we talk about maybe getting a blood test. I recommend some sleep hygiene techniques. Then I ask what he does for fun, if he gets pleasure out of anything. Work? Relationships? Kids?

'I've got my kids, my dogs, and my job,' he says. 'I like making money, and that suits me fine. And brisket. I love cooking brisket. Nothing wrong with that is there? After a long day at work I just want to go home, shut my gate, and cook my brisket, what's wrong with that?'

'Nothing,' I say. 'Sounds fine to me. Maybe tonight you should do that, cook the brisket?'

'The cooker exploded last week,' he says bluntly. 'So I can't at the moment.'

'Ah.'

'And I like riding my bike,' he says, 'but the tyre's broken.'

'Can you fix it?'

He sighs. 'Yeah, but I'm too busy. Working. Making money.'

'Maybe you should fix the tyre,' I say.

'Is that the doctor's orders?' he asks. 'Fix the tyre.'

'Yes,' I say, with confidence. 'You haven't seemed to like anything else I've suggested, so my prescription is, fix your tyre and do something you enjoy that isn't work-related.'

He looks at me.

'Thanks, chief,' he says. 'I always say, small achievable goals.'

'Well, I think that's a very achievable goal, captain,' I say, not sure whether I am annoyed or amused. 'First time I've ever prescribed a bike tyre to a patient but, hey, here in Broome, anything is possible.'

He salutes me as he leaves.

I sit at my desk, shaking my head. *Plan* ... I write in the notes. *Encouraged patient to fix his bike tyre, which we have both agreed is a small but achievable goal.*

Despite looking like paradise, Broome is a divided town, some of my patients tell me. There are bad problems here—racial unrest, maldistribution of resources, violence—and Broome has a dark history. The other doctor at work recommends I read a book called *Beyond the Lattice: Broome's early years*, written by Susan Sickert, a woman who worked at the bookstore next to the medical practice. I buy it and read it in the evenings, finding one quote that particularly resonates:

> Although there are no excuses for the crimes committed against humanity along the pearling coast, it would serve us well to acknowledge that many Australians in 2003 share racist attitudes alarmingly similar to those Australians of 1901.

Well, now it's 2021, and I wonder how much things have really changed. In recounting my travels, I deliberately haven't included some of the conversations I've overheard in pubs or the waiting rooms of clinics or, worse, from the mouths of other health professionals, because I don't want to give them oxygen. But, needless to say, this quote rings very true to me as I read it.

It also makes me remember stories I've heard in every place I've worked so far. In River Town, I was invited for dinner with a patient and her family, who told me that in the late twentieth century, so not very long ago at all, white women gave birth inside the hospital, and black women were forced to give birth on the grass out the front.

I remember a nurse in Kununurra telling me her mother didn't know her real birthday, just her 'government birthday', because at the time she was born, white authorities had just assigned

First Nations boys and girls an arbitrary date in the calendar to celebrate. I remember being at a pub and seeing a security guard come and drag out a young First Nations boy who had been sitting quietly next to me the whole evening. The guard grabbed him in a headlock and hauled him outside with the kind of sudden violence that comes from a very ugly place. I remember a colleague in another town, telling me with evident love about his parents who he missed dearly. He told me how his dad was a drover, and all about his wonderful, adventurous childhood. But he also recalled a tennis match one weekend where he'd tried to pick up a racquet only to be told he couldn't: he was black, and black kids weren't allowed on the court. He looked at me, as we were sitting at the sports club, and said, quite simply, 'People can be very cruel.' His eyes had glistened with the sheen of tears he had learnt long ago to stop from falling.

He was right. Humans, however we try to justify ourselves, have a seemingly endless capacity to be very, very cruel.

A patient comes in requesting an Implanon, the contraceptive implant. She's driven around 200 kilometres to get here because we're the nearest clinic to her town with any spots available. When I ask if she is sexually active, she tells me she isn't. I enquire about why she wants contraception now if she isn't sexually active: is there another reason—out-of-cycle bleeding? Pain? Heavy periods? She tells me, with barely any facial expression at all, that it's in case she gets raped.

I am so stunned I don't know how to respond. 'Have you been raped?' I finally manage.

She says no but that a few of her friends have. I say that that's not okay; that shouldn't happen. I try to tell her, if she is raped, to report it. She just looks at me.

I hand over the script for the Implanon, and she leaves. I wonder about the point of medicine. I can 'mitigate harm' with a prescription to stop an unwanted pregnancy, in this great modern country where we can do things like get contraceptive scripts without issue. But what happens after that?

I can sign my name to the prescription, insert the contraceptive device, manipulate and control her hormones to the point that she cannot conceive, yet I can't control what happens to her or any of my patients, or even myself, as soon as we walk back out the clinic door.

Doctors are meant to be so powerful, yet I've never felt so useless. I always help enough, do what I can, work within the lines of what's possible. But if she can still walk outside and know there's a chance she'll be sexually assaulted—and I don't have much faith in there being any kind of system to protect her from this—maybe that just makes me complicit in a house of cards that continues to collapse on people who deserve more.

Next, I see a young boy who has been having suicidal thoughts since his uncle went missing in the Territory and was found washed up on a river. No one knows if it was suicide or foul play, and no one really seems to care enough to investigate. I think about all the patients I've seen, white and black and Asian, who have strokes and heart attacks and can't access path

300

labs or decent care. WA, the state, might have the iron ore and the money, but places like this don't seem to see any of it.

I've thought about these things a lot on my travels, ever since I first saw the red dirt of the Pilbara. You can feel beauty and suffering simultaneously in this place, and never have I felt it so acutely as when I live and work in Broome. I have seen suffering all over Australia, but perhaps never seen it so sharply contrasted with a place as beautiful. One moment you can be standing on Cable Beach, in front of a very expensive resort, watching the most beautiful sunset. The next, you're driving past the main street seeing paramedics standing over the still body of a man who's been involved in a bad assault. That's Broome.

But maybe that's also the human condition. Nothing is ever one thing. And maybe when we accept that and acknowledge it, instead of denying, and denying, and denying—that's when we're able to understand the world a little better, or at least understand ourselves. Because I'm starting to realise I didn't know myself as well as I once thought, and maybe that's because I didn't really know the country in which I lived.

Just as I'm heading out to Divers one Friday night to meet AJ, my front door explodes. I stand there, covered in glass and shock.

The door just exploded, I tell myself. It actually just exploded.

I call the after-hours reception line straight away, fearing they'll think I've locked myself out, drunk, and broken in, but the lady who answers doesn't sound even slightly surprised.

'Oh, yeah, it's the heat,' she tells me, sounding bored. 'Happens a lot. Sometimes when the air-con's on and its hot outside, the glass can't take it. I'll send a bloke round tomorrow. You right with just having no door for a night?'

'I'll just, um, pull the curtains, I guess,' I say.

I look at where my door used to be, shrug, and walk to the pub.

'My door exploded,' I tell AJ as I sit down at Divers.

'Really?'

'Yeah. Something about the heat.'

'Broome,' she says, rolling her eyes.

Max and Roy somehow work around the lockdowns and manage a trip from Sydney to Broome to see me. It takes them ten hours to get here, which, as Roy points out, back in the day would have taken him halfway to Europe.

We drink and swim and have a few near-death experiences out near Gantheaume Point when I misinterpret the tides and Roy nearly breaks his leg. But with some strong antibiotics and Moontide gin we regroup and continue our cross-country reunion.

One afternoon we get ridiculously drunk, take off all our clothes in front of Cable Beach Resort and go skinny-dipping in the ocean. We are laughing and diving, with bare bottoms and free souls.

'I think this is where the shark attacks happen,' I say as we splash around.

'Who cares?' says Max. 'We're alive now.'

I imagine my patients watching me and my two other doctor mates swimming totally naked in front of the most expensive resort in Broome.

Deep down, I have a feeling they'd be happy for me. I am happy, my friends are happy, and the sharks must be happy too, because they leave us be, naked and unafraid.

I work in Broome for nearly two months. I've decided to stay in Broome for one extra week after work finishes, to try to start my book. On my last week at the clinic, patient after patient comes in to say how much they'll miss me and ask if I'll be back. I am incredibly touched. Just when I think I have finished my stint with no major catastrophes, it's time to drop off the work car.

'Hmm,' says the practice manager, who has come out with me.

'Hmm what, Sarah?' I ask, apprehensively.

'Were those scratches there when you got the car?' she asks me.

'The one on the right was,' I say confidently. 'Because I remember thinking it looked like the car had been keyed.'

'Fair enough,' she says. 'I think I remember that one too.' She walks around to the left. 'What about these, though? Have you taken it out bush?'

I have an uncomfortable memory of my accidental journey down the sand track to Willie Creek Pearl Farm.

'Not, ah, really,' I say, feeling guilty. 'But this is the Kimberley! Most cars in this car park get taken out bush and look way worse than this.'

'I know that,' Sarah says, a note of urgency in her voice. 'It's not me, it's management. When the last locum left some sand in there they charged him for a full clean. They docked his pay for it, and he's still fighting for the money'.

'Shit. Really?'

'Yeah.'

We both stand in the car park of the medical clinic in the stinking Broome heat, considering this.

'Maybe I'll go to the car wash,' I, a person who has never been to a car wash in my entire life, suggest. 'I might be able to get it waxed or something. That'd work, right?'

Sarah looks relieved. 'Good idea,' she says.

At the Broome car wash the only option is self-serve. I have no idea how to work any of it. There's a number on a piece of cardboard which I ring, but no one answers. I ask the guy next to me, who's standing at the door of his Hilux looking equally confused, but he says he's got no idea either.

I go back to the car. There's a variety of different hoses hanging off hooks on the wall of the car wash, that look frighteningly high-pressure. Still, I decide to throw caution to the wind, drive the car in, and put the coins in the slot. The water bursts out of a hose, nearly knocking me flat, and I spend my designated seven minutes spraying the car with such force that I'm sure any weird marks will surely disappear. It looks great, I think when I'm done. I stand back, pleased. Didn't even need a wax!

I decide to drive the car back out into the sunshine to confirm that it looks okay. When I do, I feel my heart sink. In the sunlight, the scratches look even worse.

I let out a big sigh, staring at the car. I briefly wonder how much it would cost to repaint the side of the car. Probably my entire two-month salary, knowing cars. I am just considering whether to 1) flee the scene, 2) start crying or 3) call AJ when I hear a voice next to me.

'Taking the car for a wash are you, doc?'

I turn around.

'That's not how you use the hose,' my patient informs me. 'You've totally fucked it.'

'Yes, I'm aware of that, mate,' I reply, never having felt so relieved in my life as I am that this patient, the man who said 'shit' with the very sharp 't' and who walked away from the clinic with a prescription to change his bike tyre, has miraculously appeared next to me. I remember that he's a builder, and probably knows things that would be very helpful in this situation, i.e. how to fix scratched cars.

'Steve, I need your help,' I tell him. 'I'm fucked.'

I explain the situation. He nods, and then walks around the car.

'This scratch is fine—you've clearly been keyed,' he says, pointing to the scratch on the right.

'Yep, that one's okay,' I say. 'Everyone accepts that was already there. It's these, ah, other scratches.'

He walks around the left of the car in silence. I am internally cringing. 'Have I fucked it?' I finally ask, timidly.

He looks at me.

'Oh god,' I say. 'I think I need to sit down.'

'This is why I never borrow anyone else's car,' he muses. 'This always happens.'

'So I've fucked it?'

'Oh no, you're fine,' he says. 'They'll come out with a buff and a polish. What happened, anyway? You take it out bush?'

'No.'

'Well, that's a lie.'

'Okay. Yes.'

'You city girls,' he says, grinning.

'So . . . can you help me? Do you think? If that's okay?'

'Yeah, course, chief,' Steve says 'You helped me. I sleep better now, since I saw you. So now I'll help you.'

I feel like Medicare might not condone this particular type of doctor–patient relationship but desperate times, etc. I could have hugged him.

'I've got all the stuff,' he explains. 'But you're going to have to bring the car round to mine. Not in a creepy way, okay? It needs a full detail; otherwise, she's going to lose her shit.'

At this point I barely care if Steve has a rap sheet and a dungeon. I am so desperately relieved I start trying to pin him down for a time—such as, like, right now.

'Listen, I've just had to sack a bloke,' he explains, 'and he's meant to come around and give me some of my tools. And I feel like when I see him we might have a bit of a blue. Nothing physical,' he clarifies, seeing my expression, 'but I don't need you there as the local doc hearing me and old mate calling each other fucking c★★★s, okay?'

'Whatever,' I say. 'Doesn't bother me, just call me when you're free. Do you like beer? I'll get you a carton. I really appreciate it.'

He looks at me. 'I've got enough beer, doc,' he says. 'Believe me.'

'I'll bring some anyway,' I say. 'You can never have too much beer.'

'From the doctor's mouth,' he says.

'Hey, these are extenuating circumstances. Plus, I'm off duty.'

'See ya later, chief,' Steve says. 'Happy to help.'

We exchange phone numbers. Always very handy, as my mother says, even in these totally gender-equal times, to know a man with a ute who knows how to do shit.

On my way back home, Steve calls me.

'I was thinking about that other scratch,' he tells me. 'The key. Look, there used to be this magic pen thingo, like, it covers up single scratches. Pretty sure they have it at the auto repairs place off the main road. That might sort that out.'

'So I just need the magic pen thingo?' I ask, with some hesitation.

'Yeah. And ask for Red Liam. He knows me, he'll help you.'

'Red Liam?'

'Yep. Looks a bit like a stoner, not sure if he is one or not. Good bloke.'

'So I just go to the auto shop, and the guy that looks like a stoner is probably Red Liam and he'll know about the magic pen?'

'Yep.'

'But—'

Steve's already hung up. I can't help but roll my eyes as I start the car and head over there. I've stayed in Broome for the sole purpose of writing my masterpiece, and instead I'm off to the auto repairs shop to find a bloke called Red Liam, who may or may not be a stoner, to get a magic pen thingo to cover a scratch that's probably been on the fucking car for years anyway. But such is my fear of my boss I go straight over. The manuscript can be written another day.

I used to have a few mates back in my ski bum days who were pretty big stoners. I'm planning on using my memory of them to help me find Liam, but as I look around the store I realise everyone looks a little like they're on the stoner spectrum. I'd like to point out here that I have no issue with stoners and never have, but as a descriptor to help you pinpoint someone, 'stoner' can be a difficult one.

I approach a man and ask a little nervously if he is Red Liam.

'What?' he says.

I clear my throat. I realise I sound like I'm doing some kind of drug deal, when all I really want is the magic pen thingo.

'Are you Red Liam?' I almost shout.

'Up the back,' he says.

I go up the back to find a bloke who looks just like the blokes down the front.

'Are you Red Liam?'

He looks at me. 'Who's asking?'

I wonder why I feel like I've stepped into a gangster movie when really, I'm just at a random auto repairs shop. But I just kind of roll with it. 'Steve,' I say.

'Steve who?'

'Well, actually, me. I mean, I'm not Steve, but Steve sent me in.'

'Yeah, Steve who?'

I realise I can't remember Steve's last name. I do know his cholesterol level, but that isn't going to help anyone.

'He's a builder?' I finally offer.

'Oh, *that* Steve. Why'd he send you in?'

I explain the situation with the scratch, and the magic pen thingo that apparently he, Red Liam, will know all about.

He shakes his head. 'We haven't stocked that for years, Steve-o should know that.'

I remind myself to question Steve about keeping his magic pen thingo credentials up to date, but I don't want to give up now I'm here: Red Liam looks like he has a wealth of scratch-covering information and the aisles are full of encouraging-looking items for fixing cars.

'Can you just come and look at the car?' I plead.

Red Liam doesn't look that enthused but kindly agrees and walks into the car park.

He takes one look at the offending scratch and laughs. 'Nah, you've been keyed. Not your fault, no pen will fix that.'

I nod. Good. We are all in agreement. This is not my fault.

He walks around to the left. 'You take her out bush?'

'Yeah,' I say. 'Stupidly.'

He shakes his head. 'Nah, you're right, you just need a buff and polish. Steve-o can sort that out at his place.'

'So, there's nothing I can buy that will help me?'

He looks at me. 'What are you after? A new door?'

'I just feel bad because you've helped me and I haven't bought anything,' I explain.

He laughs. 'Don't worry about it, mate. Steve-o buys enough from me anyway.'

For a moment I wonder if he means pot, rather than car-related things, but then remember that Steve volunteers for a variety of local charities on the side and seems pretty straight like that.

Two hours later I am in what can only be described as a bloke's paradise at Steve's place, out the back of the industrial area of

Broome. There are five dogs, a huge pig that appears out of nowhere, and about fifty thousand cars, dirt bikes and every tool a man could ever want or need.

'I should have gone into building,' I say, looking at the treasures around me.

For the next few hours, Steve and I drink low-carb beers (for his cholesterol), listen to Aussie rock and wash, buff, polish and wax my boss's car until it looks brand new.

'I never do this, even for my cars,' he muses. 'Tell her you've paid five hundred bucks to have the damn thing detailed.'

I look at the shining, glistening, positively sparkling vehicle in front of me as 'Working Class Man' blares out of the Makita radio.

In my entire life, I still don't think I have met as big a legend, who helped me just because I asked, who had no agenda and asked for no thanks, as Steve from Broome. Broome, for all its contradictions, is patching back together my soul, piece by piece.

I spend my last week in Broome living in McAlpine House. The guesthouse was originally the home of Lord McAlpine, the man who largely developed Broome into the modern sort of town it is today—beginning with the resort at Cable Beach.

The legend goes that Lord McAlpine, having fallen in love with Broome, decided to build a luxury hotel, and purchased the land on a contract drawn up and signed on the back of a beer coaster in the Roebuck Bay Hotel. Of course, the Yawuru people, the traditional custodians of Broome, had already lived here for hundreds, if not thousands of years, and still do. The traditional name for Broome is *Rubibi*.

I feel a little hypocritical sleeping here behind the white lattice (literally, the place is surrounded by it), but everything else is booked out and it's also fascinating to be here in the middle of old Broome. This part of town has the wide old street of Dampier Terrace, and the oldest outdoor cinema in the world. It's filled with pearling houses, and is very different from the newer developments out towards Cable Beach. In the centre of old Broome, this piece of time and history feels almost totally unchanged.

After I return the car to a standing ovation in the clinic car park, the crowd including two of my patients who are very impressed by its new-found shine, I hire a bike from Broome Cycles and mount my new, two-wheeled chariot.

Riding is like swimming, but even better. I fly around old Broome, down towards Town Beach, through Chinatown. It's just me, my bike, and the road. It's wonderful. There's no wind but I whip through the air, on my left the mangroves and turquoise water, on my right the sounds and experiences of Broome.

Is this happiness? I wonder, as the wheels move and I move, floating through the day. It feels like happiness, this elusive sense of everything just being right, or the absence of anything being wrong. And freedom—it feels like that too.

AJ comes over to McAlpine House after a day at the hospital and hangs out with me by the pool, where the guesthouse's dog, Llewellyn, appears, licking me.

'Good boy, Llewellyn.' I pat his head. 'Want to play with the ball?'

AJ lies on a sunbed, looking up at the sky.

'Life could be worse, you know, Son,' she says. 'Like, it really could be worse.'

'I know,' I agree.

She glances at me. 'You can't leave Broome,' she says. 'You belong here.'

I feel relatively noncommittal, but part of me does wonder if she might be right.

Steve takes me out for the day up to the Dampier Peninsula. We swim, despite the signs warning us to be croc-wise, on a beach made of white sand and blue ocean. It's so isolated and deserted here that we could be anywhere. At one point, though, a boat appears, slowly chugging past.

'Could be a drug boat,' Steve says. 'Or people smugglers.'

I look at him. 'What?'

'Yeah,' he says. 'Up here, it's so remote, this is how they all come in. I should probably report it.'

We both watch the vessel splutter along.

'Maybe gun-runners,' I suggest.

'Maybe, chief,' he says, eyeing the boat with trepidation. 'You can get away with anything out here.'

'Should we call the police?' I ask. 'Is there even a jail in Broome?'

He looks at me. 'You ride your bike past it every day.'

'Do I?'

'I did some work in there once,' he tells me, as we sit on the sand drinking beer. 'The doors are so rusted they can't shut, and the prisoners smoke outside and stuff. They go to the shops too. You would have seen them, in the prison greens.'

'What?'

'Yeah, it's on the more relaxed end, as far as lock-ups go,' he agrees.

For some reason, this makes me like Broome even more. Even in the prison, things feel relatively free.

A patient of mine who had also lived and worked around Australia said to me once that after you've been in a place like the Territory or WA, you don't see what's in front of you anymore because you're constantly looking at the horizon instead.

I now think that's true, because I find myself doing the same thing. When I stand on Cable Beach, I am completely arrested by the sand and the sky. The same way I was arrested by the red dirt of the Pilbara, and the endless line of the Tanami track. It's intoxicating, this country, once you really start to see it.

For a long time I didn't even notice the horizon. I was too busy inside the little bubble of my life. But while I was looking down, I was missing the truth of Australia: underneath this big sky is racism, injustice, lack of healthcare access—things that I didn't truly, properly see until I woke up one day, packed a suitcase and opened my eyes.

People don't like having these conversations, so we usually talk about other things instead. But politics and opinions and words and more words stop us from being able to really see.

The only way to see is to go there and look. If and when you do, ask yourself, as somebody asked me once, as I stood looking at a river in the middle of central northwest NSW: 'If you ever go, you let me know what you think, and you tell me what you see.'

I look at the horizon above Cable Beach, and I think about what I see, what I really see, now. I see a country with disgraceful health discrepancies, between both remote and metropolitan Australia, and black and white Australia. I see these differences, and then also see that, on a large scale, no one is doing anything meaningful about them, for reasons I am not certain of—at best because they simply don't know, at worst because, deep down, they don't want anything to change. Because healthy people are empowered people, and maybe we aren't quite ready for that.

I see a country that is beautiful, with land that is every colour, and every type of terrain. I see every flower and every piece of sky. But I also see a country with a strong undercurrent of inequity and unfairness. I see good people trying to make a difference, trying to drive change, but if inside the gap still sits denial and a lack of acknowledgement then these good people can't change anything, only plug the gap with tissues when it needs high-quality surgery. So, they give up and accept things as they are, with tropes thrown around like, 'It's just so complicated. It's all just so complicated.' In my life, I do not think I have met such good and decent souls as the people I meet on my journey around Australia, or seen such incredible places. But these people and places, in many respects, aside from the odd tourist advert or doco about remote Australia, are too often left behind as the rest of the country moves on. Or worse, the minerals under the ground or ocean there are helped to advance the national economy, while the people who live above them rarely see any rewards.

If you can't see it, it may as well not exist. But is that the right way to think when we are all standing under the same sky?

That evening I sit outside the pool patting Llewellyn and talk to Marilynne, who owns the guesthouse, about Broome: what it was like in the past, what it was like now.

'I knew I had to come back here,' I tell her. 'Isn't that strange? A place I should have no connection to, and yet . . .'

She looks at me.

'You know,' she says, patting Llewellyn's pelt-like coat, 'my ex-husband used to say something about Broome. That on the map of the globe, it's almost directly opposite the Bermuda Triangle, in longitude and latitude. The antipodes of Broome is the Bermuda Triangle.'

I look it up on my phone.

'You're right,' I say, almost surprised.

'Well, what he used to say,' she tells me, as the sun sets behind the white lattice, peering through the cracks, 'is that people get lost in the Bermuda Triangle, but here in Broome, they're found.'

On my last night in Broome, Kristina rings me from Denmark. She has been a constant since I left, over a year ago now, to hit the red dirt of the Pilbara. We are on opposite sides of the world but our friendship, sustained through our phone receivers, never fades. Distance means nothing for true friends.

Tonight, Kristina sounds down. 'It's all the rejection, mate,' she says to me. 'And all the fucking liars. First, my ex tries to get back in touch, even though I know he's dating someone else. Then I lose my job. And my boss tells me he's in love with one woman even though he's still married to another one. I said to him, "Are you going to leave her? Be with this other woman?" And he said no, or he doesn't know.'

'That old chestnut!', I have to laugh.

I picture Copenhagen. I picture the cold, the winter, the same people and the same feelings that Kristina has been having for the last nine months. I tell her about Broome, and the way that, without realising it, I've been asking the land for something, anything. It isn't like I ever got on my hands and knees: I didn't even know I was asking for anything at all. But there must have been something inside my soul, my cracking, poor soul, saying, 'Help me, surround me, let me breathe.'

'You need to go somewhere else for a while,' I tell her. 'Surrounded by ocean, or mountains—you need to go to a place like that. And do nothing else. Just be there.'

I then say to her what someone said to me, something it's taken me months to really understand the meaning of.

'You need to put your feet in the dirt, girl,' I tell my lost, hurting friend. 'Don't expect anything, don't know anything, don't search for anything. Just go.'

Kristina knows I am right. 'It's time to get on a fucking plane,' she says. 'I'm going to go away somewhere. I'll book it tonight.'

As we say goodbye, I think about the Broome tides. The moon, the sun, the earth and the water. Those gravitational forces way up there in the big sky that determine the ocean that I am standing in—how is that even possible? They say it's science, but I know better. It's magic. I realise, for the first time in a very long time, I am seeing the magic again.

Tears are forming in my eyes, but they aren't tears of sadness or frustration or pain or confusion—they're tears of relief that I am slowly coming back to myself. It sounds mad, but that's what happened to me in Broome.

Nothing in life is perfect. Humans are bad and good and cruel and wonderful. Terrible things have happened in Broome but the land is not responsible for those things. Neither is the sun, the moon, the water, the red earth or the rocks. I am a human made of cells and skin and blood and flesh and bone, but here I am also made of earth and fire and water and air and sunlight. I am now not so much a person who exists on the earth, but someone who exists with it.

In the light of the early morning on Cable Beach in Broome, you can see both the sun in front of you and the moon behind you. Between them is sky, and underneath them water. In Western Australia, the sun sets on the other side. And in Broome, the sun rises at the same time the moon fades. You can be there, underneath it, seeing it all. You are right there, part of that giant ecosystem.

It must be a type of magic, this disappearance of the bridge between me and the elements, the letting go of this sense that I can control everything, of the need to fit into arbitrary social boxes; I have found these things are no longer so important. Maybe that's what I've learnt about myself by taking myself so far away. Despite everything, despite my disillusionment with not just my own life but with the history of this country, and the terrible and wonderful things I have seen, Broome teaches me that about myself. That who I am is, like this country, and this town, a walking contradiction.

Who am I?

I am a doctor who still believes in magic.

# epilogue

All dog stories begin with laughter and end in tears.

Robert Genn, 'The Painter's Keys'

O f course, the end is never the end we think it's going to be. Novels have ends, but I've started to realise that lives, until we take our final breath at least—they keep going.

After I leave Broome I fly to Darwin, then all the way down to Esperance. I cross through the desert, the ocean, the lush vegetation of the south. The sun sets in the west as I slowly head back east, wondering what is waiting for me there.

It is on the plane as we fly over the Nullarbor that I go through my messages to see one I received weeks before and have been trying to ignore.

*Hi* is all it says. I stare at it for a long time, and then I delete it. In a split second it disappears, and I turn to look below me, over the red dirt, pink in the fading sunlight. Western Australia. *What a place.*

After leaving Broome and spending two weeks working in Esperance, where I spend my weekends going to the nearest national park and walking, barefoot, in the whitest sand I've ever seen, I decide to take another contract in River Town.

The plane flies through the night, and I think about the river, snaking through the top of northwest NSW. At this point, I must know, somehow, that the end of my journey is near. When I say 'my journey', I just mean a part of my life that has to close, a chapter that has to finish. A door, which was always ajar, that now needs to be shut.

Perhaps for every life to continue, somewhere there has to be a sacrifice. For me, that sacrifice was the soul that came into my life perhaps when I needed it the most. Buddy, the dog who lived, one day couldn't breathe. As it turned out, there was a giant, evil tumour slowly hijacking her little chest, a ticking time bomb that none of us knew was going to explode. Maybe Buddy knew, though: dogs always do. She did, with those big brown eyes, always seem to be clued into something that I wasn't.

It was in River Town that I got the call from the vet telling me the chemotherapy they'd promised would give her around eight months, maybe more, hadn't worked. Now, they said, she may not survive the night. I was sitting in the little medical clinic with Harry when they told me, and then it was me who couldn't breathe. There were no flights from Dubbo for days, air travel being reduced because of Covid, and we were still in lockdown anyway.

Without thinking, and with no consideration for cost, the rules or the pandemic, I rang the pilot who had flown Buddy and me from Brewarrina to Dubbo in his little plane. And so he came and picked me up, one hour later. Harry dropped me off.

'This isn't how it was supposed to end, Harry,' I said through my tears as we stood there together in the red dust of a tiny airstrip at the top of NSW. Harry, a boy who had already seen enough endings that weren't supposed to be, just hugged me, and said to say hello to Buddy.

The pilot and I flew across NSW. As the light changed, he turned to me.

'See that line?' he said. 'Where the colours change? And day turns into night? Pilots call that the terminator. The line that delineates the end of the day, and the beginning of the night.'

I stared at the purple line as we flew into it. Buddy, I knew, was waiting for me there.

We landed two hours later at the tiny airport near my parents' house. They picked me up and we began the journey home. Everyone prayed Buddy would survive the night, would stay there in the in-between mauve dusk, and not cross into the darkness. The thought she might not make it was unacceptable. I could not accept it.

She did make it. Buddy waited until I got home, and then three weeks later she died in my arms on the grass of my parents' backyard.

Buddy was barely twelve months old. The vets said the cancer was so aggressive she didn't stand a chance. I'd tried everything: two oncologists, a clinical trial, throwing money at every vet I could find. We bought her an oxygen machine and a nebuliser. I hand-fed her food recommended by a book on canine cancer. I slept with her on the floor, because she was in too much pain to lie on her back as she normally liked to on her bed, and we shared a pillow. I woke up every morning with her furry head next to mine, counting her breaths, praying the now-frail, bony little body would hold on. I wanted a miracle,

I guess. But nothing worked. Not a single damn thing worked. She slipped away from me so quickly it was almost as if she was a whisper across time itself.

On the night when Buddy wanted to die, she walked into the backyard and looked up at the moon. I sat there with her and my dad, and we held her as her big brown eyes begged us to let her go.

'She's looking for her *querencia*,' Dad said through his tears.

'What's *querencia*?' I asked him.

He explained that the Spanish talk about it not so much as a word, rather as a concept. It's a homing instinct, a favourite place. The desire to be *where one is meant to be*. And for Buddy, that wasn't going to be this world for very long. We were the same, me and my little doggy. Both searching for the place where we were meant to be.

She's always with me and, one day, we will find one another again. I always had dreams of taking Buddy to Europe, and seeing her run around with a little red scarf around her blue cattle dog neck, in front of great and important places like the Eiffel Tower or the Tagus River. Sometimes, I swear I can still hear the patter of her feet as I continue on my adventures.

Maybe she is now just cells and dirt, part of the earth where she lies. But maybe she isn't, and her soul waits for mine. Maybe she'll find me again, just like she did the first time, when I needed her the most.

There is such beauty in the unknown. It is vast, and huge, and so much bigger than me. I thought I had to see the world to find myself, but all I really had to do was put my feet in the dirt of this enormous land, and get lost enough to learn the truth. And the truth is this: there are so many things bigger than me that I have been humbled completely.

With that truth comes freedom. And in the freedom of humility, comes the chance to live a truly meaningful life.

I thought at one point, with all my escaping, that I was just a person who was going to live many lives. But now I see it a bit differently. There's a difference between living many lives and inhabiting many worlds. I am the same person I have always been, I just twist and turn through different places and experiences like a dancer.

So many patients and people asked me the same question, as I travelled across this giant place. 'Where are you from? Where is your home?'

But what is home? A place where you belong? Where, even with the blood of history soaking the land, you can still look at the sky and the ocean and the earth, and have friends you can sit and have a yarn with? Where you feel at peace, and the mess and chaos of life feels soothed? Is that home?

Then I have found many homes across this country. And if I have already found this many, then there must be more to be found.

Or perhaps a better way of putting it is that, if you truly know yourself, or at least have the courage to try learn, then home is really just wherever you happen to be.

# author's note

It's terrible to lie in chains
To rot in Dungeon Deep
But it's still worse, when you are free
To sleep and sleep and sleep

Taras Shevchenko, 'The Days Go By'

I edited most of this book while living and working in Broken Hill, Australia's first heritage-listed city. After a day spent seeing patients, I would get home, open my laptop, and read and reread the stories that had gotten me to this point. Had someone told me ten years ago, when I started medical school, that I'd end up publishing a memoir and applying the finishing touches in Broken Hill, I wouldn't have believed them. Such is the wonder of life; you really don't know where you'll end up.

During this stint in Broken Hill, I returned to Sydney one weekend to attend an event. It was hosted by the charity foundation of a big hospital. I was a ring-in; I just happened to know someone going who wanted a plus-one.

The event was packed with the crème de la crème of the medical world, and of Sydney society. While we should of course celebrate charitable donations and the people who fundraise for hospitals and medical research, I was blown away by the fact that this hospital had received 37.8 million dollars in private donations in one year alone.

As I sat listening to the speeches and hearing about the huge sum of money that the people in the room had pumped into the hospital, all I could see was Broome, and Kununurra, and the Pilbara, and River Town and Sun Town and Dingo Town, and places like them. These places are crying out for money and help, and here I was, I who had been there and seen them and come to know them intimately, sitting in a room filled with the country's smartest and wealthiest people, all of us congratulating ourselves on what a good thing we were doing. Meanwhile, no one spared those places I knew a thought. I couldn't blame them—they'd probably never been there. But for a moment, clutching my glass of champagne and listening to it all, I wanted to get up and start screaming.

Part of me knew that this hospital and its researchers and scientists and doctors needed funding, that this was a good event for a worthy cause. The other part of me knew that money, wealth and brains usually stay in the same places, circulating around the same people. Privilege, real privilege, doesn't tend to travel as widely as I have.

I flew back to Broken Hill a few days later, and met Ted, the other GP I work with, at the airport. We stood inside the tiny terminal waiting for our bags as I told him about the event. Ted's a great bloke, and he has as many good stories as me. Actually, he has better ones, because once he treated Harrison Ford, incurring my lifelong envy.

'$37.8 million in private donations alone,' I said, with some awe. 'Can you believe that?'

Ted looked at me. 'Do you know, now there are only 406

doctors covering rural NSW, and that's including hospital doctors? So GPs like us, there's barely any. From Wilcannia, and all along the Darling River, right up to Bourke, there isn't a single permanent doctor servicing any of those communities. Not one.'

'37.8 million dollars,' I said again.

Ted laughed. 'Well, it's not going out there.'

Our bags arrived as the sun set.

'You and me are two of those doctors,' he said, turning to look at me. 'You and me.'

I started this book writing about the perception I had of myself, professionally speaking, as weak. I thought that kindness and empathy, and a lack of medical heroics compared with my specialist counterparts, meant that the things I did weren't very important. I was the kind of person, who, when a beautician once farewelled me with, 'Get back to saving lives!' replied, sarcastically, 'Sure I will, one pap smear at a time.' Now I have worked and continue to work where I have, I realise that in some places there isn't a doctor to perform things like cervical screening, or check your cholesterol level, or conduct a neuro-logical examination. All these things, when done early enough, can make a huge difference to a patient's quality of life—even save it. So my little self-deprecating joke actually turned out to be not so much a joke as a Freudian slip.

I am proud to be a GP. It is a vocation that has taken me far and wide, and shown me things about my country that I other-wise would never have known. It has opened a window into the most incredible places, into the lives of the most amazing people. Through these places and these people I have learnt lessons that have improved me as a person, and did something else, too, something that rarely happens: they changed me, and I think they changed me for the better.

I did, after all that, finally make it back to Europe after Covid lockdowns ended and things slowly crawled back to a semblance of normality.

On Portugal's Atlantic coast, the sun sets in the west, as it does in Western Australia, and the moon rises over the ocean, just like in Broome. Time and space can be crossed quickly, I discovered, from one west coast to the next. Or maybe the person who told me that once the red dirt gets on your skin it will never wash off was right—maybe that was truer than I realised.

One day we drove across the border to Spain, to visit the town of Santiago de Compostela at the end of the Camino trail, which hundreds of thousands of pilgrims have walked. Europe had changed since I was there last, the main difference being there was now another war, and the Ukraine my grandparents had fled many years ago was now being pounded with missiles. I had thought so much about my identity as an Australian during my travels, and now I was faced with the other side of myself, and the confusing feelings that came with that. So perhaps, some part of me wanted to see the end of the Camino trail to find, again, something bigger than me. And bigger than this war.

Apparently, hiking the Camino absolves Catholics of their sins. I don't know about that, but it does make me think of all those other people who are getting lost to be found. As we walked through Santiago, my partner (yes, I now know happiness in this regard; it's a humble, unassuming, love and happiness, the only kind I now think means anything) turned to me and said, 'You know, it's amazing how the Europeans built all this stuff, all this infrastructure, these cathedrals, and the Aboriginal people didn't need any of these grand buildings—the land was enough.' He had come with me earlier on a return trip to Kununurra, so, like me, was revisiting the Kimberley in his mind.

It's a funny feeling, staring at a giant cathedral in the Galician region of Spain while also somehow being back in a place on the other side of the planet in your head. People can become very defensive when you speak about First Nations issues, health inequities and what I know to be the deep unfairness of it all. The truths become muddled in politics and opinions and economics and mired in controversy. But much like with the pilgrims, who go to Santiago de Compostela to find their truth, it really is quite simple. The truth I learnt about Australia came from just being there; regardless of what you read in a book or a newspaper or what conversations you have, to stand in the Pilbara and see that hostile land and know that people survived and thrived for thousands and thousands of years there—that's all you need to do to begin to understand the power of ancient First Nations cultures. You just have to, literally, go there and look, and listen. That's what our politicians should do. Whatever side of the house you sit on, when you put your feet in the dirt and experience a place and its people (properly experience, not just a few days and a few lunches), you realise how meaningless political speak is in the face of the reality of severe and prolonged human suffering.

I hope, one day, I'm able to walk as I did in the Australian desert through the black soil of Ukraine, and understand that side of myself, and my family, a little more.

That's the other thing I learnt, as anyone I think has learnt who have taken these sorts of journeys—there's always time to find the hidden parts of yourself. It may not feel like it, but for that particular quest, the clock never stops. When you travel in that way—moving across country but actually journeying into yourself—time as we know it simply ceases to exist.

I vow then and there, standing on the cobblestones in the rain in Spain, that one day, I will walk the Camino. Perhaps inspired by the pilgrims, that afternoon I speak to a locum agency and decide to take a job for a month in Ireland. Before I return to Australia, I think, I might as well experience GP life in another country.

The agency tells me it's going to be very remote, really off the beaten track. When I ask how remote, he says, in a serious tone, 'two hours' drive from Dublin'. When I stop laughing, I realise that once a wanderer, always a wanderer. Change, after all, is as good as a holiday.

Dr Sonia Henry
15/01/2023

# acknowledgements

When you find yourself on such a huge journey, you also find there are many people to thank.

As always, my agent Sarah McKenzie and my publisher Jane Palfreyman—two exceptional women I will be forever grateful for. My editors Gen Buzo and Greer Gamble, not enough praise can be heaped upon you. I handed you my life in a book and you both treated it and me with immense kindness.

Peter, Sophie, Adrian and Jasper Henry, the best family a person could wish for.

In my books there are often villainous doctors, so I would like to take this opportunity to mention the medics who have helped me, and/or their patients, a great deal (in ways unrelated to this book) and deserve recognition. Dr Damien Boyd, Dr Sandy Beveridge, Dr Cameron Holloway, Dr Ian Sutton, Dr Jennifer Massey, Dr John Rooney, Prof Bill Ledger, Dr Ed Ryan and Dr Lynne Jonhson.

My mates (some of whom who are also doctors) in alphabetical order: Alex G, Alf, Binnie, Borgs, Cokes, Daniel, Dicko, Franz, Gilles, Jaci, Jacko, Jeff, Jen, Ian, Jesso, Joules, Kazzy, Lucie, Michael, Nico, Nina, Paul, Ryan, Sally and Stevie.

The friends I made on my travels through the North West, Pilbara, NSW and everywhere else: AJ (my homie), Charlotte (Darwin, what a town!), Denise, Emily, Jarod, Kat (Uki sister), Kate, Megan, Mel, Rachel and Kenrik, Rosie M (next book's inspired by you haha!), Rob (thanks for everything, captain), Spence (can't wait to see the birth of MC mud crab), Tom M, Wes, Marcy for the good karaoke memories, Kirsten for the fishing trip of a lifetime up the Keep.

BOD and JOD, it's been wild . . . Sarah (thanks for all those on-calls together mate), Julie, Amy and Mitch. The P family (R, J, M, A) for their generosity and kindness. LB: next book to be written has to be by you, Dostoyevsky.

Special thanks to Brad Steadman of the Brewarrina Aboriginal Cultural Museum for all he taught me. Joey, D, K, BG, Nose for the whiskey which I have never forgotten, Blacky and Deb for a fantastic dinner. Gem and Sweeney. Nathan, Leanne, Charlie, Jen L and all the gang from IAMS.

Thrive Medical in Broken Hill, here's to Thirsty Thursdays, and Saskia for the beers and debriefs. The team at Kununurra library for the best writers' festival on earth. Dave, Leanne, Josh and Caro, for a great time in the Kimberley. Special thanks to Dave for the quote, and Caro for the lunches.

Marilynne, Gary and Llewellyn, not only for the good conversations but also providing a roof over my head in such nice old Broome surrounds where I wrote a lot of this book.

TC (till the next tax year . . .).

Jeanne Ryckmans for her words of encouragement. Terrence

and Helen for those great Broome breakfasts. The Wednesday wenches for really taking me in.

Pricey, Rags and Eammon, Frith and Ally, good times and many wines in Condo. Trevor from Inverell. Brett and John from Darlo Liquor aka paradise on earth. Lisa Fawkner—thanks for having my back, no matter what. Backroom Press Broome and Sara Genn and Kelly from Mushroom Records for their assistance around the use of quotes.

Ian G and G for 'weekend at Milthorpe'—a memory that still makes me laugh. Susie French, for sharing her beautiful paintings of the Kimberley. Every tour operator in Australia, but particularly Broome—can't say enough good things about my experiences there! Rob and Mark, my favourite pilots. Slam, my favourite driver.

Sophia, Georgia, Andy and Kelly—for all their help and support.

Paul Robinson, for the years of support and friendship

Keno from café Hernandez, for giving me a table to write on, and for the great coffee.

To everyone who helped me—picked me up in a taxi when I was stuck in the rain, showed me around, gave me a grin when I was really alone, said thanks for being their GP, helped me lift a bag, gave me a free bottle of Diet Coke on my birthday—I don't know all your names and you may never see this book, but thanks a million.

Katherine, James, Tiago Alexandra, Miguel and the humble art of trying to learn a new language!

Donna, Chris, and Donna.

To D. Here's to eating kebabs all over the world together. I love you.

Finally, The Sailor. This book was written in your memory.